T0365595

BETWEEN
AFRICA
AND THE
WEST

A Story of Discovery

Sahr John Yambasu

Order this book online at www.trafford.com
or email orders@trafford.com

Most Trafford titles are also available at major online book retailers.

African Shamrock Publications - www.africanshamrockpublications.com

Printed in the United States of America.

ISBN: 978-1-4907-0979-6 (sc)
ISBN: 978-1-4907-0980-2 (e)

Trafford rev. 08/14/2013

 www.trafford.com

North America & international
toll-free: 1 888 232 4444 (USA & Canada)
fax: 812 355 4082

I dedicate this book to Edwin and to Nancy
(of blessed memory), my parents-in-law.
Your unconditional acceptance of me encourages me and
reminds me of the love of God.
Your graciousness reminds me to be gracious.
Your faith inspires me.

CONTENTS

ACKNOWLEDGEMENTS

Many people have helped me during the process of writing this book: Rev. Dudley Levistone Cooney, Rev. Dr John Parkin, George Carpendale, Eleanor Mountain, Michael Armstrong and Paul Coady. Sincere thanks to you all for your kind help and encouragement. Very special thanks to Henry Carpendale, who invested an awful lot of time and thought suggesting better ways of telling this story. I benefitted a great deal from your generous guidance, Henry.

Abbie, Fayia and Sahr (Jnr.), this book is the result of your enquiries about my background. I am very grateful to you for the inspiration and courage which those enquiries gave me to investigate my origins, beliefs and values.

You have always been there for me, Clodagh. Your love, support and encouragement of me is second to none. Thanks for sharing so selflessly in my life journey.

And to my Sierra Leonean family, all my friends, and the people, organizations and institutions mentioned in this book, I say thank you. My life would have been empty and purposeless without your input.

Sincere and grateful thanks to Charles & Francisca Maduka for their contribution towards the cost of publishing and printing this book.

To God be all the glory, honour and praise.

Any deficiencies in this book are solely of my own making and should not be attributed to any of the people who have helped me in the process of writing it.

INTRODUCTION

My Heritage

This is an attempt at examining my heritage. A casual observer might equate this exercise to a desire on my part to take stock of my African ancestry, tradition, culture and society; in short, my African legacy. That would be true, but only in part.

Reflecting on my life over the years, I have come to the realization that my heritage is much larger and wider than my being African. All of the events and issues that I relay in this story arguably have profoundly impacted me and dictate my take on life: the history of my forebearers, the society and worldview that influenced their way of life, and the realities of Western power and influence. All these were ingredients of the society in which I was born, raised and educated. They pre-existed me. They dictated the values and value systems that were to become mine. And they informed the choices that I made in life. So, all of them together have come to define who I am as a person. In this regard, I can say that my heritage constitutes being a Kissi (my ethnic group), a Sierra Leonean, a man educated in Western[1] ways, a Christian, a reverend minister, a child of my parents and my village, a man, a husband, a father and a human being.

---

[1]   Throughout this story I use the word 'West' or 'Western' but only in a general way. By their use, I am in no way implying uniformity or constancy. I am aware that the West has many faces and is ever changing.

This, in essence, is what I examine in this book. In part, I do so by simply telling the story of my life. I also do so by examining my heritage, with the view to understanding its value. Some of the issues I have raised are parochial and merely informative; others are big and cross-cutting ones— perhaps even controversial. I raise both as a way of challenging what is taken for granted and which, in my opinion, should not be so. Otherwise, unaware of their power to make or unmake us, they may become our unexpected destiny.

ONE

LIVING BETWEEN WORLDS

The Worlds of Village and Jungle

O ne of the first things I learnt growing up as a child in my village was the divide between the village and what lay beyond its margins.

We were brought up to believe that while the village was safe and fine to be in, the jungle was something to be afraid of because it sheltered all kinds of wild and sinister realities. It was the place where there were scratchy leaves and large sharp thorns, for example, and where poisonous snakes, stinging insects, ghosts and other supernatural evil beings resided.

Therefore, our parents would always warn us to be careful when we left the village for the bush. Very early on in life we were taught ways to watch out for signs of lurking danger and how to avoiding falling prey to them. "Always use all your senses when you are in the bush", my dad would say to me, "so that you can smell out impending danger long before it reaches you".

The village, on the other hand, was seen as a tamed and safe place. Built in a clearing surrounded by jungle, it was populated by people we knew. Moreover, the village was governed by rules supported by sanctions for those who choose to ignore them. In that sense, expectations of what could happen to us in the village were much more predictable and so provided us with a better sense of safety and security.

As I grew older, however, I began to see that the picture painted of the village and the jungle by our parents may not have been as simple and straightforward as portrayed. I discovered that there were sinister elements in the village too. There were men and women living in the village who practised witchcraft and terrified even the bravest of hearts with the stories of what they could get up to in the spirit-world as they sought to harm other people. There were also men and women in the village who were greedy and quarrelsome; liars, adulterers, fornicators and drunks. More often than not, these were sources of much fear, conflict, pain and suffering to people living in the village community. Sanctions were needed to curb malevolence from such people also.

On the other hand, I began to see that the feared jungle had within it enormous potential for good. Much of our fruit, food, meat and fish, for example, came from the jungle. But we had to take the initiative to explore the jungle for what it had in store for us. We needed to develop and employ skills to do so. Otherwise the jungle remained both a looming symbol and reality of chaos, suffering, destruction and the fear generated by these realities.

The jungle also shaded us from the hot African sun as we walked miles from one village to another in the absence of other forms of transport. It hid us from our enemies in times of local wars or trouble. It provided us with a suitable place to be taught various life skills upon which our continued successful existence depended. In the jungle we practiced hunting and war games without endangering the life of anyone in the domesticated village setting. As a child I spent hours every week with my friends playing war games, setting traps to catch animals and birds and hunting for food. From the jungle too we gathered firewood for cooking our meals.

That was not all. The rites of passage into adulthood for boys and girls also took place in a remote part of the jungle. There, boys and girls were taught separately valuable lessons in how to exploit and put to profitable use the resources of the jungle. There were lessons in what it meant to be a mature and responsible adult member of society. Separate clearings in the jungle away from the village housed different groups of boys and girls almost every year as they were being taught everything they needed to know for full participation in life in their village and society. From the womb of the jungle those young boys and girls were reborn in the village community several months later as newly approved and confirmed adults, trained and qualified to defend their people and to practise their way of life. In short, the jungle equipped and prepared me for a fulfilled life in the domesticated village community.

So, very early on in my life, I was able to see the good and bad in both the village and the jungle surrounding it—the tamed and the wild. As I lived my life between the world of the village and the world of the jungle, I was able to see that the divide between them was fairly porous.

Other Worlds

Gradually, I became aware that my village was in some significant ways not just like any other village. We, for example, spoke a different language from some other villages not more than six miles away. While our cultural practices were similar to those of those villages, they were not identical. We certainly had different leaders; and this was true even for those other villages near us in which the inhabitants spoke the same language as we did and had identical traditions, cultures and practices as ours. Some of them even lived outside the borders of my country and, so, outside the jurisdiction of the government of my country. But we all lived so close to the people of those villages that we could not, as it were, avoid living in their social and cultural worlds—neither they in ours.

At the same time as I was becoming conscious of living in these different worlds, I was introduced to the world of the West as Western political administrators and Christian missionaries gradually spread their influence throughout my country. Gradually, that world was to lay claim on me as I on it.

What's in a Name?

So today, when I attend a meeting and I am asked to introduce myself, I find the exercise a little bit simplistic. Who am I? Where do I start from? Is there enough time to answer properly? These are the sorts of questions that quickly run through my mind when I find myself in such a situation. "My name is Sahr Yambasu", I start when it is my turn. Over the years, I have come to know that names are much more than just words. Like any label or sign, names are pointers to a whole lot more than the person carrying them. They are, for example, about those who chose them, where, when, and why? As such, names have histories, evoke memories, and conjure up familiar and not so familiar worlds that are often not so easy to reconcile. I have often wondered whether or not my listeners at meetings heard more than just words when I announced my name.

Sahr, for example, is not a name chosen for me. I was born with it. It precedes me in as much as its origin is in the tradition of my people. And tradition, for my people, translates as a practice coming down from God. In our tradition, every child of a family is born with a name indicating where he or she comes in the family. So I am called Sahr because Sahr is the name of the first son of every family. When my parents named me Sahr, they had no choice in the matter.

I have not always been officially known as Sahr Yambasu. It was not until nineteen eighty-eight that this was the case. Before then I introduced myself as John Yambasu. I once asked my mother why I was given the name John from birth, as that name was not native to the area in which I was born. She told me that my father had a friend named John who had travelled to visit them. My mother did not know where exactly he came from, but reckoned he came from a town 'a great distance away from our village'. That was my mother's way of saying that it was so far away in her imagination that she never even bothered to ask.

I was born, my mother told me, while John was staying with them. My father decided to name me after him. That is all I know about this passing stranger, John, whose name indelibly became mine. Was he a Christian? Did he know he was carrying an English form of a Greek name? Who gave him that name and why? What did he do for a living? Was he married and did he have children of his own? Where did he actually come from? How did my father get to know him? I never met him in my life and it was probably the last time my mother met him. So, all these questions about him cannot be answered.

Who am I?

There is also the fact that each of us is defined by many 'I ams'. Whenever I introduce myself in the formal settings of a meeting or conference, I more or less automatically go on to make these seven 'I am' statements about myself: "I am originally from Sierra Leone . . . I am a Christian . . . I am 'a property' of the Methodist Church . . . I am married to Clodagh . . . I am a father of three lovely children . . . I am living in Ireland now . . . and I am living at present in . . ."

As with my names, each of these 'I am' statements constitutes for me a world of experience which is unique and replete with stories. To have been born in Sierra Leone, for example, means that I am African and, so, from a continent which in many ways is a world of its own. Africa is a continent like no other on planet earth in terms of her size, number of countries, and wealth of landscapes, peoples, languages, cultures, mineral resources and diversity of land and sea creatures.

The stages of definition that Africa has gone through in history also reinforce my view that Africa is a world of its own. At first, Africa was believed to be only the ancient Roman colonial province in present-day Tunisia and Algeria. Then Africa became only that area south of the Sahara inhabited by Black people. Today, most people would accept, at least notionally, that Africa includes the whole of the continent bordered on the north by the Mediterranean and including the Berber and Arab lands. This would define Africa as having fifty-five recognized states, about thirty square kilometres (larger than China and India put together, and large enough to absorb the acreage of all the imperial powers that have ravished or conquered her throughout the centuries), over one billion people, at least two thousand known languages, and hundreds of dialects.

One of the things I am often conscious of when I define myself as an African is that all definitions of Africa available to us do not come from either Africans or people of African descent. Instead, all definitions of Africa were imposed by non-Africans and often through institutionalized academic, military, political, economic and psychological violence.

Accordingly, the community of those called Africans has its origin in their common suffering as a result of violence inflicted upon them by outsiders. Difficult and uncomfortable though this reality is, nonetheless, it is one certainty that unifies all the peoples of the continent.

Sierra Leone is no different. A small country of about seventy-one square kilometres and with a population of about five million people, Sierra Leone got her name from non-Sierra Leoneans. Historians date her name back to 1462, when a Portuguese explorer who sailed down the coast of West Africa named the country 'Sierra Lyoa' (Lion Mountains). His name was Pedro da Cintra. There is no agreement, however, about whether it was because the mountainous coastal regions looked like sleeping lions, or he thought the thunderstorms over the mountainous peninsula sounded like the roar of a lion. Be that as it may, between 1462 and 1787, Pedro da Cintra's 'Sierra Lyoa' had become 'Sierra Leoa' for 16th century English sailors and then 'Sierra Leone' from the 17th century until the British officially adopted that name in 1787.

I find it amazing that even in this short story of how my country got its name, so many otherwise unrelated people, places and things play a role. This story reveals that with a stroke of the pen and a word from strangers, about a dozen and half disparate groups of ethnicities, cultures, and languages was turned into one country. The new world which this action created was to become subsequently a battleground between indigenous and foreign ideas, resources and ways of life. The propagation of Christianity played no small role in this battle.

From the early sixteenth century Roman Catholic missionaries were active in the coastal regions of Sierra Leone. By 1804 Protestant Christian influence had commenced through Anglican, British Methodist, Baptist, United Brethren in Christ and other traditions. In those early days Protestants spread the gospel largely through freed black slaves or slaves who, after slavery had been banned and declared illegal, were liberated from slave ships. This brief history gives a small but important insight into how my country came to be linked inextricably to the global forces which define her place in the world today.

Born in a country and village shaped by such diverse realities, histories and interests in many ways explains the kind of person I turned out to be. It explains, for example, why I am a Kissi by ethnicity, why I am a Christian and not of another faith by profession and life, why I am educated in Western ways, why I married the woman I married, and why I ended up becoming a 'property of the Methodist Church'.

Describing myself as a 'property of the Methodist Church' is my way of alluding to what most non-Methodists do not understand about being a fulltime Methodist Minister. Most Methodists do not experience the state of being the property of the Methodist Church either. It is a reference to the undertaking I made more than three decades ago when I offered myself to the Church for fulltime ministry. That undertaking was to go wherever the Church sent me and whenever the Church did so. Therefore, in this regard, being a Methodist minister is arguably a signing off of one's life to the Church.

When, in introducing myself, I say "I am living in Ireland now", that may not be strictly correct. Yes, I have my wife and children here with me; I physically live and work here. But I am also aware of the myriads of times when I am living in my home country mentally and emotionally. This is in addition to yearly visits and weekly telephone calls to family, friends, and communities with whom I am involved in projects. This has been the case since I arrived here in Ireland in August 1995, escaping from a civil war in my home country.

Each of these aspects of my life has afforded me experiences which I may never have had had other paths opened up to me. I have often wondered about this. What, for example, if my country was never influenced by the West? What if I never went to a Western school? What if the only form of Christianity that was brought to my village was Roman Catholicism? What if I never became a Minister of Religion? What if I never married and had children? The list of 'what ifs' could go on. All I can say is that I would be a very different kind of person today with different sets of experiences and different takes on life.

Stories of Life

Who, what and where I am today are unalterable facts of the story of my life thus far. What led me primarily to consider telling it in writing are my children. More often than not they have desired to know about the world and relations and decisions which have shaped me into the person I am today.

By writing this story I hope to address some of their questions and reflect on them.

At one level, this is a story of my life so far. At another level, it is also a story of those who gave me life and brought me into this world. For, who and what one is, is also determined by where one comes from. Among my people, we confirm this with the saying, "If you do not know where you are going, know where you come from". This is also a story of those with whom I have interacted in my life. Consequently, retracing my steps in this story means telling the story and experiences of the people and place I come from and the stories of the places and peoples I have encountered on that journey. Therefore, this is essentially my story of living between and experiencing different worlds I have journeyed through: physical, human, social, cultural, spiritual, and emotional.

I invite you to come with me on this journey. I hope it will open up windows for you through which you can take a glimpse into the strange and familiar worlds of the reality of being human.

If I may say one more thing before we embark on this journey, it is this: continue dreaming and daring to deal with challenges you may face on your journey towards being truly human. And, to prevent you from abandoning the journey for fear of not getting to your intended destination, realize that this is a never-ending journey. The gift of life is primarily in the travelling, rather than in the arriving.

TWO

AS IT WAS IN THE BEGINNING

My Ignorance Exposed

"**W**hat was the name of Mama Abbie's mother? Where did she live? Does Mama Abbie have any sisters and brothers?" My daughter Abbie asked me one day about my mother—after whom she is named. "What about *Keke*?"[2] She continued. "Who are his real brothers and sisters?" Her questions reminded me of the importance of passing down from generation to generation the stories of who we are, where we come from, what we believe and why. That is how histories and traditions are preserved.

But when my daughter and her brothers started asking me very specific questions about my background I realized

---

[2] *Keke*' with the '*e*' pronounced as the 'e' in 'bed' is Kissi for daddy. From hearing me use that word when I refer to my present daddy, the children adopted the same to refer to him. *Nde* is the kissi word for mum.

suddenly how very little I knew. My children's questions also reminded me again of the obvious sharp difference between the culture I grew in and that of my children. For, when I was growing up in my village, children were not allowed to ask questions like the ones my children asked me. Inquisitiveness was frowned upon. The best we were expected to do was to be silent and to do what we were told. That was what being a good child meant.

I was also brought up to consider anyone of my mother's age as my mother and of my father's age as my father. The same applied to those who were of the age of my grandmother, grandfather, father, sister and brother. As I grew older, listened to and participated in adult conversations, I came to discover the wisdom behind that reasoning. My people believed that encouraging questions like the ones my children asked laid foundations for treating people that were not one's real relations as less important and so with less regard. In a society in which everyone at one time or another would depend on others for their social welfare and in many cases survival, it made sense not to sow such seeds of discrimination in children's minds. "I am because we are" was the philosophy that informed life in that society. Everyone was believed to belong to everyone and so was accountable to everyone. Consequently even bringing up the children in the village community was the responsibility of all the adults in it. After all, were they all not our grandmothers, grandfathers, mothers, fathers, brothers, sisters, and uncles?

What this way of approaching life did to people like me was that we were never quite able to know with absolute certainty who our parents' real fathers, mothers, brothers, and sisters were. I remember in my early teens travelling with *Keke* from village to village visiting. We would arrive in Bokodu, my mother's village, and he would introduce at least a dozen people to me as my mother's mothers, brothers, and sisters. Then we would go to Seidu village where he would introduce me to more of my mother's brothers and sisters. In Kakaydu, Kamabobu, Ngirima, Mofindoh, Sandaru and Kongonani he would introduce me to other groups of people as his own sisters and brothers. This was in addition to those who were in our own village in Lalehun. And this was just in Sierra Leone. At other times we would go to Kpangbaya, Sandia, Yibema, Basaydu, Koosodu and Kamakuma in neighbouring Guinea where I would be introduced to more of my mother's and *Keke*'s relations. Not allowed to ask specifically who the blood brothers, sisters, mothers and fathers of my parents were, I was, with a few exceptions, unable to find out. And polygamous marriages made relationships even more complex and difficult to decipher.

Dissatisfied with this state of affairs and planning to write a book in which I would tell the story of my life as a way of answering some of the questions my children continue asking me, I decided to find out. So, at home on a holiday from Ireland, I sat my mother and *Keke* down and asked them, "Tell me about Kissi people and their customs, my grandparents, uncles, and aunts. My children want to know and I want to be able to tell them with certainty." This was in Freetown where my parents were living for several years after they fled the decade-long brutal civil war.

A Long Lesson in History and Culture

"Yangasa was your grandfather. His wife's name was Nyande. They both were born in Sandia where they lived for many years. It was home for their forebearers for as far back as they could remember. It was also home for the people and language called Kissi to whom we belong. In fact, long ago before any encounters with White people, Sandia was a very tiny part of what was known as Kissi Country. In those days countries were determined by and named after the dominant ethnic group that settled a particular area. So, Kissi Country was the country of Kissi people, ruled by Kissi people, with Kissi language as the predominant language of communication. Brave Kissi warrior kings like Kailondo and Ndawa fought victoriously many a fierce battle against their enemies to protect the interests of their people, extend Kissi Country, increase their free labour force, and extend the influence of Kissi people and their culture. So Kissi Country then included all the areas where Kissi people in Guinea, Liberia and Sierra Leone live today. And Kissi Chiefs had absolute authority over their country and people."

As I listened to *Keke* I was reminded of one story I read long ago when I was doing my research in Christian missionary work among Mende people—another ethnic group in my country. It was about a Chief in what was known then as Mende Country. His name was Nyagua. Britain had already colonized the Freetown Area of Sierra Leone but her influence had not yet impacted much on the peoples and systems of the interior. The Hut Tax War which the British won against the rebellious Chiefs and peoples who refused to pay the British imposed tax had not yet been fought. It was during that time when two English Christian missionaries Vivian and Sage decided to go inland from the city of Freetown on a preaching tour. They hired hammock bearers to carry them.

A few days into their journey, news of their approach to chief Nyagua's Headquarter town reached the chief. Accompanied by a couple of his wives, Nyagua walked out of the town towards the approaching missionaries. As he got closer to them, he was shocked to see that these missionaries were been transported in a hammock; for only the chief was allowed that sort of treatment in his Country. On reaching them, he stopped the hammock bearers and asked the occupants to get down. One of them had a rifle in his hand which Chief Nyagua took off him and gave to one of his wives for safekeeping. He then sat in one of the hammocks and asked to be carried back into town by the hammock bearers while the missionaries and his wives followed him on foot. This action of the chief Nyagua gave me an interesting insight into the exercise of power and authority by chiefs in the days that my mother and step-father were talking about.[3]

"Farming was the way of life in those days." *Keke* continued. "A man's status was determined by the number of people under his control and by the size of his farm. Not infrequently, the desire for these invaluable assets led to wars. Slaves, wives, children, dependents, and other relations in a household were symbols of wealth for their owners. Human capital is what we call it

---

[3]   See my Dialectics of Evangelization (2002:88-9). Accra: Asempa Publishers

today. They provided the labour that was needed to produce food and to transport commodities from one place to another. Their presence deterred potential enemies from attacking him. They were his eyes and ears in and outside his village.

Polygamous and inter-ethnic marriages established alliances within and between societies, giving an increased sense of security to the man who enters into them. The bigger and more diverse the number of people under a man's influence, the more powerful he was considered to be. The members of his household were often treated with deference as a result. Demonstrating his prowess in amassing and exerting influence in this way was a convincing indication of his ability to lead. As a result, such a man was easily entrusted with positions of leadership in his society.

In addition to people, land was the other most valuable asset. After all, Kissi warrior kings, their chiefs, elders and people had fought and shed their blood to possess and retain the land. It was for Kissi people as a whole that they made that sacrifice and so Kissi land and Country belonged to all Kissi people. It was an asset to be held in trust for the use of the entire community. It was not for sale. Slaves, strangers, and Kissi people alike living in Kissi Country had right to land to live on, grow food, hunt, and enjoy its resources. To ensure that everyone was given equal access to its resources, special activities like planting, harvesting, and fishing the streams were regulated by the king, chiefs and elders who set dates when it was legal to engage in them. Violators were seen as selfish and greedy people and were punished by a fine imposed on them by the king, his chiefs and elders.

Valuable services were provided by specialized men and women. Community priests and priestesses were responsible for leading communal prayers. These were organized for special occasions. The beginning of the farming year was preceded by a ceremony of symbolic washing of farmland in which the entire community took part. Using water specially blessed by the priests, the community walked behind the priests on the main roads leading out of the village. As the priest walked he sprinkled the water on the bushes shouting '*fofain*'."

My nieces who were nearby listening to our conversation burst into laughter as they saw my father trying to demonstrate with his hands and voice how the priest did it in those days. '*Fofain*' is a very old Kissi expression which I did not understand. So I asked *Keke* to tell me what it meant. "Be clean! Be freed from any curse or impurity", he replied. "You see", he continued, "it was forbidden for a man and woman to have 'that' in the bush. The earth was believed to be the wife of the sky. When the sky rained on the earth the rain fertilized the earth and the earth in turn conceived and gave birth to the plants which provide us with food. Having 'that' on the ground was believed to defile the ground and breach the sacred relationship between the sky and the ground. If anyone had committed that offence unbeknown to the community, the washing ceremony of farmland was to remedy that problem and repair the damage that may have been done. After the ceremony which was accompanied with prayers and eating and drinking, the community was assured that the rain would fall again to water the land and help plants grow." Realizing that *Keke* was avoiding using the word 'sex' and, instead, referred to it as 'that', I smiled. He made me realize the vast difference between the world that shaped him and that in which my children now live.

"The end of the farming year was celebrated by a communal thanksgiving ceremony", he continued. "It was to thank the ancestors and *Hala Meleka*[4] for protecting the people during the farming year and providing for their needs through the harvest they had gathered. It was a great time of celebration amidst drumming and dancing, eating and drinking. It lasted for at least two days. A few days before the ceremony began, the whole village went hunting together and caught a lot of animals. The meat was divided between all the households equally. The priests and elders were given generous good portions in gratitude for their services to the community. Women went to the surrounding streams with their fishing nets to fish together. Chickens and goats were slaughtered if need be. Every household and family had plenty of rice, beans and vegetables. In those days nobody bought rice. It was in plentiful supply. The able-bodied men of the village tapped a lot of palm and bamboo wine, enough for everyone in the village who wanted to drink. So there was plenty of food, meat, and drinks for everyone. Even children who at other times were allowed only bony portions of meat were given meaty portions at this ceremony.

"Why were children not allowed meaty portions on other occasions? Was that not considered cruel of their parents?"

---

4   This is the long form of the name of God for Kissi people. The shortened form is 'Hala' or 'Meleka'

I interjected. *Keke* laughed wryly. "My son", he said, "it was not a matter of cruelty. Our parents believed in people waiting for their turn in everything. They believed that it was good for children to have something to look forward to when they grow up and are adults. This was one of many such things. You see my son, if you do everything you want to do in life while you are still a child what will you do when you are an adult?" "I see where you are coming from *Keke*." I responded.

"Community prayers are also said just before initiation ceremonies of the children of the community. If you can still remember we did the same thing in the years you were initiated. You were probably too young to remember it happening for your circumcision ceremony. But you were old enough to remember it happening when you were to be initiated into the *tomaporndo*[5] It was the year your mother and I had to take you out of school for a while to allow you to be initiated along with the other boys."

"Yes I do remember that time alright". I assured *Keke*. I was attending school in Sandaru then. I still recall arriving back in our village on the night before I was going to join the others. Worry was written all over mother's face. That did not help my own nerves either. "You see, *Keke*, a whole week before returning home for that initiation ceremony I had been worrying not knowing what the initiation process involved. And you know the scary stories adults tell children about the ceremony. So I still vividly remember the days before that ceremony."

---

[5] This is the name of the society into which young Kissi boys are initiated to prepare them for adulthood in their community.

"Those pre-ceremony community prayers were for a trouble-free initiation ceremony and a safe return of all the children into the community". *Keke* continued. "And they were led by the village priests. The priests, however, exercised no monopoly in religious matters. Every household had someone who was responsible for leading family religious ceremonies. These were often the oldest men or women in each household. Because of their age, they were seen as further on on their way into the next life and deemed to be spiritually more knowledgeable and powerful than other members of their households."

I was reminded from subsequent conversations with *Nde* and *Keke* that though death was considered a traumatic event by Kissi people, it was not viewed by them as something to be avoided by all means. Instead of a permanent separation, it was seen as a moving on into another realm of existence, only better. In that realm, I was told, the adult dead especially were still in daily contact with their living relations showing the same kind of love and concern they showed towards them in their previous life. The living on their part continued to venerate them if they had made valuable contributions to the society and had sons before their death. These were known and related to as 'the living-dead'. But the dead who added nothing of value to society and or produced no sons were considered truly dead and so were not venerated.

"In those days", *Keke* said, "there were no hospitals or schools like those we have today. But there were men and women who knew the medicinal value of some herbs and used them to heal people of their illnesses. They were people who had special knowledge about barks, leaves and roots of trees that had healing power for different problems. Some were given this knowledge in their dreams; others spent years working as fulltime apprentices with people who had this knowledge. You remember my father Kolokpasie? He spent ten years of his time being trained to become a healer. He had to leave Basaydu village where he and his family were to reside with the man who trained him. During those years he provided labour for the man and his family. That was the way people paid for their training then. And at the end of the ten years, his parents took a container of palmoil, two white cocks and some rice to the man who trained him to thank him for training their son." "Did the cocks have to be white?" I asked. "Oh yes. It was a way of saying to the man that their hearts were clean and pure towards him. It was after his training that your grandfather left to go and create Kayeima village just a few miles on the east of Kailahun town.

This is what healers usually did. Their patients would travel to go and consult them. Those who had serious illnesses that needed a long time to heal stayed in the village of the healer. In some cases members of their families also stayed with them there. Some of the patients with their relations would decide to stay in the village even after their problem had been solved. This is how those villages grew. All the people who stayed in them were believed to be living under the healing and protecting power of the healer whom they revered greatly. Before long he would be known far and wide as stories of his healing powers were spread by those he had healed and who had moved to live in his village.

There was another group of people who were closely related to healers. They were generally known as 'medicine' men. These were fortune tellers, sorcerers, or witchdoctors. Like healers, Kissi people still believe them to have supernatural spiritual powers. They were revered because it is believed that they have mystical powers to know and reveal unknown secrets concerning people and can cause them to fall ill or even die.

"To this day all medicine men are believed to have the capability to use their powers for good or evil", my mother decided at last to contribute to the conversation. "That is why all medicine men are feared greatly. While some medicine men always choose to use their powers for good, others are believed to use their powers to inflict illness on people or even kill them. There are always bad people who use all their time and powers trying to harm others. That is why our people believe that every illness, misfortune, and death is caused by evil people. These are witches who do not work in the interest of other people."

"Excuse me *Nde*." I interrupted her. "You remember what I told you was wrong with Fayia when we took him to hospital in Ireland to be operated on? The doctors told us that he was born with a blockage in his urethra. If he had lived in our village and died as a result of that illness, would people not have been wrong to say that he was killed by witches?"

"Not at all!" *Nde* replied. "People would have wanted that doctor to explain why it was that no other woman in the village gave birth to a child with that problem except my daughter. They would also want to know why my daughter died in the process of giving birth to Fayia. Have you forgotten that before my daughter gave birth to her son, she had spent over five months with us? Her husband's second wife hated her and because her husband loved the other woman more than her she was forced to leave her marriage home to come and live with us. How would you know that she or somebody in her husband's family did not have a hand in what happened to my daughter and her son?"

I detected in her voice at this point that she was trying hard not to cry. "Witches have only one aim in life: hurt, maim, and kill", she angrily told me in a matter of fact way. "That is why our people detest them. And that is why when they are found out by a witchdoctor or, for whatever reason, they confess their deeds, they are brought to the public square by the chiefs to face the whole community. And it does not matter what their status is when they are brought to face the community. They are made to publicly confess all the evil they have done. Insults are hurled at them by everyone beginning with the youngest to the oldest. Do you remember what Dennis told you last week about the people in our village who recently confessed they were witches? They were all found out by a witchdoctor before they confessed they were witches. All of them were publicly humiliated as a way of punishing them. That is how witches have always been treated by our people. People like that often run away because they cannot handle the shame of continuing to live in the same community." Mother concluded her outburst against witches.

As *Keke*, *Nde* and I continued our conversation, I remembered that *Keke* had mentioned earlier about a different kind of school Kissi people had before the new system of schooling that was now in place. *"Keke"*, I said, "tell me about the kind of school you had in those days".

"We had *tomaporndo* for boys and *tomabondo*[6] for girls" he told me. "Before people were considered to be adults they had to be initiated first into one of these societies as a rite of passage. The period of initiation was spent in a clearing in the forest. There the candidates were taught, trained, and prepared for adult living. Once the initiation ceremony was over and the candidates were graduated into the village community again, they were from that time on considered to be members of t*omaporndo* and *tomabondo* and so adults. From then on they were held squarely responsible for violation of any of the rules of our people because they had been taught them and could not plead ignorance. Until then if any of them broke a rule it was always overlooked after a reprimand. This is because prior to being initiated they were considered and treated as ignorant children. That is why our people don't treat those who are non-members of these societies with the same amount of respect as they would those who are members. In fact, they essentially treat them like ignorant children no matter what their age. It is why non-members of these two societies are not made chiefs by our people.

The first non-Kissi people who ever came to live among our people were *Feniah*. We called them so because they told us they came from a faraway place called *Fene* in Guinea.

---

[6]   This is the society into which girls are initiated to prepare them for adulthood.

25

We didn't quite know where this place was but we accepted them to live among us. Our people discovered shortly after accepting them that they were Muslims who were both traders and clerics. They came with bourbon sweets, jewellery, salt, sugar, and medicated oils and rubs. They also came with their religion. They settled among us and learnt to speak our language. Their way of life was pretty strange to us. We'd often see them either reading from a book, or washing their feet, their ears, mouths, and hands right up to the elbows, or praying. At first we used to laugh at the way they prayed, bending, bowing, kneeling, stretching their hands up with the palms opened towards the sky, sometimes muttering and other times shouting out 'Allah Wa Kubaru'. They were a pretty quiet, reserved, and reflective people with beads in their hands always and whispering things to themselves.

As time went on our people began to admire especially their persistent repetition of these activities several times a day, every day, week, month, and year. It was not too long before they began to tell us about a new way of praying to *Hala*. They called *Hala, 'Allah'*; and this *Allah*, they said, had told his intentions for human beings to a man called Mohammad. According to them, Allah's intentions were contained in 'the God Book' which they called *Koran*. From the book they would read in a strange language and translate what they told our people were the instructions of Allah to humankind. From what they told us it seemed this new religion was not really too different from our ways of life. We could marry several wives, make sacrifices to *Hala*, or practise medicine like their medicine men did. We too could carry on our bodies or keep in our homes or farms charms provided by medicine men to protect ourselves from witches who may have wanted to harm us in one way or the other. In the same way we were allowed to have charms to increase our luck, influence, or wisdom in whatever field we wished to excel ourselves. Some of the Muslim clerics themselves were believed to have even used portions of their God Book to harm people. The really distinctive new thing about this new religion was its Book and language. Our people did not know how to read and they did not understand the language in which the Book was written. There was also another thing. Those clerics were always men but were not members of the *tomaporndo*. This meant that our people would neither fully embrace them nor readily embrace their religion."

"As you rightly mentioned", I teased Keke, "Kissi people's religion did not have 'a God Book'. How did our people know what *Hala* expected of them?" "I don't know." He thoughtfully replied. "But our elders told us that long ago *Hala* used to live very close to them. So *Hala* used to hold conversations with the people to tell them how they should live. The people on their part used to tell *Hala* their problems. At a certain time, however, *Hala* decided to move away from them into the sky because *Hala* was angry that every time the women were pounding something their pestles hit *Hala* and every time they threw dirty water out from their huts on to the ground outside it splashed up and dirtied *Hala*. But before *Hala* moved away *Hala* instructed them to sacrifice a chicken anytime they wanted *Hala* to come close to them and listen to their concerns.

What our ancestors learned from *Hala* at the beginning they passed on to their children through stories, parables and ritual practice. That is the way things have been since. Because they practiced what they believed, our people were able to pass down their beliefs and practices to their children. That is one of the reasons why we treat our ancestors with great respect. It is because they took on the responsibility to teach us the ways of *Hala*. Practising what they taught us is one way we show our appreciation and respect for them."

At this point, Harry, the youngest of my siblings who was also listening in, asked, "And what exactly did the ancestors say *Hala* told them to do?" After a brief pause *Keke* exclaimed, "N*amu naa*", meaning 'our traditions'. Pressured to name them, he went on to list the initiation ceremonies for boys and girls, not having sex in the bush, venerating ancestors, not using supernatural powers to harm people, honouring one's parents and elders, welcoming strangers, respecting women and girls, paying a dowry for a woman you want to marry, regarding your maternal uncle as one whose blessings you need and whose curse you should avoid at all costs, . . ."

"Let me ask you another question." I said to *Keke* and *Nde*. "You know I am a Christian and Minister in the Church, right? I became a Christian because long ago some white people, like the Muslim clerics you told me about just now, came from their countries and told us about what they believed and asked that we adopt their beliefs and practices. Now I do the same, hoping to get people to become Christians. Was there ever a time when Kissi people went from place to place to tell other people what they knew about *Hala*?"

"Not that we know of." *Nde* responded. "But I doubt it. Our forebearers would have told us if that kind of thing happened; or we would have at least known people who were involved in such work. You see", she continued, "our people believed that what *Hala* told them was for them alone. If *Hala* wanted to tell something to other people *Hala* would tell them. So that is why I think our people never bothered to go round telling people about their religion."

Nde, however, added that nothing suggested that Kissi people ever denied anyone the right to know or practise Kissi religion if they chose to. Neither did she or *Keke* hint at anytime during the long conversations I had with them that Kissi people stopped other people from telling them their own stories of what *Hala* may have told them. In fact reading between the lines of what *Nde* and *Keke* said, I gleaned that Kissi people liked listening to such stories and had the goal of adding to their knowledge and practise of spiritual matters.

Reflecting on the Lesson

As I listened to *Keke* and *Nde* over a few days telling me about Kissi people, their customs, practices, and approach to the world, it began to dawn on me that Yangasa and his wife lived in a very complex world. This world had its own rules for living informed by its beliefs. Its government, social and economic systems were dictated by its needs and aspirations. Its people lived close to nature and respected it. They were patently aware of nature's almost predictable rhythms and so arranged their own activities to fit in with the requirements of those rhythms. Rules were put in place to check selfish individualism and rituals were conducted to address imbalances to nature and relationships caused by human failings. Old age was equated with knowledge, wisdom, and authority. So, old people were given the role of giving advice to, praying for, and blessing their people. In turn they received honour, care, and protection from the community if they lived honorable lives. No important decision was made in the family or by the community without consulting with the ancestors.

Reflecting on much that they shared with me, it began to dawn on me gradually that the world in which my ancestors lived had value systems, a simplicity of life, and an earthiness about life which I could only imagine and long for. But it was also a world ravaged with debilitating fear, ignorance, discrimination, and the abuse of power. The reality of jungle was ever so present with them both in their village communities and outside of them.

Yet, the seemingly unsophisticated and precarious world *Nde* and *Keke* depicted seemed to have mastered the art of living with contradictions. Singularly supportive of communal interests over individual pursuits, it nonetheless had room and respect for people who wanted to better their positions. While its people were open to new ways of seeing and living in the world, age old customs and traditions determined the changes in attitude and practice they embraced. Strangers were welcomed; but to be truly integrated and considered as fully one of them they had to go through the initiation rites for acceptance as adults in Kissi society. Kissi people were not unfamiliar with drawing boundaries that excluded; but they were not incapable of embracing outsiders. It was a world which had a lot in its favour but still had a long way to go. How far it was willing to go no one could predict. One thing though was certain. Life in Kissi Country was set to become even more complicated and challenging.

THREE

PEOPLE ON THE MOVE

Founding New Settlements

It seems from what *Keke* and *Nde* told me that Kissi people were not afraid to dream for a better future for themselves and their children. For whatever reasons, Yangasa, they told me, became dissatisfied with life in Sandia. Believing that he could do better in another place, he persuaded his wife Nyande and some other close relations to leave. His intention was to go to the other side of the river Meli to found a new settlement there. There were Kissi people already living across the river who were relations of Yangasa. Kobba, Ndoli, Fayia and their families had moved there from Sandia and Yibema and Kpangbaya many years earlier. There they had created a settlement of their own called Lalehun, and had become its main leaders. Kobba even prospered enough to become the first and only person to ever build a two storey house. This was something no other person in Kissi Country had done before. Yes, it was built of mud blocks and timber walls and floors, but it was a unique achievement that many admired and talked about long after he died.

So, when Yangasa and his relations decided to move across the river they were neither pioneers in this venture nor were they being foolhardy. They had examples that inspired them. Besides, they knew help would be available if they needed it. The result of their venture was Folodu village, situated about ten miles up the river from Lalehun. There, Yangasa, his wife Nyande, their two sons and a few relations settled for many years to come under Yangasa's leadership. They successfully ran their own lives, acquired control over large areas of land for agricultural production, and pursued their interests. Life in Folodu offered them new opportunities and responsibilities.

This did not, however, mean a severing of relationships with their roots. Yangasa and his Folodu family frequently paid visits to other extended family members in Lalehun, Sandia, and other villages. They attended family meetings, initiation, marriage and funeral ceremonies, and even worked on farms of relations when there was need to give assistance. "One tree cannot form a forest" is a Kissi saying that always reinforced in them the need to cultivate relationship.

Father Leaves Home for Sandaru

The younger of Yangasa and Nyande's two sons was Yambasu Yaniwah. If there is any truth in the saying that 'what goes around comes around', the Yangasa family certainly proved it. "One day", *Keke* told me, "Yambasu came to his father

Yangasa and asked for permission to leave Folodu. His intended destination was a town called Sandaru. Sandaru was in Mende Country about seventeen miles west of Folodu. A much bigger and long established settlement, Yambasu discerned that there would be much better prospects there of improving his lot. A certain Nyaley, an aunt of his, was married in the town and had lived there for many years. Yambasu had heard about her from his father and begged to be released to go and visit her. Seeing life in Sandaru confirmed what he had believed, and he decided to stay there with his aunt. You see", *Keke* continued, "Yambasu had heard that white people had introduced new ways of life where aunt Nyaley lived. So when he arrived there and saw for himself what was happening he liked it and did not want to return to Folodu village."

British Colonial Influence

I recalled that years before Yambasu had made his decision, the scramble for Africa by Europeans had taken place. At a conference in Berlin[7] European nations had divided between themselves the African continent and each nation proceeded to take possession of the areas it allocated to itself. Consequently the political system that had held Kissi people together for centuries as one country and people was ended. Using rivers as borders between countries the colonial system that was introduced created serious problems for Kissi Country. Kissi

---

[7] This conference started on November 15, 1884 and ended on February 26, 1885

people ended up split between the three artificially created countries called Guinea, Liberia and Sierra Leone and under three different political jurisdictions and systems of rule. The rivers Meli and Moa formed the boundary between Sierra Leone and Guinea, and the river Manor formed the boundary between Sierra Leone, Guinea and Liberia. Consequently, Sandia, my grand parents' home village, came under French political rule in Guinea while Lalehun, Folodu, and Sandaru came under British political rule in Sierra Leone. So by the time Yambasu moved to Sandaru it was already experiencing the impact of British indirect rule.

Under this system the whole of Sierra Leone was divided up into four regions: the Western Area, and the Southern, Northern and Eastern Provinces. The Western Area which was composed of Freetown and its surrounding villages was called the Sierra Leone Colony and the three Provinces were known as the Sierra Leone Protectorate. While the colony was divided into Wards, the Protectorate was divided into Sections, Chiefdoms, and Districts.

Sections were made up of several villages and towns and were headed by Sections chiefs, speakers and elders. These were men and women who had proven they had the ability and competence to be leaders and so were elected by their peoples. Often they were essentially those who had held leadership positions among their people before the advent of British rule. Chiefdoms were made up of Sections and had Paramount Chiefs to administer them. A number of Chiefdoms constituted a District which was placed under the administration of a District Commissioner. And a number of

Districts together constituted a Province which was headed by a Provincial Secretary.

The selection of Paramount Chiefs was often closely monitored and influenced by colonial officers. This was deemed to be necessary because Paramount Chiefs were key power holders who could make colonial control of the Chiefdoms impossible if for any reason they decided to do so. In the Kissi language a Paramount Chief was known as *Masalelengdo* which roughly translates as 'ruler of the land'. So for Kissi people the Paramount Chief was the real ruler of the land. His name reflected his importance and it spoke of the legitimacy and authority of his rule.

Paramount Chiefs were always natives of the area they were elected to rule. They wielded a great deal of economic, political, and religious power. In fact the first port of call for any visitor in any Chiefdom was and still is with the Paramount Chief or his/her Speaker.

I read a story once about Christian missionaries who visited a Chiefdom Headquarters town in former Kissi Country. The missionaries in question, however, failed to report their presence and mission to the Paramount Chief of the territory. As they were about to start preaching to the people they were summoned to the Chief's Court. On arrival they were asked to explain their action in front of everyone present. After answering many questions and apologizing for their misconduct the Chief took a white Kola nut out of his pocket, offered a portion to each of the offenders against native custom as a sign of forgiveness and reconciliation. The Chief and the missionaries ate their parts of the nut to seal the pact. In front of the gathered people the Chief declared that the white men and himself were henceforth friends, and that his people were theirs. The missionaries were then allowed to hold their preaching meeting. Thus it was that those Christian missionaries had to experience Kissi people's forgiveness first before they could preach their gospel of forgiveness to them. The sinners in that case were the missionaries who stood in need of forgiveness and reconciliation. And it was granted them.[8]

Life in Sandaru

Sandaru, the town Yambasu had relocated to from Folodu, was the Chiefdom Headquarter town of Penguia in the Sandaru Section. It was in the Kailahun District in the Eastern Province. At the time Yambasu arrived in Sandaru the Paramount Chief was Gulama. Sandaru housed the Native Authority Court Clerk, the Chiefdom Police and Chiefdom Prison. There, as Yambasu found out, there were clear signs that British colonial rule was already taking deep roots. It was this new world with its new resources of power that Yambasu saw and wanted to be a part of. In Sandaru he believed he would be better positioned to have access to at least some of the new resources and the power and influence they brought with them.

---

[8] See my Dialectics of Evangelization (2002:89-90) Accra: Asempa Publishers

How right he was! "Living with his aunt", *Keke* continued, "Yambasu proved to be a very hard working and diligent man. Small as communities were in those days, people quickly got to know him. Over time, Paramount Chief Gulama, being a distant relation of Aunt Nyaley, also got to know of him. Yambasu Yaniwah soon gained the admiration of the Chief, even though he was not aware of it."

"One day", as he once told his Folodu family while on a routine visit with them, "he got a message from his aunt that the Chief wanted to see him. Apprehensive, confused, and agitated, he wondered what crime he might have committed for the Chief to want to see him. Despite aunt Nyaley's assurances and encouragement, he worriedly made his way into the Chief's very large compound and then into his big house. It was his first time ever into the compound. On entering the Chief's house he could hardly believe his eyes. It was the biggest and most beautiful house he had ever seen. It was built with mud bricks, the walls inside and outside plastered with cement and painted golden green. The roof was made of corrugated aluminum sheets. In the house was a very large room with cement concreted and uncarpeted floors. It was in this room that people who came to visit the Chief were received. The room had many large windows letting in a lot of fresh air and keeping it cool all the time."

'Sit down over there', one of the Chief's elders directed him to a seat against the wall directly opposite where the Chief was seated. Frightfully anxious and with his legs barely holding him up, he slowly walked over to the seat facing the Chief who was flanked on both sides by a number of elders.

'The Chief says he has heard a lot about you' one of the men told Yambasu. 'He has heard how you came to live here and how you have carried yourself in this community. He has called you here to let you know that he is pleased with your behaviour and courage.'

Yambasu told his family that he listened intently but did not utter a word, except for a nervous nod of his head. 'The Chief has decided that you should become one of his court messengers. Your job will be to fetch to court people whose complains are brought to the Chief. This will mean travelling to where they live and bringing them back here with you.'

For a while he said he sat dumb-founded, and then he summed up courage to speak after getting over his initial shock and disbelief. 'I have heard you, Chief, and thank you from the bottom of my heart for offering me this job. I am your subject and am ready to serve you always.' That was all he said he was able to say. After a brief period of silence the same elder said to him that he was free to leave.

Greatly relieved, but amazed and unsure that he was not just dreaming what he had seen and heard, Yambasu slowly edged his way out of the Chief's presence, out into the open big compound which held other much smaller and less beautiful houses. Those houses housed the Chief's wives, children and other relations. After making sure that no one was looking at him, he took a deep breath and almost ran home to share the good news with his aunt."

Nde told me that it was not too long after before Yambasu became a well known personality throughout the Chiefdom. "People regarded him with great respect and fear", she said with great satisfaction and pride. "He was respected because of what people believed he had succeeded in achieving; and he was feared because anytime he visited a village people knew someone was being summoned to the Chiefdom Court, and that it could be them or a loved one."

"So," I decided to ask *Nde*, "what about your side of the family? So far nothing has been said about your people." After what seemed to me to be a long silence thinking about what to say, she finally began, "My father and mother also came from across the river from a place called Kolomba, about ten miles east of Sandia where Yambasu's dad originally came from. My father Sovula and his two wives Yawa and Norwoh came over and built Bokodu village. While there my father's wives between them bore him seven children: Josiah, Alieu, Ngawuja, Nabieu, my two sisters Nehma and Mattu, and then me.

I was the only child to my mother Yawa and she died when I was only about five years old. I don't know what she died of, but after she died *Nde* Norwoh was saddled with the additional responsibility of taking care of me. It was not an easy task for her having six other children to rear, and as a result I sometimes suffered from discrimination and neglect." At this point I detected that her voice was shaky. She took a long pause trying to fight away the tears. "But my brothers and sisters were very kind to me. Josiah and Ngawuja eventually moved to settle in Seydu after they got married, while Alieu and Nabieu remained in Bokodu. My sister Nehma got married to the famous witchdoctor Fayia Kormenday in Guinea."

Then *Nde* switched the conversation back to my father Yambasu. "Your father did really make a name for himself in his job as Native Authority Court Messenger. Earlier in the job, he married two wives for himself, Amie and Satta. Both Amie (the first and older of the two wives) and Satta were not originally natives of Kissi Country, even though they eventually learnt Kissi. I believe they were natives of Mende Country from somewhere in the Kenema area. That is what your father said anyway and we did not bother to ask him to tell us exactly where they came from. You see", she continued, "in those days even a place twenty miles away seemed like the end of the earth and was not worth one's time and energy to find out where exactly it was. All that was important was that he met, married, and brought them to live with him in Sandaru. As we were saying to you yesterday, in those days the way a man's success was measured was not just by the size of his rice farm, plantation, and house. It was also measured by whether or not he could win a woman's and her parents' hearts for marriage. The way a man sometimes knew he was successful was when parents offered their girls to him to marry. Families who did so were often making strategic and calculated decisions, knowing that in times of need—and there were many—they could count on the support and protection of their daughters' husbands."

As *Nde* spoke, I realised how, in a society like theirs without any formal system of social welfare, having such a support system could have been extremely important. I also recalled how in an earlier conversation they had hinted that many wives and large families were also an important source of labour, creating and increasing the wealth and power base of a person who acquired them. That was when *Keke* told me about the old saying that "He who has a large and extended family has many ears and eyes." When I asked what the saying meant he told me that a person with a large family is guaranteed to hear and see many things including the secrets of his enemies. The reason for this is plain, he told me. "Members of his or her family and extended family become his eyes and ears and because they are so widely dispersed, they can hear and see many things that he may not be able to see and hear." I remember thinking to myself then, "In a society without daily newspapers, radio, television, or mobile phones, I can see the advantage of this social system."

"So", *Nde* continued, "Yambasu was privileged to marry three more women—Matta, Mattu and me, in that order. Mattu was my older sister, as you know. You see, your father was unlucky with his first two wives because none of them were able to provide him with children. This became a matter of grave concern and dissatisfaction to him and his parents, because children were a symbol of fecundity and a source of wealth. Apart from the fact that this lack of children from his two wives undermined his already achieved success and posed a serious challenge to his manhood, it also meant that he had no sons to carry on his name and family line. Girls, our people believed, eventually got married, took on the family names of their husbands, and left their own homes and families for the homes and families of their husbands. So it was important for a man not only to get married and have children, but to especially produce sons, because at home or away from home sons were believed to always preserve the father's name and family line. In return they were rewarded with the privilege and responsibility of inheriting all the assets of their fathers.

In order to help Yambasu have his own children and sons and, so, keep him happy, your *Mama* Amie first allowed him to marry Satta. But when Satta could not bear him any children Matta, his own native Kissi girl was married for him. Matta bore him five children—three girls and two boys. Only two of the girls (Kumba and Lombeh) and one of the boys (Tamba) survived. But Tamba was born a long time afterwards. Still wanting to have at least a son Amie, Satta, and Matta together helped him marry my older sister Mattu who bore him four children two of whom died in infancy. The other two, a son Sahr Borbor and a daughter Sia Amie, lived. With the birth of sister Mattu's Sahr Borbor, Yambasu got the first son that survived. It was after that that my sister Mattu encouraged him to marry me. I bore him another four children, first your sister Sia Messie, then yourself, followed by your brothers Tamba Sheku and Fayia Emmanuel. Matta's son Tamba Steven was born a year before your brother Fayia. So you were Yambasu's second son", *Nde* told me. "On the morning you were born", she continued, "Sandaru was filled with shouts, shrieks and songs of joy by the women. A second son has been born to Yambasu", they announced loudly, "by Sia Abbie of Bokodu."

As *Nde* told me about the cooking, eating, drinking and partying that took place that day, I tried to imagine how the other two childless wives of my father may have felt especially on a day like that. "No wonder" I thought to myself, "Satta eventually left for her home. She must have realised that there was little she could look forward to in her marriage." And yet, I still remember my mother often privately instructing us her children regarding *Nde* Satta. That is the way we addressed her because we addressed all our father's wives as our mothers and his eldest wife as *Mama*. To do anything different would have invited unfavourable attention to say the least. *Nde* told us to never do anything that would remind *Nde* Satta that she was childless. "If N*de* Satta asks you to do anything for her", she often warned us, "be sure you do it immediately. Even if you have work to do for me or for another person, be sure to attend to her request first." The other wives of my father privately told their own children the same thing regarding *Nde* Satta. And all of us children acted towards her exactly as we were instructed to do.

Thinking about it now, it seems that nothing anybody did to lighten her burden was enough to keep her in the marriage and family. But *Mama* Amie stayed and even outlived my father. For most of my early childhood days I was brought up by her. She had, through allowing my father to marry other (and younger) women, promoted herself to the status of mother to the other wives and grandmother to all the children born to my father. The other wives treated her with deference, saving her the trouble of daily exerting and tiring physical tasks of rural farming life. It was because of her age and status that all of us children of the family addressed her as M*ama* Amie. As she grew older and older, she took on a nickname for herself. It was *Mama Nyamui,* meaning 'bad grandmother'. It was her way of telling us bratty children that she was a 'no nonsense' grandmother.

Feeling a little bit left out of the conversation, *Keke* noted that long before I was born he and the other nephews of my father used to live with their parents across the river in Basedu, Sandia, and Yibema. But they too had left with their parents to found a settlement about five miles from Bokodu. They called it Yandehun. But after living there for years most of their parents and guardians died, leaving them to fend for themselves. So a year before I was born, *Keke* Yambasu invited them all to join him at Sandaru where he believed they would be better looked after and cared for. As a result Yandehun was deserted.

But little did *Keke* Yambasu know then that his days in Sandaru were somewhat numbered. For when Kobba his relation in Lalehun became Section chief there with Ndoli as his deputy, both of these men wanted *Keke* Yambasu to leave his job at Sandaru and join them in Lalehun. "You have to bear in mind", *Keke* reminded me, "that while uncle Yambasu was working as court messenger he had been exposed to ways of life and resources that people in Lalehun and Folodu knew nothing about. So Kobba and Ndoli believed he could be of invaluable help and support to them if he returned to stay with them. After much persuasion uncle Yambasu accepted their request, bid Chief Gulama goodbye, packed in his job, and left to go and settle in Lalehun. He brought with him his wives, children, and nephews Isa, Joseph and me. His other nephews Sundifu and Samuel were already away with distant relations attending school. So though uncle Yambasu had gone to Sandaru as a single man, he returned blessed with a large family of his own."

Life in Lalehun

"By the time uncle Yambasu returned home to Lalehun", *Keke* continued, "his father Yangasa and mother Nyande had passed away and the other inhabitants of Folodu relocated to Lalehun. Once in Lalehun, he was shown land to farm for his and his family's needs. With our help, he also built the three bedroom mud walled house roofed with corrugated iron sheets which as you well know existed until it was destroyed during the recent civil war. In one room he lived, in another *Mama* Amie lived, and the third room was reserved for visitors. This was no mean achievement in those days when less than a handful of houses in Lalehun were tin roofed. For us it was another public demonstration of uncle Yambasu's success in life, and we held him in high esteem because of this. A big round thatched mud house was also built. This was to house the rest of his wives, each of whom had her own bed in it. Each of us his nephews also built a hut for ourselves."

The houses *Keke* was talking about no longer exist, but growing up in them I knew them very well. Directly in front of each wife's bed in the big round mud thatched house was a fire place where she prepared her meals. The house was approximately thirty feet in diameter. In the middle there was a round mud seat, about two feet in diameter with a large wooden pillar in the middle supporting the roof of the house. That was the seat that was often offered to visitors. Children and their mothers often sat on small cane seats round their fireplaces. Behind this mud seat facing the only door into the house, four big round mud water pots sat against the wall on a raised platform. These always had fresh supplies of cold water for all.

Not surprisingly, especially at night time when everyone was home from the farm, this house was often teaming with activity, and boisterous conversations were going on in every section of it and all at the same time. While my mother and her children conversed in their section of the house, the other mothers and their children did the same. Living and growing up in that environment as children, we had to learn quickly and develop the skill and capability to listen to all the conversations going on and make sense of them. Mothers, children and visitors shouted information, questions and answers to each other across this one big room of a house. We quickly learned from seeing what the adults did then that one had to seize the initiative to say what one wanted to say and not wait until one was asked to speak, as this seldom happened.

Except for festive days, day times were mostly quiet because most of those who usually lived there were out on the farms. Only children who were not old enough to go to the farm, our M*ama* Amie, a few elderly relations and an odd visitor would be there during the day. The same was true of the rest of Lalehun village.

Mama Amie always spoilt us her grandchildren with kindness and good food. We got everything we asked for and as quickly as possible. I still remember times when I was a little ill with a headache or something else. *Mama* Amie would bath me in warm water using home made black soap, rub burnt palm oil all over my body, and let me lie down on her bed. She would then cover me up with lots of cloth. Now and again she would suggest this or that food to me and ask what I wanted to eat. She would then go away very quickly and prepare it: pepper soup, rice and palmoil soup, pineapple, rice pap, and so on. On such occasions I exaggerated the illness as much as I could because I knew the more I did so the more attention I got from her. The longer I let it go on the more pampering I enjoyed. *Mama* Amie's other grandchildren were no different. There were times at home when falling ill was like a competition between each of us grandchildren one trying to outdo the others for attention and pampering. But she never seemed to be tired of us.

Thinking about it now I think she knew what we were up to and was somewhat entertained by our little machinations. Not surprisingly we all were a lot fonder of our *Mama* Amie (especially in the earlier years of our growing up) than we would have been of our own mothers of whom we saw very little because they left home early in the morning for the farm and returned late at night when we were already tired and ready to go to bed.

A Village Doctor

Nde recalled one of the periods in her life she told me she would never forget. "Just over two years after we arrived in Lalehun from Sandaru", she said, "you took seriously ill. You were so ill and pale that I feared you might never live. Your dad decided that we take you to Sandia his original home to see a family healer there whom he believed might be able to sort out your problem. But I think he had resolved that if you did not live it would be better for him that you died where he was born.

"I spent many weeks with you in Sandia as the healer tried you on different herbal mixtures. There were days when I thought you might never live to see another day. I spent such days sobbing interspersed with loud weeping. During the time I was staying with you there, your father Yambasu lived between Lalehun and Sandia, risking crossing over to Sandia and back to Lalehun every evening and morning most days. It was during the rainy season and Meli was often dangerously flooded. As time went on and your condition had not improved I continued to fear for the worst. For many days and nights I had little or no sleep afraid that you might die while I slept.

"Then one very early morning the healer walked into the mud hut where I lived with you. I was worried when he came in thinking that he had bad news for me. But he looked very calm and confident as he greeted me and told me that he had been directed overnight to try another herb which he believed would help reverse your condition. I never asked him who directed him. But the excitement on the man's face and the calm confidence with which he spoke told me that he was on to something significant and not merely trying to calm my fears. 'Something definitely important has happened to this man overnight', I thought to myself.

"As he left me he told me he'd be back after a short while. True to his promise he was back by the time everyone else in the village was up. He came in to me with some leaves which he handed me to boil. He instructed me that you should drink some of the water in which the leaves were boiled and then bathe with the rest of it. That was it. It was as simple and straightforward as that.

"I immediately did exactly what he told me to do and laid you down by the fire to sleep. As usual I then sat down watching you. Suddenly you woke up vomiting violently and before long round worms started coming out of your mouth and nostrils. I was afraid you would choke on them so I shouted for help. The healer was the first person on the scene. I believe now that he was expecting it to happen. He took you away from me and held you face down tapping your back gently. When you stopped vomiting he handed you over to me and I wiped you clean and laid you down again. He told me to prepare some food for you so that it would be ready before you woke up.

"How absolutely right he was!" *Nde* said. "When you woke up from your sleep in the early afternoon the first thing you asked for was food to eat. I was overjoyed when I heard you say those words because for many weeks you had eaten only what little had been painstakingly forced down your throat. But that day you asked for food yourself. That was a sign for me that you had passed the point of dying. And you know", she looked into my eyes, "I was right. From that day on you gradually increased in health and strength, and about a month later you were completely well again. Oh! I nearly forgot to tell you that the day after you vomited the worms you also passed out some worms through your stool. "Huh!" She sighed stretching both her hands towards the sky and saying, "Sometimes when I see you I still do think of that man who healed you. But for him you probably would not be here today."

From the time *Nde* told me this story I have often wondered what special guidance that healer received the night before he decided how to treat my illness. By whom was he guided? Was he a dreamer and visionary too? Did he possibly have the powers to journey between the seen and unseen worlds? I have asked *Nde* what guidance he could have received and from whom, but she did not know and never bothered to ask him. I have often been baffled by her decision not to ask. Nonetheless, I have never forgotten her response to my inquisitiveness. "My son" she said after reflecting for a while, "Only *Hala* knows. There are things in life that we will never know", she continued. "We are not meant to know everything." After saying this she left me pondering her reply to my enquiry. She went to attend to a neighbour who had come to see her. I resolved after a while that I would never ask her or anyone again about that incident. Like a student to a master teacher, I decided to remain silent at her feet and continue to reflect on the probable truth of her statement.

Unanswered Questions

As I continue to ponder the stories of my people that *Keke* and *Nde* told me there are still many questions that I do not have any answers to. Who exactly, for example, were Kobba,

Ndoli and Fayia who founded Lalehun? How were they related to grandfather Yangasa and then my father Yambasu Yaniwah? Where did *Mama* Amie and *Nde* Satta actually come from? Who were their parents? Did they have siblings? And how in the name of fortune did my father meet them and where? I knew *Keke's* father and mother. But who were the mothers and fathers of my father's other nephews? Why did they, Kobba, Ndoli, Yangasa, and Sovula decide to settle across the river away from their original homes? To these and many other questions *Nde* and *Keke* were not able to provide me clear answers. Maybe these are some of the things in my life that I am not meant to know and will never know. And in some strange way I have come to accept that.

Desiring Better

People on the move? Yes, leaving home, separating from loved ones, clearing jungle forests, building new homes, establishing new relationships of love, and keeping links with the past in order to address present needs. These stories have given me a sense of a people who were at once at home and away from home, displaced sometimes by choice and at other times by circumstances. These stories, I have concluded, are stories of the need for a better life. For in them I have discovered the human ability to dream and dare to risk following dreams, a deep desire and an innate hunger for more, and the human need of others to help them feed their hunger. In short, they are stories of human beings seeking to tame the jungles of life and living.

Whatever reasons my people had for leaving home in the first place, one thing I now know was certain. They were men and women who had and used their power to decide who and what they wanted to be. Their decisions changed their lives forever. Dreaming to be free of whatever it was they believed threatened and diminished their existence, their dreams led them to domesticate physical and human jungles. The process in turn changed them into the people they were not before they decided to leave. Yet their search for the ideal life was never over. Perhaps for them getting what they dreamed of was not as important as having the dream and embarking on a journey they believed would lead them to the reality of what they dreamed. And, while I may never know why they did or said or thought certain things, I am no longer in doubt that they somehow enlisted me on the journey they embarked on. As to where exactly that journey would lead, I am not certain. I do not think my people were either. But, like them, the desire to venture out must be attended to, trusting that one is not alone on that journey and that help will be available from fellow travellers.

FOUR

MEMORIES OF MY FATHER

A Desire to Learn New Skills

One of the earliest things I remember as a child is that *Keke* Yambasu often had more food than he could eat alone. With five wives, he was always guaranteed five dishes of rice and sauce, one each from his five wives. But he also had many mouths to feed. There were his nephews, children, other relations, many friends, and visitors. Meal times were often interesting times, especially just before they started. "Aisa!" *Keke* Yambasu will call one of his nephews. "Go down to Bana's house, see if he is there, and invite him to join us for food."

Bana was more than just another rural village subsistence farmer. In addition to everything else he was and did, Bana was also what was known in the village as a 'Saw Man'. He was one of about eight men who had acquired the skill of producing the timber needed by those who wanted to build modern type houses. *Keke* was one of those 'Saw Men', and I later learnt that he and the others were trained by Bana. So Bana was held in very high esteem in the village.

Until relatively recently, I never really found out where Bana learnt the skill. I had concluded that he did not learn the skill in our village. But on asking *Keke*, he told me that Bana learnt the skill from Bakalie who in turn learnt the skill from someone in his village of Buyeidu over sixty miles west of Lalehun towards the now Liberia and Sierra Leone border. Bakalie's village was part of the pre-colonial times Kissi Country. "He had travelled that far", *Keke* told me, "because he was looking for better prospects elsewhere. Reading between the lines of my discussion with *Keke*, it seems that there were many 'Saw Men' in Bakalie's village then. So he decided to venture out looking for a place that would need his skills and services. That is how he eventually arrived in our village carrying with him his eight feet long steel saw blade and settled there. It also seems that he had some money with him when he arrived because the first thing he did was to start buying and selling local and non-local products. After he had lived in the village for a while, he trained Bana and Ellie how to produce timber.

On several occasions I visited *Keke* and the others when they were engaged in the process of splitting up huge logs to produce timber. It often would take anything between a week to three weeks on one log depending on the size of log and the type of tree. Whoever they were working for was responsible for feeding them during the period. There were no real time limits set for any requests for timber to be fulfilled since the

'Saw Men' were full time farmers and engaged in timber production only on days they could afford to do so without affecting their farming work in serious ways.

On my visits to the site of production I was often fascinated by what I saw. The process of production was started by cutting down a big tree. This was chopped up into acceptable lengths and a log at a time mounted on a platform of between eighteen and twenty feet high built of sturdy smaller logs. The job of mounting a log always required the help of many strong men recruited by the person who commissioned the production of the timber. Once mounted, the log was tightly tied in place. The 'Saw Men' would then bring their steel Saw blades, a rope liner, black ink-like liquid into which the liner was dipped for lining the log for the different widths of the timber required, and wooden pegs of different sizes to start their work. The rope liner was used for ruling the log. This was done by dipping it into black ink-like liquid first. The rope was then run along the whole length of the log in a straight line and held tightly at both ends by two people. A third person would then pull it up while it is still being held tightly and let it go so that it hit the log leaving a straight black mark along its length. This was done several times until the black line could be seen clearly. It was this line that the 'Saw Men' followed as they sawed the timber.

The sawing itself was done by two men at any one time while the others watched and assisted in any other way needed. Of the two men engaged in sawing, one balanced himself on the log holding on to the handle of the top and broader part of the Saw. The other stood on the ground holding onto the handle of the bottom and narrower part of the Saw, vertically aligned with one of the black lines that had been earlier made on the log. As the one on the log pulled the Saw, the one on the ground push it up. This was followed by a coordinated reverse movement. The simultaneous pulling up and pushing down movements by both quickly settled into an almost predictable rhythm. As a child visiting *Keke* at those sites, I still remember making my own musical sounds to coincide with the seesawing sound that the 'Saw Men' were making and its echoes in the forest. Now and again the sawing would stop for wooden pegs to be inserted in appropriate places along the sawn portion. This was done to help ease the seesawing movement of the Saw. Now and again the Saw was oiled; and when it was needed, the Saw was also filed.

Bana was one of *Keke* Yambasu's about half a dozen close friends in the village. As I grew up and began to understand the interactions between the peoples in my village, I came to realize that *Keke* Yambasu and his friends characterized their relationship in terms of brotherhood rather than friendship. This was another contributory factor to the difficulty I had deciphering who my parents' real siblings were.

As Aisa was setting out on the errand to call Bana, the other two nephews Robert (my *Keke*) and Joseph would be sent out to invite other friends and relations. According to *Keke,* the nephews were often less than enthusiastic about running those errands. They knew that more people at meal times meant less food for them. I have been told stories of what they sometimes did to avoid actually inviting the people they were sent to invite. Sometimes they, on leaving the house and supposedly going to deliver the invitations, would stand in the dark for a reasonable amount of time (if it was at night time) shielded from sight, and then returning panting with the message: "He is not at home." There is a famous true story about Aisa who, when sometimes sent on such errands on rainy nights, just went out of the house, stood on the edge of the veranda for a while with his head in the rain, walked back in and reported: "He is not there." It was not the rain that kept Aisa from going, of course. It was the worry that he might not have enough to eat if all those my father wanted to join them came.

The Many Roles of Food

Among my people, food was important for more than its ability to satisfy hunger. Eating had its own rituals to observe. A bit of the food was always thrown to the ground accompanied with words of thanksgiving and an invitation to the ancestral spirits to join the living in the meal. This was often done by the host or the oldest person present before the eating started. This was followed by all of the food to be eaten being put into a large round bowl and all the sauce poured over it. Everyone present then washed their right hands in one bowl of water, sat round the basin, and then dipped their hands into the bowl now and again to take a handful. There was a difference between taking a handful and being greedy, and it did not take long for a culprit to find out when they had crossed from the acceptable threshold to the unacceptable.

Everyone had to be careful to observe the etiquette. At the beginning of a meal, for example, young folk were not allowed to dip their hands in the bowl before the older folks. During the meal, they were also not allowed to freely venture towards the meat or fish. The older folk would in the course of the meal push directly within the immediate reach of the younger folk the bits of meat and fish they wanted them to have. That was a nod to say they could have those bits. Older folk on their part were expected to stop eating before all of the food in the bowl was finished. This gave the younger folk the opportunity to make up for what they may not have eaten as a result of fear of not overstepping the expectations placed on them.

Food was used to communicate the presence or otherwise of love and relationship. You showed people you loved them by inviting them to eat with you from the same bowl. Strangers knew they were welcomed by the amount of food they were given, the frequency of its offer, and the amount of time that was given to its preparation. Welcomed strangers were never allowed to go hungry. That is why they were always served separately. As early as possible, children were discouraged from eating alone and by themselves. My earliest memories of meal times in our household were of girls eating with their mothers and boys eating with their fathers from the same bowl.

Food was also a medium for bringing people together and nurturing relationships with the living and the living dead. When strained relations between two people or groups of people were mended, eating food together was how they demonstrated they no longer had any bad feelings for each other. Eating food together in such circumstances was a powerful sign of reconciliation. That was why food was often cooked at the end of disputes for the disputing parties to partake in with the rest of the community who sought to reconcile them. Ritual ceremonies of thanksgiving and prayer were also always accompanied by sharing in food. Consequently, food was always at the centre of my people's life, either as a mere satisfier of hunger, or as a means of building up and sustaining community within the living and with the living dead.

Growing up within that society, I quickly came to realize how important it was that chiefs and elders often made sure they had plenty of food and shared it with others. I came to understand as well why many meal times were held in open communal spaces; and why people who always ate on their own were considered as antisocial, greedy and strange. With time, *Keke* told me, he and his brothers got to learn that this was the way to live as community, and embraced it. They realized that their little tricks to discourage *Keke* Yambasu's practice of inviting outsiders to share in their food would change nothing.

A Disciplinarian of Sorts

Keke Yambasu was a disciplinarian of sorts, but a man of principles as well. 'Spare the rod and spoil the child' is a saying often associated with traditional societies. Yet I do not remember my father ever hitting any of his children. Instead, he had several ways of making us know we had incurred his anger. Standing in a corner for a period of time and putting up your hands, pumping (squatting and rising up in quick succession), and holding up something for a period were his ways of punishing us.

Being quite a stubborn child, I often spent the hours before my bedtime standing in one of the corners of my father's parlour. There were times when I would almost be dropping down with sleep before he would release me to go to bed. "Come here", he would say to me, "and go lie down." By this time his anger would have subsided or gone completely. I would then open the back door and walk sleepily down the steps towards the round house in which my mothers lived. Once inside, *Nde* would ask how I was and offer me food. "Take your mat, spread it over there and go to sleep", she would say to me. "Over there" was sometimes the head, foot, or front side of her bed depending on which areas around the bed her other children were already occupying. Living in a house with other mothers and their children meant that almost every place in the house was a bed at bedtime. One therefore had to be very careful not to step on others when going outside during the night for whatever reason.

Attending church services was not an option for anyone living in *Keke* Yambasu's home. It was one of the practices and disciplines I and all the children of our home grew up with. The children were responsible for cleaning the church, dusting the seats, ringing the bell to summon people to church, lighting the kerosene lamp, and sometimes fetching people to church under orders from *Keke* Yambasu.

How Father Became a Christian and Started a Church

Later in life when I sought to know when and how Christianity came to our village and why *Keke* Yambasu was so involved with it, the youngest of *Keke* Yambasu's nephews sat me down and told me the following story. "Uncle Yambasu became a Christian of sorts in 1958 and started a church here", Samuel started. "I say 'a Christian of sorts' because uncle was a polygamous man as you know. He was also unable to read or write in his language and any other language. It meant he could not read the Bible . . . . ."

The story of how my father became a Christian and a pioneer Christian agent in our village has never ceased to intrigue me. In those days, according to Samuel, there were no outlets nearby for selling one's farm produce. So anyone who had farm produce to sell had to travel miles away to do so. My father used to travel about twenty-five miles to Manowa which was the nearest commercial town. His nephews who accompanied him helped carry his farm produce on their heads. They would often leave our village very early before daybreak to make the long and physically exerting journey over the hilly and mountainous ranges. Because the journey used to take a whole day, they always had to stay overnight and return home the following day after selling the produce.

"During those overnight stays", Samuel continued, "uncle Yambasu used to go and listen to a white man who used to come to Manowa to tell people about *Hala*. Although brothers Aisa, Joseph and Robert saw the man on one or two occasions they never went with him to the meetings because they were so exhausted after walking for the whole day carrying heavy loads. All they wanted to do was to go to sleep. So they did not know what he heard from this man. But it was as a result of whatever he heard and understood from him that he decided to become a Christian and to start a church in our village.

At this time the missionary in question knew nothing about what change he had influenced in uncle's life and uncle never said a thing to him. But one day, while back in our village, he approached the chiefs and elders, told them about his new found faith, and asked for permission to start practising it in the village. At first the people were bemused. They wondered why anyone in their right minds would want to do what uncle was proposing to do. You see, they believed that the way of worship handed down to us by our ancestors was enough.

But after reminding themselves of his earlier exposure to some foreign ways, it all began to make sense to them. Nonetheless, they still asked him a few questions about what his new found religion entailed. They were especially keen to ascertain from him whether or not it involved practices that would go against the ways of *Hala* as passed down by the ancestors. After they received assurances from him, the elders and chiefs gave him permission to carry on. So uncle started Christian Meetings with members of his own family and in his house."

As I listened to Samuel tell this story, a few questions surfaced in my mind. Why was my father so sure that his new found faith would not undermine the ways of *Hala* as received from the ancestors? What did he actually tell his family at those so called Christian meetings since he could not read the Bible? Even if he could read, my father did not have a copy of the Bible in his own language or in another language. These and other considerations began to reinforce my feelings that my father was perhaps incredibly naïve about the implications for himself and his people of what he had decided to take on. Curious to know at least what those first meetings involved, I asked Samuel to tell me what exactly he told them at those meetings.

"He told us about the white man he met at Manowa. This man, he said, had a motor car. He used to travel from place to place. He had also built a school for the children of Manowa to learn how to speak the white man's language, write, and do all the things that white people do. With his help the people had also built a house in the town where they and their children met to sing songs about *Hala*, pray, and hear the words *Hala* has spoken which were recorded in a big book. He said the white man also told them about a man called *Yesu* whom *Hala* sent into the world because *Hala* loves all human beings. When this man came God offered him as a sacrifice to free us from the punishment of our bad behaviour. He said that if we come to this man and believe in him, *Hala* will forgive us any bad things that we do. He said that *Hala* also wants us to love one another and not to do anything to anyone that would harm that person."

That was it. The Gospel according to Yambasu Yaniwah! Curious about what was happening in his house, people started eavesdropping. Some listened in and went away after a while never to return; others after a few visits listening in from outside decided to stay and joined our group. The numbers continued to grow until there was no longer enough room in his parlour to hold everyone that came to the meetings. So the group decided to build a mud-walled and thatched meeting place in the centre of the village where they regularly met to pray to *Hala* and *Yesu*. It was only after that that my father decided to tell the white man that he and his people wanted to be Christians.

"I still remember what brother Aisa told me about that trip to Manowa when uncle Yambasu was going to tell the white man about his decision. They did not bring as much to sell that time round because he wanted them to be with him when he went to see the white man. When they went into the building where the people and the white man had gathered to pray, all the men were sitting on one side and all the women on the other side. They sang songs in Mende, prayed, listen to the white man talk about *Hala* and how *Hala* expected people to live. There was a Mende man there who interpreted what the white man was saying. Everything they saw and heard was very similar to what uncle Yambasu did and said at his meetings in Lalehun."

"So", I interrupted him, "how come Kissi people were singing in Mende?" Samuel laughed in a way that suggested he knew I was just bothering him about something I already knew. "They understood and spoke Mende. It was like that in those days. Mende, Kissi and Kono people lived so close to each other that many could understand and speak their neighbour's language. I am sure you know this. But there were people who, though they could speak a language pretended not to if they did not want to afford someone a favour he or she was asking. You must have heard the story of a lady from Kono Country who visited a man in Kissi Country asking to buy some of his rice."

"No. Tell me it". I said. I knew the story of course, but I wanted to know if his version was different from the one I knew. "It was in the middle of the rainy season when food was really scarce. Most people's food reserves from the previous harvest had been depleted and they lived on wild fruits and roots while waiting for the year's harvest. But because this man did not want to sell his rice to the lady, he pretended not to understand the Kono language. So the lady spoke to him in Mende making the same request. Again this man pretended not to understand what the lady was saying. Finally, the lady made her request in Kissi. As she did so she detected a little softening of attitude on the part of the man towards her even before the man responded to her. After a brief silence the man smiled broadly and told the lady to take a seat. He then went on to tell her about the increasing numbers of people calling on him for food and that he was afraid his supply would run out if he was not careful. He confessed to the lady that he did understand all three languages but had resorted to doing what he did because he did not want to sell anymore of his reserved rice. Pleading with him that her six children at home had not had any food for a few days the man sold her some, warning her not to return again or tell anyone."

Samuel's version of the story was the same as mine. After apologizing for interrupting him unnecessarily, I asked Samuel to tell me what happened after the church service in

Manowa. He then went on to tell me that at the end of that meeting *Keke* went to the man who was interpreting and told him he wanted to talk to the white man. In the presence of the interpreter he confessed to the missionary that he had been attending the meetings for some time, even though he did not live in Manowa. That night, he told the white man about where he came from, his own conversion and the church he had started in his village. Before letting the white man go he invited him to visit his people and take charge of the church. But it was not until a year or so later that a missionary visited him and his church, introducing himself as a Methodist missionary from England.

I wondered if the words 'Methodist' and 'England' meant anything to my father and his village community then. For them, perhaps, it was enough that this man was a white man with a new religion. But eventually *Keke* Yambasu, in consultation with the chiefs, elders and entire village community, asked the missionary that a school be opened in our village.

Subsequent meetings with the missionary led to further Christian teaching of *Keke* Yambasu and some members of his church and to baptism. So it was that *Keke* Yambasu providentially became a Methodist Christian and all of his family after him. I say providentially because had the first Christian service he attended in Manowa been a Roman Catholic one, he and his family with him would have become Roman Catholic Christians. His decision was not based on any theological reasoning. The same was true for the rest of his family who became Christians. But his decision influenced the building of a Methodist church and school in Lalehun which subsequently led to many more in the village becoming Methodist Christians and, to date, four Methodist ministers and a Pentecostal pastor.

Once when I told this story of *Keke* Yambasu to a group of Christians in Ireland one of them asked me, "How could a person like your father have been a Christian? How could he have been used as an agent of the gospel of Christ?" As I looked at the faces of the others in the room before attempting to answer his question, I was in no doubt that this person was voicing a question that most of them had on their minds. "I don't know" was my reply to the question. "May be it was a case of God using the weak and foolish things of this world to confound the strong and the wise."

It is understandable that to a Methodist Christian, like to my audience in Ireland, my father who had five wives was not the ideal Christian. How could a polygamous man like him be considered a Christian when Christianity requires that a man marries only one wife (monogamy) or one wife at a time (serial monogamy)? Could such a man be considered a convert to the faith?

The Dilemma of Christian Missionaries

My father and many others in the exact same position did in fact make Christian missionaries ask many such questions and forced them to provide answers. How should a Christian missionary deal with such a person? What about the many other people who wanted to be Christian but had already entered into polygamous relationships? Should they be asked to choose one among the wives if they wanted to be considered Christian? Which one of the wives should they keep and which ones should they let go? What would the criteria be in deciding? What would happen to the rest of the women and their children? What about a woman with a husband of more than one wife who became a Christian? Should she leave her husband? Who would repay the dowry in that case? Would it be the church, missionary, or the woman's parents? Would a missionary be doing more harm than good if his policy led to the abandoning of women, the annulling of age old relational alliances, and the division of peoples who had lived together for considerable amounts of time? To avoid this, should categories of Christians be created? Should Christians be categorized into the ugly, the bad, the good, the better, and the best Christians?

In *Keke* Yambasu's time and long after, this was what happened. People were divided into enquirers, those on trial, catechumens, full members, and pagans. Enquirers were those who had just started attending church and finding out more about Christianity before they decided whether or not they wanted to convert. Those were promoted to the 'on trial' category when they had decided for Christianity. While in this second category, they were taught the basic tenets of the Christian faith as represented in the Bible, the Methodist junior catechism and the Lord's Prayer. People were also closely watched to make sure that they were behaving as they were required to. The successful completion of this period was marked by a ceremony of baptism held, more often than not, in a stream outside the village. Maximum use was often made of this ceremony seeing it as an opportunity to witness publicly to the rest of the village community. Consequently, baptismal ceremonies often took a whole day, beginning with preparations of enough food in the morning. Churches from neighbouring villages were often invited to participate in the occasion and many saw it as an obligation to go and support their fellow Christians. Enough food was prepared in the morning for them too. This food was left in the homes while all went to attend a church service in the village where the baptism was taking place. Candidates for the baptism were given their final instructions at this service, and all present were encouraged to support those to be baptized in their Christian journeys.

Then the candidates for baptism were lined up outside the church to process to the stream through the village accompanied by the entire Christian community and amidst Christian songs. At the stream, the rejoicing continued as each candidate, having been dipped into the water, was being brought back up again. Naked to the waist before baptism, the newly baptized were then dressed up in pre-made completely white robes to underline the fact that they had been washed of their past sins and were now a new and holy people of God.

Amidst further great singing and rejoicing, all went back into the church for the third and final part of the service. During that time, words of congratulations were extended to the newly baptized, thanks to all those who came to support them, and prayers were said for all including those who were believed to be still living in the darkness of sin that they may be converted to see and live in the light of *Yesu*. The day concluded with great feasting with deep satisfaction that great public witness to the gospel had been borne. Those who had attended went back to their homes, telling the news to anyone they met on their way.

The newly baptized were promoted to the class of catechumens. Here they were taught the beliefs and doctrines of Christianity in a highly condensed form but in much more detail and depth than what they were taught previously. The senior catechism and the Apostles' Creed formed the basis for this teaching. As when they were in the 'on trial' period, they were closely watched here too to make sure that they were behaving according to allegedly Christian principles. Membership of so called 'Secret Societies' (rites of passage for girls and boys into adulthood), soliciting the help of traditional healers, sorcerers, and fortune tellers, having more than one wife, sex before marriage, drinking of alcohol, participating in Muslim festivals, and ancestral veneration were some of the crimes that were high on the missionaries' list of the forbidden for Christians. Anyone caught committing any of these crimes could be stopped from continuing with the classes.

Graduating from this class to become a full member of the church required one to pass the oral exams on what one had been taught and that one should not be caught doing any of the things listed as forbidden. Only those who satisfied these two conditions were recognized as full members of the church at a service arranged for that, allowed to partake of

Holy Communion, and given certificates as proof of their full membership of the church of Christ. They were allowed to bring that certificate with them anywhere they wanted to show that they were now full members of the Christian church. Only such were allowed to hold positions of leadership in the church. This is because Christian leaders, it was taught, should also lead by example.

As might be appreciated, this was not very easy for both missionaries and their converts. How, for example, were missionaries to know how my people obeyed the externally imposed rules of Christian life day by day when the missionaries always lived either miles away from their village congregations or in secluded compounds away from the rest of the people? And for converts among my people, how could they belong to a society and not practice the culture and traditions which they have been brought up to believe were handed down by their ancestors from *Hala*? Little wonder that converts often had to live a lie when it came to participating in at least some of the practices they were banned from. Interesting true stories abound among my people illustrating the naiveté of many a missionary that served them.

One is about a catechist who did not only conduct church services himself but also used to accompany the missionary when he was going round the villages taking services. One day the missionary arrived at this man's home unannounced and wanted the man to accompany him to a village where he had planned to take a service. Unfortunately for this man he had earlier, before returning home from his farm, drank a lot of palm wine. Palm wine is locally produced alcoholic beverage from a palm tree. Not wanting the missionary to come too close to him and notice from his breath that he had been drinking, the man decided to keep a safe distance as he spoke to the missionary. Suspecting that the man was behaving strangely, the missionary tried, unsuccessfully, to get closer to find out why. After a period of the man and the missionary going round in circles, the missionary gave up.

But on their way walking to the preaching post they came to a one log bridge over a reasonably wide muddy stream. Suddenly the man realized that the missionary was going to need his help to cross the bridge. He was going to have to carry the missionary on his back across the stream because this is what he had always done. Realizing that he was not going to be able to hide his little secret any more, the man asked the missionary to climb on his back. Just as they were approaching the middle of the bridge the man unavoidably belched and the missionary caught a strong whiff of the alcohol from his carrier's breath. Suddenly, and as the man expected, the missionary began to rebuke the man for drinking alcohol. Using the only power he had over the missionary at that particular moment, he threatened to throw him into the stream if he did not stop giving out to him. "You are a little boy" he said to the missionary. "You have no right to dictate to me an older man by far what to do. We don't tolerate that kind of behaviour here and I will not take it from you." As he said these words he stood still in the middle of the bridge and began to slightly loosen his grip on the missionary. Shaking with fear the missionary did not utter one more word until they got to the other side of the stream.

Another story tells of a group of full members elsewhere who were once caught by another missionary participating in the ceremonies of the boys' rite of passage into manhood. It is said that he was so furious that he threatened that the next time he caught them doing that he would remove his baptism from their heads. "Ridiculous!" You might say. "How can one remove a baptism from someone's head?" But it is the kind of dilemma missionaries sometimes created for themselves when they turned the gospel into a 'do's and don'ts' list of externally imposed rules. And perhaps equally important was the fact that the list often reflected more of the missionaries' own cultural stances than it did those of Christianity.

Keke Yambasu was in many ways like the people in these stories. He too went through the staged process of being made a follower of Jesus but not without cost to missionary ideals of Christianity. Mindful of the context within which they were operating, it soon became clear to missionaries that they would never have any Christians (and so any church leaders) if they insisted on their prescriptions of who and what a true Christian was. Moreover, their actions, if they were to insist on their ideals, may have resulted in doing more harm than good. Consequently, missionaries settled for people like *Keke* Yambasu being accepted as make-do Christians, full members, and possible church leaders as long as they refrained from marrying additional wives.

The Beginning of New Things
in my Village

In our village, *Keke* Yambasu had influenced the beginning of a spiritual and social movement into which many, including outsiders, would buy. By becoming a Christian and influencing the building of a church and school in his village he helped start something that had the potential to change his people and community for better and for worse. He could never have been aware of the full implications of his actions. No one in his situation could have been expected to. One thing though is certain. His was an effort towards taming the jungle he perceived in his life and in the life of his community.

In a significant way he probably had no choice. The Hut Tax War between Britain and the peoples outside the colony area had taken place in 1898. This was because the latter opposed a tax they believed was an unfair imposition. Payment meant accepting unsolicited foreign interference in their lives. In any case, why were they being asked to pay for living in houses which they built for themselves, on their own lands, and with their own money, energy and materials? Their sense of outrage and decision to fight off this foreign imposition notwithstanding, they had been defeated in the war. Many people had been killed, and some of leaders had been captured and imprisoned.

A British Protectorate had soon after been firmly established to oversee and control the affairs of the rest of the country. From then on everyone one, who was eighteen years old and over, was forced to pay a Hut Tax to the colonial administration every year to offset the costs of administering the system. This had introduced unprecedented levels of change in the mindset of most people throughout the country. Chiefs and elders of most communities outside the colony had embraced colonial rule and the new educational, economic, health, religious, court and policing systems that came with it. As a result, Western educational, health and administrative systems had been proactively sought after and established by many.

My father was aware of this. He had come into direct contact with some of these systems while in Sandaru, in his work as a court messenger and also in his travels. Two of his nephews Sundifu and Gbewa had even got places in schools in other parts of the country. He had seen or heard of Chiefdom towns that had benefited greatly as a result of their Paramount Chiefs embracing Christian missionaries, their religion and system of education. Some of the towns had even opted for purely academic schools systems opposing, through their chiefs and elders, the industrial schools systems that were initially introduced. The practical skills training offered through the latter, they had argued, would not give their children as good an access to the white man's knowledge and power as the former. My father had also seen traditionalists and Muslims alike convert to the white man's religion and take the opportunity of sending their children to Western styled schools.

Had my father and his village elders and people come to the conclusion that the ways of life *Hala* revealed to the white man were better that those revealed to the black man? Or better still, had they reasoned that it was expedient to buy into the white man's way of life so as to exploit the benefits of both theirs and his? Had the black man decided in the face of his defeat by the white man's guns and goods to live and let live? Had the black man, confronted with the reality of obvious power and influence of the white man's resources and value systems, come to the decision that the black man's future survival lay in the embracing of both his and the white man's worlds?

Although in 1961 the country had gained its independence from Britain, my father had most probably come to the conclusion against the background of his experiences that Western systems and resources were a significant part of the way forward for the country and its peoples. This is probably why he and his people had negotiated with the Methodist missionary the building of a Western school system in their village in addition to the church.

I do still remember going to church with *Keke* Yambasu, *Nde*, *Mama* Amie, *Keke* Yambasu's other wives, his nephews and other children when I was only about eight years old. In those days the church had a register into which the names of all those who attended were recorded under their different categories. There were two church services held every week, one on Wednesday nights and another on Sunday nights. The nights were preferred for services since most people normally left for their farms early in the morning. It was at Wednesday night services that a roll call was made and members were expected to pay their class dues. "Present two cents", or "present nothing", or "sick", or "absent" or "absent nothing", or "absent one cent" were the responses shouted out as names were called from the altar by the catechist who was leading the service. But when it came to the Yambasu family, there were often long sighs from other members of the congregation. These sighs were invariably followed by laughter. This was because the list of Yambasus seemed to go on forever. So by the time the roll caller was on, say, number five of twenty five Yambasus, the sighs and laughter from the congregation would begin. Some members of the congregation would even sometimes leave the church for a while and return a little while later for the closing song and prayers. This was not done out of spite or be-grudgery though, but purely to make fun.

Mediators of New Ways

Reflecting on the facts of *Keke* Yambasu becoming a Christian with his many wives, children, and dependents enrolled on a church register illustrated patently to me how people like my father embraced new ways but often on their own terms. Perhaps this was made easier for him and other Kissi people because missionary success in evangelizing them depended a great deal upon the cooperation of people like him. People like my father were the real evangelists, preachers and teachers of their people. They lived with them, they knew them very well, and they lived like them. So the people followed their lead.

Missionaries on their part were few and far between. They were often seen only a few times in a year. Given this situation, it seems to me that people like my father who accessed them and their resources must have had and exercised considerable power and influence among their peoples. This must have also been the case in their relationship with missionaries. And in both cases they must have determined in significant ways the outcome of Western encounters with their people. As mediators of those encounters, I would imagine that they probably essentially became power brokers between local and external powers. In that way they became change agents and change stoppers for the worldviews, knowledge and practice of their people and also for outsiders.

The order of the alleged content of *Keke* Yambasu's introductory Christian meetings in his house has also often intrigued me. Why, for example, did he start with referring to the white man's motor car and the school and church the white man had helped build in Manowa? What role if any did the material and social advancements connected with the white man's religion play in the pull my father experienced towards Christianity? Did these lead him to dream of what his people could benefit from if he aligned himself with this man's religion? Did my father also opt for the white man's religion because he detected in the white man's teachings principles handed down by *Hala* through the ancestors?

I can only guess the answers to these questions. What is certain however is that it was as a result of the role *Keke* Yambasu and his people played in embracing new ways of thinking and living that their small, remote and unexposed village placed itself in the way of change as it had probably never contemplated. A church, a school, white Christian missionaries, motor vehicles, teachers of Western ways and ideas, the Bible, books, football games, English language, and many more competing ways of life were added to features of life in their village's cultural, social and moral landscape. These set a wheel of change in motion that would usher in a pace of change that was probably not possible before. This was especially so for their children.

But what was happening in *Keke* Yambasu's village was only a small indication of what was already happening on a wider scale in the rest of the country. Most communities in the country had already been experiencing significant changes in their moral, cultural and social landscape as a result of the presence and activities among them of white men and women. These men and women were engaged in a secular or religious mission to convert. The religious missionaries used both secular and religious means to help them succeed in their mission. For both types of missionaries it was great cause for rejoicing and hope because they believed heathen, savage, uncivilized, Dark Africa was being tamed, domesticated, civilized, and humanized at last, albeit gradually. My father's endeavours were only a tiny cog in that powerful wheel of change, but an important one nonetheless.

FIVE

THE BEGINNING OF THE END

Schooling

I was nearly five years old when my father decided to send me to school. By this time the older of his sons born to his fourth wife Mattu was too old to start primary education and the youngest too young to begin. So my father decided that *Nde* Mattu's daughter Sia Amie who was less than a year older than me also started school with me. This was quite a remarkable move on the part of my father and a few others in our village who decided to send their daughters to school. More often than not, sending girls to school was not considered a smart move. Most people, frankly, did not think it was a better use of resources to educate a girl because they believed she would eventually end up becoming some other family's property.

For all of my first school year, though, *Mama* Amie often had to carry me to the school which was housed in the village barrie. She would always have a supply of bananas and oranges to leave with me in the school to encourage me to stay. Often, though, when what food she left with me was finished, I would escape back home to her for more whether or not it was break time. So there were times when in one school day she had to take me to school more than once. In the four years when I attended the school I was very stubborn, *Nde* often reminds me. School in those days started at 8.00am and finished at 2.00pm. In the first two years I was expected to join my *Mama* Amie at home immediately school closed. That changed in the last two years when I was considered to be old enough to join my parents on the farm and do a few jobs there. It is what every child of my age upwards who was in school was expected to do. Not infrequently, however, some of my school friends and I just ignored that expectation. Instead we would go into a forest to make toys from stems or branches of trees, hunt for wild fruit, birds, and rodents, or just simply play in the woods until nightfall. Then we would gingerly walk back to the village very fearful and anxious about how our parents would react and unsure about what excuse would earn us a desperately needed reprieve. It was in those earlier years of my life that my love for the forest and its wildlife was born and nurtured.

Arriving home on such nights, my seemingly well rehearsed excuses amounted to nothing confronted with my parents' reasoning abilities and fury. In addition to not doing what I had been told to do, I had also caused them unnecessary concern and worry about my whereabouts and wellbeing. Consequently, they made crystal clear the ridiculousness on my part of even thinking about the idea of mounting a defense in the form of an excuse. The result in the end was always the same: my lies were exposed and this was followed by one of *Keke* Yambasu's tried and tested ways of punishing his children. But *Keke* Yambasu did not just punish me. His discipline was always tempered with mercy. At the end of my punishment he would often give me some of the food that had been given to him either by his wives or neighbours. He would then warn me to always do what I was told and not to rely on my excuses to save me. He did not have to remind me about the latter. I had arrived independently at that conclusion myself. While I did take his warnings seriously though, this often lasted only for a period until some really interesting adventure plan was hatched by another school friend again. The whole cycle, needless to say, was repeated again.

I was nonetheless very fond of my father and we were very close. In the early parts of the night at the end of each day when everyone has returned to the village from the farm, the big round house of my father's wives was always buzzing with activity amid great noise coming from all sections of it. It was the one time when all the mothers and their children were together in one place and so could share stories of the day and talk about plans for the next day while cooking and eating their evening meals. It was often at these times that my father would call me away from there to join him in the barrie where he and other men-folk of the village would be gathered talking for hours about religious, farming, hunting, community and local political issues.

Looking back now, I understand why my father wanted me and his other sons to be where he was. He knew it was by being with him and listening into these conversations that we would learn more about the culture, traditions, history and politics of the society into which we were born. We would also learn about the nature of relationships within the community and between our community and neighbouring communities. But it was not all talk. Sometimes local games were played too. Sometimes, too, we were given the chance to learn by taking part.

Learning by observing, listening and taking part! This was one of the significant ways all children in our society were groomed into adult life in those days. Ours was a society which had no concept of children not having a childhood because they were doing what only adults were expected to do. As early as six years old, for example, I used to go with my dad to the farm at weekends, stand by him to see what he was doing, and was given a toy tool made by him with which I would practice doing what he was doing. A couple of years later my toy tools were replaced by semi-real tools made to size and blunt enough for me to be able to use without causing myself much hurt. Adult supervision was also always at hand to teach, guide, and protect. My sisters were no different with their mothers. At an early age they too were encouraged to start learning through observing and participating in what they would be spending much of their adult lives doing.

A Rite of Passage

In those days, as today, male and female circumcisions were a must. Traditional men and women whose job it was to carry out such operations in society used small and very sharp but unsterilized knives produced by the village blacksmiths for such operations. Circumcision ceremonies were often huge public occasions. Relations of parents of candidates far and wide were invited and often came. Huge amounts of food and drink were provided and consumed. Men and women spent the whole night before the ceremony dancing while the candidates were hidden away in a special house at the edge of the village with the trusted performer of the operation. There the boys too and the operator enjoyed their own share of the good food.

When I went through the process myself, however, I discovered that all of us boy candidates did not really enjoy the food as much as we might have done if we did not have to worry about what awaited us on the following morning. While none of us really knew what was going to happen to us, we gathered from snippets in some of the songs men and women sang and also from the anxious looks on the faces of our parents that what awaited us was not pleasant.

Recalling my experience of that event, I now suspect that the operator may have been in a very similar position as we the candidates were. While he knew what we the boys were in for, he did not know, however, whether or not his operations on sixteen boys the following morning would go problem-free. What if anything bad happened to any of the boys? Perhaps even death from bleeding? Later in my life I learnt there have been times, even though not frequently, when a boy or a girl has died after undergoing such an operation. Recalling now what his face looked like on that night, I have had to question my initial reading of his face as that of a man who was doing his best to convince everyone that he was a serious and an important person with mystical powers too. I suspect now that the reason why he too looked the way he did was because he was scared stiff. Why else did he eat very little of all the good food that was brought to him in that little and least conspicuous house on the edge of the village? And why did he spend most of the night up in the dark corner of the room, his back against us, and muttering hardly audible prayers to *Hala* and the ancestors? Like us, I suspect now that this man equally did not know what was awaiting him on the day of the ceremony. Doctor and patient, it seems to me now, were in the same boat on that occasion, threatened by the same storm: fear. That was the enemy he and us had in common, in whose grip we were, and whom we had to face up to in order to earn our respect as true Kissi people. Through the songs of the many jubilant and some anxious singers outside our dimly lit secluded house who were aware of these realities, the whole community was joined in urging and encouraging us to be brave and courageous as we faced up to our fears.

Early at dawn on the day of the circumcision, the boys or girls would be dragged by pre-appointed people through a big crowd of shouting men or women into a clearing in the bush where the operator would already be waiting. There and in haste each candidate after another was blindfolded, made to sit on his/her own stem of a banana or plantain tree prepared on the previous day, legs forced apart by adults who were present, and circumcised. I still sometimes hear the shrieks and shouts of some of the boys I was circumcised with and sense the palpable fear I felt as I waited blindfolded in line for my turn. I can still clearly hear the anxiety the fathers felt as it came through their hushed conversations with relations as each of them stood close by his son.

Not knowing how the operations went for their sons because they were forbidden to visit the clearing, our mothers would wait anxiously with bated breath in the village to secretly hear news about the operation from their husbands or older sons. The same was the case with husbands when their girls went through the ceremony. It was forbidden for anyone to openly divulge anything that happened in the clearing to the opposite sex. And it was totally forbidden to tell anything to uncircumcised boys or girls. It was often weeks later and well after the wounds have completely healed that the circumcised will graduate back into the village amidst great rejoicing and dancing. Until that time circumcised boys or girls lived in a clearing in the bush outside the village. It was the beginning of the end of my fear of the utter blackness of darkness with its creepy and eerie sounds from nocturnal creatures. While the circumcised remained in the place of seclusion, their parents were obligated to send enough food to the clearing twice everyday for both the circumcised and those who were looking after them. And, from the time they were graduated back into the village and onwards, it was forbidden for the circumcised to be seen in public naked.

I once had a privileged conversation with *Keke* about the banana tree stems on which the candidates sit on the morning of the circumcision. Another ceremony was coming up in our village and people were discussing it. I wanted to know why banana tree stems were used as seats for only this occasion and no other. "You know, don't you", he inquired, "that our people peel a bit from a banana tree stem and tie it around their neck and wrist when somebody close to them dies?" "Yes, I do", I answered. He continued. "Our people associate a banana tree stem with death. I don't know why but it is one of those traditions our ancestors handed down to us. So boys and girls for circumcision are made to sit on the stem of a banana tree because it is at circumcision that they first experience their own death. A part of their body is cut away, dies and is buried by the person who performs the circumcision. Their life blood spills into the ground to the ancestors to inform them that it is only a matter of time before they would join them. So sitting on a banana tree stem at circumcision is a way of teaching our children from the time they are young that death is inevitable and is no respecter of age."

How my Father Died

It was at one of these male circumcision ceremonies in 1966 in a neighbouring village that *Keke* Yambasu suddenly took ill. It was at the end of my fourth year in primary school. He had been invited there by a relation; and while he was there his food was allegedly poisoned. By the time he was brought back to our village his face had already been so swollen that it was difficult to see his eyes. Two days later, on the way to the missions clinic in Sandaru where he was been carried in a hammock by his nephews for medical attention, he died.

The night before *Keke* Yambasu died I was sitting by him on the bed he laid on with my left hand in his hands. Sundifu his nephew who was by this time a school teacher in Sandaru had come home and was in the room with us. So was my mother, *Keke* Yambasu's other wives, his other nephews, and a few other relations. Then *Keke* Yambasu, aware that he might not survive his illness, said to his school teacher nephew: "Take care of my family and my children when I die. You are the only one in the family who has learnt the white man's ways and language very well and now work for him. I thank God that I helped you get to where you are while I was able. Do whatever you can to help my children in school. And take care . . ."

Before he finished the sentence I was dragged away from his hands by my mother who was already frantically yelling. Those were the last words of my father in my hearing and they still ring in my ears today. Every time I recall that incident I cannot but cry: cry for *Keke* Yambasu who had given so much to us and still had so much to give us; for the youngest of my father's wives, my mother, all of whose children were still so young and who was left with such a huge burden of taking care of us; for myself who was cheated by death stealing from me someone I loved so dearly and at such an early age, and leaving me with a gaping hole which has never been filled.

"*Keke,* don't leave us", I cried with my mother as she led me away into the dark at the back of *Keke* Yambasu's house holding me tight to herself. "Who will take care of the children?" my mother yelled. "Who will provide for me? Who will clothe and feed your children?" she continued to cry aloud her questions and dilemma. Those questions also told me how much faith and trust my mother had in *Keke* Yambasu as a caring and loving husband and father.

My Mother's New Husband

In those days a wife bereaved of her husband almost always remarried someone in the family of the husband. This was the only way she was entitled to any of her deceased husband's property. So my mother remarried *Keke*. His actual name was Fallah. Robert (pronounced in Kissi *Lorborti)* was his given baptismal name. *Keke* Lorborti is how we called him whenever we needed to distinguish him from *Keke* Isa, *Keke* Joseph, and so on. Otherwise he was just known to us who were my mother's children as *Keke*.

Keke never spared anything to help us and *Nde* in our times of need, even though he was materially very poor. He had the responsibility of helping *Nde* take care of four children she had with *Keke* Yambasu. Our sister who was the eldest of *Nde*'s children was not yet married and was living at home with us. So, even though my *Keke* spared nothing to look after us, taking care of us was getting more and more difficult for him. Now and again *Nde* did ask and receive help from her brothers at Bokodu village. But this was only a little help since they too had their own often taxing responsibilities. This meant, in reality, that by the time I was ready to go to secondary school *Keke* and *Nde* had already incurred quite a few financial debts. These they were trying to repay either in cash or kind. In the latter case they offered physical labour, palmoil, rice, coffee and kolanuts in exchange for the monies they owed different people.

When *Keke* Yambasu died there was an inheritance row over who should get the proceeds from his plantations and which portions should go to whom. Consequently, nothing my father left was of any use to help *Nde* care for us. The proceeds from the coffee and kolanuts *Keke* harvested from his own very small plantation could only settle some of the debts he and *Nde* incurred.

Because *Keke* became well known in our village for producing and selling palmoil to provide for his family, people nicknamed him 'wasp'. They believed his waist had become as thin as a wasp's due to constant use of a climbing rope to harvest palm fruits. He also became a laughing stock of the village for taking care of children that were not his and who, many believed, would never acknowledge him as their father. Though this was sometimes said in my *Keke's* hearing, he never ditched his responsibility towards us.

Some Experiences of Primary School Days

For most of the remaining years of our primary education we joined the other boys and girls from our village and neighbouring villages who commuted to and from Sandaru every day. The reason for this was that we could not just handle living away from our parents and missing the fun of constantly being with those we grew up with in our village. We considered walking seven miles each way to and from school every day as nothing compared with having to live away from home. So we readily accepted the early morning rise, the gathering in the village centre of us all, and the long journey to and from school five days a week every term time!

While demanding, these were days filled with great fun and memorable incidents. By this time a kind of road had been cut through the forests and hills to our village from Sandaru. This made it possible for some vehicles to be driven into it. I remember one very early morning when we thought a driver who had come to the village with his lorry and was returning to Sandaru would give us a lift. Some of us who were up went quickly round waking up the others and gathering as usual in the centre of the village. After he had loaded his coffee, palm kernel, rice, kolanuts and palmoil and was about to leave, we all walked to him and begged for a lift. To our dismay, he refused, insisting that he be paid before carrying us. Since we had no money to do so, he left us all standing there and drove away. Having discussed among ourselves what to do, we decided that since it was not too far away for dawn to break we should start walking to school. So we did, not realizing that it was still a long way away from dawn. We had no watches in those days and so discerned time from the length or position of our shadows, or the position of the sun and moon in the sky, or the noises of certain birds and insects, or the crow of cocks.

This particular morning, and for whatever reason, we all misread the time. It was after walking about half the way to school that we realized what had happened. So at the junction of where the road from our village and that from a neighbouring village met, we decided to lie down and wait for the morning. We broke leafy branches off the trees near the road, spread them on the ground, and lay down to sleep. It was a hunter who, early at daybreak, as he was returning home from his nightlong hunting expedition, woke us up shocked and surprised to find us there. We told him our story as he listened with great sympathy. When we finished, he urged us to continue our journey, reminding us that we might be punished if we got to school late.

Return journeys home at the end of the school day were no less eventful. The older boys would sometimes organize fights to determine who is stronger. While a fight went on, others stood and cheered. When someone in the fight was been defeated or hurt, the older boys would intervene and stop the fight. All the time and throughout the way, we scavenged for wild fruit and palm kernels to eat. Sometimes we decided to have a swim in one of the many streams on the way. Thinking about it now, I wonder how we survived doing this for five days every week of school time. But we did and without much bother really. Whatever hardships we endured, they were not as bad, we believed, as having to endure hard daily chores on the farm.

But in the year Amie and I were to take our Selective Entrance Examinations for entry into secondary school, we had to give all of that up to go and stay with teacher Yambasu. That was how *Keke* Yambasu's nephew, Sundifu, was commonly known. It was a year of a lot of serious studying for the exams. Our head teacher who had the task of preparing us for them was very strict and took no chances with any of us.

He demanded that we lived in Sandaru for that year so that we would give the exams our best shot. Throughout that year he used to visit the homes of all candidates for the exams in the nights unannounced. To be found not studying when he visited incurred his anger. He often called out of assembly the next morning any such pupils, sternly reprimanded them, and gave them twelve lashes for letting themselves down. Some night times that year, Amie and I resorted to studying outside in the moonlight because we had no money to buy kerosene. Once our head teacher came round and met us studying there. He was very angry and went into the house to tell teacher Yambasu off for putting us through that inconvenience. But his visit did not result in much change.

Amie and I were the only two *Keke* Yambasu sent to school before he died. We were both in the same class. One day, during one of Rev. Richard Jackson's visits, teacher Yambasu introduced us to him. Rev. Jackson was an English Methodist missionary responsible for my home area. As they talked, he told the missionary about *Keke* Yambasu, the role he played in building a Methodist Church and school in our village, the circumstances surrounding his sudden death, and the financial problems we were having with regard to our education. Rev. Jackson listened carefully and, after discussing a few more church related issues with teacher Yambasu, he drove back to his house which was about a mile outside the town.

Mother and Child Pray in Desperation

For many years after *Keke* Yambasu's death, *Nde* always talked about him, especially when life's problems were choking her. One such time I clearly remember. I had just passed my class seven (eleven plus) exams to go to secondary school. It was in late July during the summer holidays when I got my results. By this time I had been transferred to the school in Sandaru which had up to seven classes. It was in the year that *Keke* Yambasu died that I first started school there. At last the time had come for me to proceed to secondary school after three years of schooling there.

The Wesley Secondary School in Segbwema which I had been advised to select a few months before the exams was about fifty miles away from my home village. But when I came home with my results the celebration of my success was very short-lived. It suddenly dawned on *Nde* and *Keke* that they would not be able to afford to pay for my secondary school education. While *Keke* had never spared anything to help take care of us, secondary school fees and related expenses amounted to much more than he could manage.

One day as my mother and I walked to the farm alone, she suddenly started talking to my deceased father as if he was right there with us. "*Fallo*⁹ Yambasu, you left these children with me and look at the problems I am going through trying to look after their needs. If you were still alive I would have had no problem with your son's education. But, still, don't forget

---

⁹   'Mr'

us." '*Fallo* Yambasu' was the way my mother always addressed
my father, and this is still the case. It is an address both of
endearment and deference. My mother was a lot younger
than my dad when he married her, and so she reckoned
'*Fallo*' a much more appropriate way to address her husband.

As I listened to her words and prayers on that quiet four miles
stretch of road through the forest to the farm that day, I was
moved to make my own request to God. Quietly, I prayed
under my breath, "God, if you help me to go through my
education, I will spend the rest of my life serving you." That
was it. But I meant every word of that simple childlike prayer.
My education prospects had reached a crossroad. There were
many in my village who had already dropped out of school
for lack of fees—especially girls. With my prospects seeming
very dismal, it seemed there was only one other option
left: God. "If God was the one who turned my father into a
Christian, the same God must surely be able to find a way of
paying for his son's education", I reasoned in a child-like way.
By the time I came to myself my mother and I were already
on the outskirts of our farm. Consequently the focus of both
our attentions was switched to the tasks that needed to be
completed that day.

That summer holiday, Rev. Jackson had travelled back home
to England on furlough for three months. It was in his absence
that our Selective Entrance Exams results were published.
But just before schools reopened in September that year, he
returned to Sandaru to learn that I had passed my exams but
might not proceed to secondary school because of financial
constrains. Teacher Yambasu had many children by his two

wives. The responsibility to educate them was his alone. Then there was my sister Amie and I into whose care we were placed by *Keke* Yambasu before he died.

Our Prayers Answered

One morning, as my parents and I were getting ready to go to the farm, a messenger arrived at our home from Sandaru. He had a letter with him from Rev. Jackson asking me to go and see him immediately. *Nde* would, however, not let the man return before he had something to eat. So she set out to prepare him some food. *Keke* decided to go on ahead to the farm while my mother did that. Later on that morning the messenger and I left for Sandaru, arriving at Rev. Jackson's by midday.

As we walked to Sandaru that day, little did I know that I was on the verge of something I would subsequently only describe as a miracle. Seated in the office of this missionary preacher, he opened a drawer, took out something which looked like an envelope, and handed it over to me. "Open it and read the underlined paragraph", he said. There, in the envelope, was a letter he had received months earlier from his brother and his brother's wife in England. The summary of that paragraph was its last sentence which simply read, "My wife and I have decided to pay for John Yambasu's secondary school education." At the end of the letter were signed the names Derek and Gill Jackson.

I hardly believed what was happening to me. What had happened, as he explained to me later, was that from the time he was told about me by teacher Yambasu, he had contacted his brother in England and asked him and his wife to consider the possibility of sponsoring me through school. They, in turn, had agreed to do so and had written back to him informing him about their decision. "My brother and his wife will help pay for your schooling for as long as you need help" he told me. "You can now go back to your parents and tell them the good news", he concluded. Overjoyed to the point of crying, my voice trembled as I said, "Thank you sir".

Off I left walking back to my village. Did I say walking? I actually ran for most of the seven miles knowing the importance of the good news I was carrying with me. Rev. Jackson and his wife had given me two large slices of bread with marmite to eat on the way.

That evening, my parents returned from the farm to the village a lot earlier than usual. They had spent the day wondering why the missionary wanted to see me. On arrival home and seeing them sitting round the fire where my mother was cooking, I ran to them shouting, "I can go to school now." They both stood up and ran toward me. "What do you mean?" they asked. "The white man says his brother and his brother's wife will pay my school fees."

The joy in our home that night and after was indescribable. We all knew that a most unbearable burden had been removed from our shoulders and we had been set completely free. Had God actually answered the prayers of an eleven year old boy?

Had my father also been interceding for his son? "The answer to both questions must be 'yes'", I thought to myself. "Is that not what my people believed? Did I not once overhear my father saying, 'my family that first came and settled here continue to look after us?' But they were long dead, so how come he said they still looked after us?" As these questions were going on in my mind, it suddenly dawned on me, "That's why my mother continues to speak to my father as if he was besides her, alive and kicking and still caring and able to help her and her children as he did while he was still physically alive." Gripped by this discovery, I thought to myself, "Well, love's caring never really ends does it?" That was, of course, long before I was introduced to any refined and sophisticated Christian theology.

Another Rite of Passage

It was two years before all this took place that I was initiated into the society which boys went through in order for them to graduate into true and proper manhood. This is the rite of passage *Keke* referred to before when he was telling me about some of the Kissi customs and traditions. It was a must for every boy who was born in our society. It still is for most areas in my country. Though it was called a 'secret society' by white people, it was not by my people because every male person in that society eventually got initiated into it. I had gone through the circumcision ceremony the year my father died. This rite of passage was the final ordeal I had to go through before I would be accepted as a fully fledged man in Kissi society.

During it I was taught the things I needed to know in order to fully carry out my responsibilities as a man in my society: farming, hunting, fishing and warfare techniques. There I was taught the history, traditions and culture of my people including the need always to respect those who are older than me and the responsibility for me to perpetuate that tradition of respecting elders. The responsibilities of marriage life and how to relate to women in general formed part of my training during that time. Other things I was taught included the need to be my own best friend, to face situations of hardship and persevere through them, to keep confidence, to be careful not to be too predictable in my relationships so as to avoid being taken for granted or, worse, becoming an easy target of enemies. These I was taught as being among the qualities a proper man has. And I was not just taught them by word of mouth. I was often put in situations during my time of training in the forest where I was forced to practice them. It was during that rite of passage that I received much of the training for life that I still trust and draw upon today.

A Reservoir of Blessings at Eleven

So when at eleven years old I left home and family in 1970 to go to Wesley Methodist Secondary School in Segbwema and look after myself, I already had a reservoir of skills, rules and resources that I would call into play to see me through those challenging but exciting times. There was, for example, what *Keke* Yambasu had given me. By his life he had taught me about daring to be open-minded, to reason, to dream dreams, to act to bring about what one believed in, to serve one's people well, to be generous, to love, to discipline with love, and to cautiously trust people. If he was poisoned as it was alleged, he died in the course of being available to members of his community when they needed him. To this day I stand or sit for a while in front of his grave every time I visit my village. I do so not because I believe he is there. But sitting or standing there reminds me of the life he lived and inspires me to follow his example.

Then there was the inspiration of *Keke's* commitment to responsibility when he took *Nde* and us on. His is a commitment that has lasted for a life time. In addition to everything else he did, *Keke* used to accompany me half of the way back to secondary school at the end of every holiday. The nearest and cheapest place where I could catch public transport in those days was about fifteen miles from our village. Carrying most of the food I needed for the term on his head, *Keke* would walk with me for nearly a day while I carried my very few clothes and books. He would stay with me until a vehicle was available and I have boarded. Then he would start the journey back home again in rain, sunshine, heat or darkness. I remember one such occasion when about a third of the way through our fifteen miles journey I discovered that I had left my school prospectus, booklist and result back in our village. There and then *Keke* handed me over to a family in the village where we had been taken a rest and walked back home to bring them for me. I felt so bad putting him through that situation. In later life when I asked him how he coped he simply said to me: "What has to be done has to be done." His dedicated commitment to family has always inspired me.

To be sure, *Keke* was not a saint in all his ways. Nobody ever is. Unlike *Keke* Yambasu, for example, he had a very short temper and that sometimes resulted in him having almighty rows with *Nde* and hitting her. On one such occasion I was still in primary school. I cannot remember now what exactly happened. But I still recall coming home from school one day and not meeting *Nde* at home. It was one of those days when there was an all-village community ceremony on and people did not go to their farms that day. Even before I got into our house I had suspected something was seriously wrong because there was a huge commotion around our house. I was immediately told by *Mama* Amie why *Nde* was not where I expected her to be. She had been taken away from *Keke* by some elders and locked away in another house.

As she explained to me, I saw *Keke* running down a small hill towards some houses in that part of the village. He had found out where *Nde* had been hidden. He ran full speed towards the door of the house, jumped and smashed into the house with his two feet, and grabbed *Nde*. It was a terrifying sight; and as I watched what was happening, I began to cry. But the elders were eventually able to free her from his grip and calm him down. I still remember the sad and angry look on his father Kolokpasie's face as he said shaking his head disappointingly, "One can give birth to a child but one cannot guarantee giving birth to one's heart." Grandpa Kolokpasie was a quiet and non-violent man, and wished his son *Keke* took after him. He obviously did not. But *Keke* had his own good qualities. From him I had learnt the value of doing what has to be done. He has also taught me the truth that everybody is beautiful in their own way.

My mother? She had taught me to trust in God. Even when her children were not given their share of the inheritance, *Nde* never begrudged anyone. Instead she always prayed and did what she could to address her family's needs. She would always refer to *Keke* Yambasu by the endearing and respectful title *'fallo* Yambasu, and talk to him with fondness as though he was still alive and present with her. I have often wondered whether or not this was where she sometimes got a significant amount of her strength and courage in difficult circumstances? Our people believe that their living-dead continue to live in the form of human Spirits before and near God. So they believe them to be in better stead to intercede to God on their behalf.

Nde's difficulties never stopped her from being generous. One of the big problems *Keke* has often had with her is to do with her undiscriminating and unrelenting generosity. Even in those difficult days when they were struggling to raise us, she would give a portion of food her family did not immediately need to another needy family. When *Keke* queried her she would respond saying, "We have something to eat today, but that poor lady and her kids have nothing. We surely cannot let her go and watch her children suffer today just because we want to eat tomorrow!" On hearing that *Keke* would get even more furious with her. At such times she would change the conversation and that was that. *Nde* had taught me to be mindful of the needs of other people even in my own poverty and need.

Mama Amie had taught me that in every circumstance I may face in life there is always a way and that quitting is not an option. Uncle Nabieu Sovula of Bokodu taught me that blood is thicker than water. *Nde* Satta, *Keke* Yambasu's second wife had taught me that disappointments are a part of life and that we can neither avoid them nor wish them away but deal with them as best we believe and could. She abandoned her marriage to *Keke* Yambasu because she was unable to have her own children. Teacher Yambasu had taught me the principle of returning a good turn. Amidst personal economic difficulties of his own he still took on Amie and me. Then there was what Rev. Jackson had taught me about the important place of connections in human life and their use to advance the cause of humanity. The humane generosity of Derek and Gill towards someone to whom they were not related gave me my first insight into the art of building, nurturing and sustaining the universal human web of relationships. They never reneged on their promise. In fact Derek and Gill used to help improve my English and writing skills by correcting mistakes I made in my letters to them and, with their reply to my letter, posted my letter back with the corrections. Over the years this helped me in no small way. By the time I left my village for secondary education I had begun to learn from the Jacksons the crucial importance of connecting people and building bridges across races and cultures and continents.

And then there was what my people had taught me through the way they lived in general and through the different rites of passage they made me participate in. They taught me the need to know and cherish my roots and the value of community. They taught me that people can be both noble and savage and that the world in which I was born and was living is at the best of times unpredictable and at the worst of times hostile.

They also taught me that time is important only in terms of events it marks and activities one carries out. Above all they taught me that people were more important than things and that I should tread carefully and responsibly on mother earth and her children because they are the ones who have given me the life I have. Undergirding all this was my people's deep belief and conviction that all life lived in this world must have a spiritual basis. I had been taught this approach to life by my people long before I had any contact with Christianity. There was nothing we ever did without first acknowledging the spiritual reality of our existence through conducting a religious ritual. In essence my people had taught me that all of creation including myself come from *Hala* and that I will return to *Hala* when I die.

As I grew up and made a personal decision to follow Christ, I found the idea of this world and humanity as chance occurrences more difficult to believe than the belief that they are creatures of God. And the life and teaching of Jesus—especially the example of his life—are what initially drew me, and still does, to Christianity as the best representation of who God is. The God of grace at the heart of Christ's teaching and lifestyle became, for me, what distinguishes Christianity from all other forms of religion. That is why I chose to become a Christian and will remain to be so in a world which is often characterized by a divide between those who merit our love and those who do not. That, I want to believe, was also partly what my father heard, saw and related to in the life, teaching and preaching of the missionary that introduced him to Christ. And grace is neither Protestant nor Roman Catholic. It is simply 'the grace of our

Lord Jesus Christ and the love of God . . .' That is why, for me, I care less about the fact that I became a Methodist and not a Roman Catholic or a member of some other Christian denomination.

Looking back now I can say without doubt that of all I had been given before leaving home for secondary school, Christianity was the best. In addition to that, the rest of what I had received from my father, mother, *Keke*, *Mama* Amie, Uncle Nabieu, *Nde* Satta, teacher Yambasu, Rev. Jackson, Derek, Gill, and my people constituted in no small part my arsenal, as it were, in the battle of life in secondary school and beyond.

SIX

SWIMMING UPSTREAM

Enrolled to Swim

S almon are said to lay their eggs upstream. So every year they make that difficult and often hazardous journey to lay their eggs. But once they have successfully done so the adult fish die and their offspring undertake the less difficult but, nonetheless, hazardous opposite journey down stream.

I have often likened people like my father to salmon swimming upstream to lay eggs that would be hatched into a future generation. What I and others after them did was, in a sense, like swimming downstream buoyed by currents they had already initiated. To be sure we, too, in our own life times would also need to make our own upstream journeys in order to lay our own eggs for new lives.

By the time I started secondary school, about a dozen boys and girls had already gone on from the primary school and church in our village to a Methodist secondary school and church in Kailahun, our District Headquarter town. For one reason or another some were not able to continue in school. Others did and, like salmon, embarked on the somewhat inevitable upstream journey to lay eggs. But all became and remained Christians in their own ways. And, because of those who successfully continued in school, our village was becoming very well known to others in and outside our Chiefdom.

The influence of the white man's ways in the forms of social and cultural realities was already too much with us. Were those ways different from or the same as Christianity? In those days we did not even know there was any difference between the two. But our ignorance made no difference one way or the other to the reality that we were embarked on a downstream and upstream journey on which our forebearers had enrolled us.

Sometimes we journeyed with great fun and excitement, enthused by the dream of good fortunes that lay ahead. At other times we did so with great trepidation aware of, and trying to avoid, the dangers that might undo not only our dreams but perhaps even our lives.

That was why before I left home for secondary school my parents did three things. A week before I left, *Keke* and my mother brought me to a medicine man in Guinea to 'work' for me. For Kissi people this meant that the man was to provide me with medicine that would have power to protect me from evil people and their powers to harm me in any way whatsoever. This man was *Nde*'s sister's husband, Fayia Komende. He and his wives and family lived in the neighboring Republic of Guinea. In the two days we spent with him in his village I was fed on herbs he had prepared with rice. He also gave me some preparations to rub and to eat while away at school, and a small normal handkerchief size white cloth knotted at one end. I was told that what was contained in the knot had power to ward away witches from me by blinding them to my existence. On returning to our village a ritual was conducted during which prayers were said to *Hala* to protect me from all harm and danger. Appeals were made to *Keke* Yambasu and all those relations who departed before him for their continued concern for my wellbeing. This was followed by a big meal of chicken stew and rice which had been prepared for the occasion and shared in by all the members of our household.

I have often tried to understand these three undertakings of my parents in terms of a Kissi people's trinitarian practice: a visit to the medicine man, pleas to ancestors and prayers to *Hala*. The powers of the former two were and still are believed to derive from the latter one. The knowledge and practice of the medicine was handed down by ancestors who initially received it from *Hala*. With the demands for protection of all three of these met on my behalf, my parents were happy and ready to release me from the burial place of my umbilical cord.

Among my people the remains of the umbilical cord of each child after birth were buried under a kola nut tree. It was that child's testimonial that s/he was born in that place and, of right, legitimately belonged there. That was, however, more than just a symbolic act to say the person was born in that place. It was also a statement that the person was rooted in the traditions, culture, community, and history of that place. So for me, as for other students, leaving such a place behind for another meant also leaving a host of relationships, memories, and emotions that had given meaning to our lives. Not surprisingly, therefore, my journey away was not taken or felt lightly.

Nde's actions on the day I left home for secondary school put this reality into proper context for me. My bag had been packed, a sack of food expected to last me until half-term put together, and a little pocket money handed me. *Keke* and I were ready to start the fifteen mile journey on foot to where I could catch public transport to Segbwema. *Nde* drew near to say her parting words. As the words 'goodbye my son' left her mouth, they were immediately followed by a string of questions about how I would manage on my own in a strange land among strange people that neither she nor I had ever met. "Who will cook your food? Who will wash your clothes? Who will take care of you?" With these questions welled tears in both of our eyes and we fell into each other's arms sobbing uncontrollably. As I was being dragged away from her by *Keke* who was desperately trying to save himself the embarrassment of shedding tears publicly, my mother handed me a parcel of cooked food to eat in the middle of the day when I would be tired and hungry from the long journey. She knew it was going to be the last meal cooked by her that I would eat until I returned home again in seven weeks. I had been told I was going to live with a distant relation neither *Nde,* nor *Keke*, or I had ever met, who lived in this town we had never visited. I had also been told I would be responsible for myself to make sure I attended school and did my school work, prepared my meals, washed my own clothes, and organized my meagre resources to last me until when I would return home again. It was in one way a downstream swim of *Keke* Yambasu's hatched egg. But it was certainly also going to involve an upstream swim on my part if I had any prospects of laying my own eggs.

The New World of Secondary School

In Segbwema, we first visited the school, paid our fees and bought our books and uniforms with the help of teacher Yambasu. He was the only one who knew our hostess and where she lived. When we arrived, she was waiting to welcome Amie and me. After the usual formalities of greetings and questions about how everybody was, teacher Yambasu formally handed us over to *Mama* Hannah with everything we had brought with us. She was a relatively old woman probably in her late sixties. "Put your things in my room here", she ordered us, "and we will sort things out later." Teacher Yambasu then left to stay with a teacher colleague he had studied with a long time ago who was now living and teaching in the town.

It did not take long before we found out that there were already a few more students staying in this household, all of whom were older than Amie and I. So sleeping accommodation was quite tight. That night we were given food to eat, water to bathe, and a sleeping place on the floor of the parlour in the house. We had brought mats with us which we spread down and went to sleep. The honeymoon period ended the following day when our hostess instructed us to assume the responsibility of looking after ourselves and managing our own affairs. "All I promised to offer you is a roof over your heads and a little guidance now again if and when needed", she said to us in a matter of fact way. "As you can see for yourselves", she continued, "I am an old woman now and depend on my son and others to take care of me."

Almost everything I saw in Segbwema indicated that I was now in many respects in an entirely different world from the one I had lived in before. There the new world and way of life that we had only read and dreamed about in primary school seemed patently present. The town was at least fifteen times as big as my village, and populated with people from almost every ethnic group in the country. It was bigger than any place I had seen before. Public transport vehicles of different shapes, makes sizes and colours conveying people daily to different parts of the country were present all along the one main street in the town. Assistants to their drivers shouted out the names of the places they were heading for and tried to woo intending travellers to join their vehicles. Private cars, Honda bikes and bicycles were also seen everywhere. At least a third of teachers of the only two secondary schools in the town had a private car, or motorbike, or bicycle; and those who had cars and motorbikes were especially highly admired by their pupils and the wider community.

It was in Segbwema that I first saw a train. By this time trains were being phased out by the then Head of State Siaka Stevens. He had planned to replace them by buses promised by the German Government to our country. The sight of this very long snake-like structure slowly edging its way into the station through rows of houses on both sides was simply mesmerizing. The sight of it approaching the station as teacher Yambasu, Amie and I walked to school the morning after we arrived in Segbwema left me open-mouthed until it crawled across the main road which led towards the school. "This is a cargo train", teacher Yambasu told us. "It is mainly used to carry things for the government and traders", he continued. "Passenger trains used to come here as well, but they no longer do because train services are being phased out." For the rest of our journey to the school I could not get out of my mind this huge moving structure I had come across on the way.

When that early evening Amie and I decided to walk the short distance from the house in which we were staying to the main road, it was to take a closer look at the huge tall mushroom shaped silver tank we had seen as we arrived in the town the day before. We later learnt that it housed the main terminal from which the pipe water for the whole town was supplied. The tank stood on the grounds of the only police station in the town. Across the way from it stood a tap at which there were at least a dozen children and women standing by their buckets and waiting for their turn to get water to take to their homes. Coming from a village where a river, streams and wells were our sources of water, the sight of water pumped out into a bucket through a pipe was a novelty for us. In fact we waited until everyone at the tap left so that we can try our hands at pumping the water ourselves and drinking straight from the tap. As we were engaged in this exciting task, we suddenly heard a very audible and big lorry-like noise coming from what looked like a very large compound across the road with many large concrete built and nicely painted houses. As we stood up to find out the source of the noise, we suddenly saw the whole compound light up. Amazed and scared we asked a bystander what it was. "It is electricity", he said. The light is coming from that machine making the noise down there. In there is the Nixon Memorial Methodist Hospital."

As we thanked him, we walked gingerly into the compound towards the houses curiously staring at them. Walking by one building after another through long meandering corridors, we peeped into the wards and whispered information on what we saw to each other. The wards were wide and long—each holding about ten beds on each side. First came the men's ward, followed by the women's and children's wards, and then the maternity ward. We then walked out past the main hospital building and dispensary, seeing on our left hand side a chapel, some of the doctors' residences, the nursing school, female nurses' hostel, canteen, the African staff quarters and the generator house. On our right was the outpatients' department and the private ward. Over the whole compound were well cultivated trees, flowers and fruit trees. We learned later that male students of the nursing school resided in privately rented rooms in the town. We also discovered that the staff quarters of the African staff were a lot smaller than those occupied by white staff.

Later that night as I lay down to sleep, I thought to myself, "A very different world indeed, this one into which we have been brought to live! Cars, lorries, motorbikes, buses, trains, tap water, electricity, a hospital and schools with black and white people working together, even bits of tarred road which reminded one of the days when the white man ruled the land, you name it. Everything was here. "In Segbwema", I said to my self, "we are definitely face-to-face with the white man's world".

My excitement and admiration of what I saw then played no mean role in increasing the desire I had to succeed at school. I too wanted to do the kinds of things other educated African men and women were doing and live the kinds of lifestyles they were living. As it were, my early experiences of Segbwema helped settle my mind and resolve on the upstream swim to birth my own future.

An Offer of a Scholarship

On the day school started I found out that my sister Amie and I were the youngest and smallest students in the school that year. Standing out on the green just outside the principal's office, a crowd of students stood around us commenting on how small they thought we were. Besides, the tailor who had adjusted my second hand acquired school shirt did not do me any favours. He had done it so badly that the badge sown on the pocket of the top left hand side of the shirt actually went into my shorts after tucking the shirt in. "How embarrassing", I thought throughout that day. It was even more so when the first words of the principal at assembly that morning was about the school uniform: "When you come to school, wear the full school uniform. And remember this. Anytime you wear the school uniform, you are representing the school. Anyone who sees you will know that you belong to this school." So my first school day was filled with mixed emotion—pleased with the admiration of others that I was one of the youngest in the school and embarrassed that I was dressed so funnily.

On the last day of that first week in school, the principal, Mr. Patton, a long bearded English Methodist missionary, came into our classroom during our last lesson before lunch. He had a piece of paper in his hand. Our teacher immediately stopped teaching, sat down and gave him the floor. "Yes sir, carry on", he said to the principal. "May the following pupils please see me in my office at the end of school today: Charles Amara, Florence Kanneh . . . ." As we all listened intently, I suddenly heard ". . . and John Yambasu." The list ended with my name as every other list almost always did.

My blood started to race faster than normal. My heartbeat increased dramatically. Fear and anxiety set in. My legs started knocking against each other under my desk and my hands were slightly shaking. Within that short period of time I started perspiring. "I hope nobody is aware of what I am going through!" I thought to myself. I tried to disguise things as best as I could. But this was no small deal. "How could this long bearded and fearful looking white man just walk into our class and ask just a few of us to see him and not tell us why? And this is no ordinary man. He is actually the principal of this school", I pondered. "Could we have committed a crime, broken a rule or rules of the school? But I can't recall doing anything wrong since I started school. But just in case I have without knowing, what punishment could be dished out to us? Detention at the end of the school day accompanied with manual labour? Or could it even be suspension? What else? But please God whatever it is let it not be suspension. It will bring a big shame on me and on my entire family in the village." The lesson had long resume but with the conversations going on within me I did not hear a word of the rest of that class. "Will the following pupils please see me at the end of school today". The words of the principal kept ringing in my ears for the rest of that day.

"Gbolong, gbolong, gbolong . . ." the bell rang announcing the end of the school day. Off we tiptoed to the principal's office: four pupils from my stream and several other pupils from other streams of that year's first formers. It was only then I realized I was not alone in the feelings of anxiety I was experiencing. "Stand in alphabetical order besides the door all of you", the principal came out of his office and ordered us. First person, next, next . . . . and so on it went. As usual, I was the last person in the queue. It seemed I was there for the whole day. Finally my time came. "We are offering government scholarships to all the pupils who got over 350 points in their selective entrance exams", Mr. Patton informed me. "But this will cover only your school fees for the next five years you are going to be here. We will be sending letters to your parents about this." He stopped for a while, looked at me again and asked, "Do you have any questions?" "No sir", I timidly replied looking at a pile of books sitting on his big desk behind which he sat and taking care not to look in his face. "Then you may go", he said. Phew! Thank God this is not as I thought it would be. "Yes", I punched the air immediately I was out of the principal's office. Joy and excitement replaced the earlier anxiety I had experienced.

Then it suddenly dawned on me: "I prayed that God helps me to continue my schooling. I got help from a couple I am not related to and have never met. And now I have been offered a government scholarship? Wow!" Was *Hala* trying to tell me something? With the two sources of help available to me I was well placed to help Fayia Emmanuel, my second younger brother, to start school. The one immediately after me, Tamba, was too old by then to do that. Fayia was a bit old too but he was not past it. "Thank you God that you have provided for me and my brother to go to school", I murmured. As I walked home that afternoon I sang quietly to myself:

> "Praise, O praise, our God and King,
> Hymns of adoration sing:
> For His mercies still endure,
> Ever faithful, ever sure."[10]

These words of Henry William Baker written in the nineteenth century have, indeed, become true for me about a century later", I thought to myself.

---

[10]   Henry F. Lyte (1834)

A Tragic Incident

A typical school day worked out as follows. We were up at 6 o'clock in the morning, went to the water tap about four hundred yards away from the house to get water to bathe, got ready for school, and walked about three miles to school. The school assembly started at 8am at which all pupils were expected to be present. Assembly consisted of a Christian hymn sung, prayers said and announcements made by the principal and other teachers. Classes started at 8.30am and went on until 2.00pm with a fifteen and thirty minutes break times mid-morning and lunch times respectively. Sometimes when we could afford it, we bought a snack to eat during our lunch break from the local stalls pitched near the school by local women traders. Other than that we each were totally dependent on the one large spoonful of cooked bulgur wheat with vegetable oil provided by the school. These were supplied to schools then by USAID and prepared by a school cook, Madam Lahai, and her assistants. The school administration provided the other condiments.

A tragic incident in connection with the distribution of this food to pupils in my stream once took place. As usual, we had all queued in front of our classroom with our class head at the top of the queue facing us with a bucket load of cooked wheat standing beside him. In his hand was a big oval-shaped silver spoon. One after the other he dished out into the two joined hands of each pupil a spoonful of the contents of the bucket beside him. Not infrequently the food would prove insufficient for the thirty-five pupils of a stream. So there often was quite a lot of a little more than jostling for the top places in the queue since the food was served on a first-come-first-served basis. The further down the queue one was, the less it was guaranteed that one would have a portion of the food. On this particular day Seidina Bockarie, who was desperately hungry, joined the queue late. Peeping from the back and realizing that by the time his turn came there would be nothing left in the bucket, he became very angry, broke away from the queue, and walked right to the front where the class leader stood beside the bucket. Looking into the bucket he confirmed, to his utter dismay, his fear. There was in fact hardly any food left in the bucket. Bitterly disappointed and angry, Seidina got hold of a stick that was lying on the ground, and hit the class leader on the head with it. Momoh fell to the ground, blood gushing out of his head like water from a tap. By the time one of the school's American Peace Corp teachers arrived on the scene there was already absolute pandemonium as Seidina tried to run away from the scene.

I will never forget the agitated look on Seidina's face, nor the bad English he spoke in defense of his action. "Leave me, Mr. Dale, I will judge". He shouted to the Peace Corp who by this time had caught him by his shorts. "He first nacked me on the head." He continued his defense. "Then I myself I turned round, took a baobao tree, and nacked him on the head. Leave me Mr. Dale, I will judge." As he concluded his defense, all the school was already at the scene and everyone booing him, I think more so for his bad English than for what he had done. Within what looked like minutes the principal's car arrived at the scene to carry Seidina to the police station and Momoh to the hospital. A few weeks later Momoh was discharged; but he was never again able to speak normally.

I have often wondered what considerations resulted in the release of Seidina from police custody a couple of days after he had been taken there. But I clearly recall all of us pitying Momoh then as a victim of a senseless attack. Thinking of that situation now, however, I do clearly see who the real villain in this story was. I believe now it was not Seidina as we had all thought then. It was poverty and hunger. Both Seidina and Momoh, like many of us then, were the real victims of these two very closely related villains.

After School Hours

In those days, when the school day was over, my sister Amie, two other boys from our home area and I would walk back home again, passing through the local market to buy what we needed to cook our meal that day. When we returned home we would take off our uniforms, put on our house clothes, and go to help work on the rice farm of the man whose mother we were staying with. It was our way of showing appreciation for having a roof over our heads and for which we were not paying. On returning to the house in the evening we would prepare our food, eat, and do whatever homework and studying we needed to do. A kerosene lamp was among the things our parents provided money for when we left our village. Our night studies were done by one of these kerosene lamps which we lit and placed on a long raised platform going right round the veranda of the house in which we lived. Our days would then end with going to bed about midnight to rest. The whole routine would start again the next day.

A Mother's Love

And my mother? For each day of the first seven weeks I was away at school, she dropped a piece of live firewood in a stream on her way from the village to the farm, stood to see the fire go out and its smoke disappear, and prayed for protection from any danger for her son until he returned home again. She lovingly showed me the huge pile of sticks lying down on the bed of the stream on the first morning after I returned home for half term break. "I have been missing you a lot my son", she said to me as we stood side by side looking at the pile of sticks. "I am always praying that no harm would come your way in the strange land." How right she was to constantly pray for me. I needed every one of her prayers because school days away from home were quite trying times. It often demanded a little more courage and perseverance than was needed living at home with one's parents and family. Many left school not necessarily because their parents could not afford to pay the fees, but primarily because they were not able to cope with the struggles of survival away from home.

Habits Die Hard

While I did sometimes find the reality of living away from home and being exposed to other peoples and ways of life daunting, I also found it quite rewarding in other ways. There was, for example, the freedom I enjoyed living away from the closely watchful eyes of not only my parents but also the village community as a whole. Disciplining young ones in the village was a community task. So, as children and young people growing up in the village, we felt we were constantly living under the watchful eyes of 'big brother and sister' adults who reprimanded us without hesitation if we did or said something that was against the norm. But away from home with the different kinds of freedom it offered I found life in that respect very much like a downward, effortless, swim of young salmon.

But this freedom often came with its costs. I had been introduced to smoking in my last year in primary school when I was living away from my village with teacher Yambasu. So by the time I went to secondary school my casual smoking adventures had developed into what seemed an unbreakable habit. The last thing I did before setting off to school every morning, for example, was to light a cigarette; and the last thing I did before going to bed was smoke. At school the bell announcing break and lunch times was heard as a welcomed invitation to go for a smoke in the boys' school toilets. These were simply holes dug in the ground. I am horrified today when I think of one of the boys in our group who once fell halfway through into one of these pit latrines as he pushed through to get hold of a lit cigarette that was going round from one person to another. But for the fact that he was trapped by his hands, this boy would have fallen right down into to the pit and died. This incident, nevertheless, did not stop us from going into the toilets to smoke.

'Habits die hard', it is said. Habits are also costly as I found out. More than half of my pocket money went towards feeding my smoking habit. It developed to a stage where I would sometimes bring my school uniform into a cigarette trader on a Friday afternoon and leave it in for a loan of a twenty pack cigarettes. The next day I would go and break wood in the forest to sell or work on somebody's farm for a wage. Most of the money I earned from these activities went towards settling my cigarette debt and redeeming my school uniform before school started again the following week. Whatever money was left over went towards buying more cigarettes for the week, kerosene, laundry soap, and food items to augment what I had brought from the village. So while some of my weekends at school were spent helping out on our guardian's son's farm, or washing and ironing his family's clothes, or milling his rice in a mortar by hand, others were spent getting fire wood from the forests a few miles outside the town, or undertaking daily wage labour for somebody, or growing vegetables and some other food crops for myself. On at least two occasions I went round the Methodist Nixon Memorial hospital English doctors in residence and asked for weekend work for pocket money. On both occasions I was successful and spent some of my weekends washing and ironing clothes, moving stuff from one place to the other, scrubbing floors, and doing some gardening. Some weekends were spent with one of *Nde*'s uncles who lived with his family nine miles away in a place called Daru. *Nde*'s uncle Sheku was a tailor by trade and a Muslim. Every time I visited, he sent me round the surrounding villages with pillow cases and bed spreads that he had made. So my Saturdays in Daru were spent hawking. Some of the money I made was given to me to cover my bus fare back to school and a little pocket money. So my secondary school days were never boring. They were full of activities—and too full to be bored. Often, however, by the end of mid and full term when I went home to my parents, I had also managed to save a little money to enable me to buy the family a small present or two I knew they would appreciate.

Missing Home

But there were times when I missed the freedom of living and growing up at home in the village, spending time in the forest hunting and not having to worry about whether or not there would be food for the day or kerosene for studying and so on. Those were concerns I was glad to leave *Keke* and *Nde* to worry about. Not so in my new world and state of so called freedom. Its bills were my responsibility to settle. So I had to work hard to do so, even though it was not always possible to satisfy all my needs. I remember my first involvement in the school's sports. I had been selected by my sporting house master to do high jump and hurdles. While I did pretty well during the practice times, it was not so on the day of the competition. Unfortunately our food supply had run out the night before and I had gone to bed hungry. On the morning of the sports day I managed to buy a couple of doughnuts with the little money I had. But that was hardly enough to sustain and enable me to compete well. It was the high jump event that I was down to take part in first. By the time it started my legs were so weak that they could barely hold the rest of my body up. As a result and to my disappointment and shame I did very badly. Annoyed with my performance, or should I say non-performance, my house master called me on the side to give me a good telling off. It was during that time that I took the opportunity to tell him the reason for my poor performance and asked that someone else replaced me for the hurdles later that evening. Poverty and hunger: the common twin enemies of many of us pupils won again on that sporting day. In that case and as always, I was the loser. One of the things we learnt quickly in those days to beat hunger was to add a lot of chili peppers to our food. This made us drink a lot of water as we ate so that by the time we were finished eating the little food we had our bellies were full.

Fun and Serious Times

But amidst these problems, there was also plenty of fun. There was the fun of school sporting activities and competitions. We had our own school sports competitions and also sporting competitions with the only other secondary school in the town. This was an Irish Roman Catholic school called Holy Ghost Secondary School. The competition between them and us was always not only very keen, but also often ended in fierce acrimony. This came to a time when both schools had to travel and participate in their athletics and soccer competitions in the Daru army barracks. There, as the army officers warned us, we engaged in any thuggery to our own detriment. And we never did because we knew quite well that they would match their words with action untempered by mercy.

Friendly football matches with schools further afield often yielded even much more fun and pleasure. Played in the town field, they also gave the local non-school population the opportunity to watch the games. Some of us enjoyed much more than the football match on those occasions. There was, for example, a local man who always came to see the matches. We nicknamed him 'Korlayman', literally meaning 'admiring man'. This man always gave us a lot of fun because he moved his foot or some part of his body with every movement of whichever player was in possession of the ball. He did this so absent mindedly and automatically that we used to pile stones directly in front of him close to his feet waiting for when he would move his foot to kick the air. We used to do all that without him noticing what was going on. That was how much engrossed he was in the game that was going on. And within minutes of setting our trap, he usually was caught. On kicking the pile of stones, we would burst into laughter, and the poor man would chase us up and down the side of the pitch. After a while he would give up and then go back to watch the game. Cruel little brats we were in those days!

The fun often continued in the evenings after the games. A dance was organized in the town court barrie for those who could afford the entrance fees. But since the dances were always advertised long beforehand, we often had managed to raise the necessary money. They were almost always staged on Saturdays so we never bothered about going home in time because we knew there was going to be no school the following morning. Some of the money I earned from selling my garden produce, or doing weekend jobs for missionary medical staff, or daily wage tasks for local farmers, went towards paying for such fun nights. That was fun at school!

Then there was the fun on holidays back in our village. Having our own soccer games at home, organizing soccer matches with accompanying after-game dances with neighbouring villages, playing in the moon light, telling stories around the fire, and visiting relations in neighbouring villages in and outside the country were among some of the fun times we had on holidays. Often when I was home for holiday, I visited aunt Nessie and her husband Pornorwabeh in Kamakuma village in the Republic of Guinea a few miles from Sandia where I had my miraculous cure earlier in life. *Nde* Nessie, as I call her, is one of *Keke's* sisters. It was through visiting her that I came to know many more of my relations in Guinea. She would take me round to visit them when I stayed with her; and for a long time I knew Guinea more than I knew Sierra Leone. *Nde* too used to bring me round to visit her own family in Bokolu, Saidu, and Kosodu (in Guinea). For both of my parents, these visits were also times of great pride. They were bringing round their son to show him off as a story of their success in striving to have a foothold in the white man's world.

My elder sister Sia Messie Komeh and I were very close. Often she waited for me to return home so that she could share the grievances she had with our parents and other members of the community with me. "When my brother comes home I will tell him what you have done to me", she would often warn them. And tell me she did. She would find time shortly after arriving home to sit me down and tell me everything. She did this not only because I was her brother and we were very close, but also because she knew those she threatened did take account of me. Whenever she shared what and who was troubling her, I visited those people with her, investigated in to the problem, and tried to find closure to it. But I would also warn whomever was responsible for her trouble that I would not stand back to allow anyone to take advantage of her. That often seemed to work and my sister was happy again. I have often asked myself why anyone listened to a young, relatively inexperienced, and in many ways inconsequential person like me in those days? But they did. I sincerely believe it was because I was seen, like my other school going friends, as someone growing up into a person to reckon with and they did not want to be in my bad books. All this and more made me believe being in school was a rewarding opportunity. What made it more so was the deference with which I and others in my position were treated by our people. Aware that we were much more exposed to the outside world and especially to the ways of the white man than they were, everything we did was viewed with great admiration. Even when we participated in the ordinary farming tasks that everyone else did daily, we were greatly admired as if we were doing something very special.

Every year throughout my secondary school days, for example, I farmed my own plot of swamp land. The best time for growing rice on that sort of land is in the summer months. Knowing I was keen on growing my own rice crop during the summer holidays, *Keke* would always get my machete and farm bag ready before I came home. I would then spend much of the holiday season clearing and ploughing the plot, followed by transplanting the rice seedlings nursed beforehand. I also spent many hours in the bush setting traps, hunting, and fishing for the family. Then off I went at the beginning of the academic year to go back to school. *Nde* and *Keke* would harvest the rice in my absence, store it, and polish and sell it when I needed money to get something special. All this earned me a great deal of admiration and respect in our village because my people believed I did not look down on their ways even though I was deeply involved in the ways of the white man. The same was true for any of my school going colleagues who engaged themselves with similar activities during holidays in the village; and we all very much relished this deferential treatment.

When we spoke even broken bad English, everyone believed we were very highly educated. So, girls in the village who wanted to get our attention tried to also speak some English, often with hilarious consequences. I remember a girl once trying to beg her boyfriend not to be angry with her. In Krio this should have been said as, "Bo, nor vex", meaning 'Please don't be angry'. But instead of that the girl said, 'Bo, nor vek'. All of the mates of this boy just erupted in laughter. Obviously this boy was embarrassed; so was his girlfriend. But we just could not stop ourselves from laughing. Oftentimes I thought we were really, in many ways, like the proverbial one eyed man among the blind. Needless to say this sometimes went to our heads. I, for example, remember once introducing *Keke* to a friend who had come home with me on holiday. Sam and his family came from another area of the country. I had met him in school and became friends with him. Introducing him to *Keke*, I just simply said, "Sam, this is my father." "What is your name, *Keke*?" Sam asked. To which my *Keke* answered in Mende, "Nya lei mia a Lorborti Yambasu" ("My name is Lorborti Yambasu.") Embarrassed by the way he pronounced his name, and trying to let him know that I knew the proper English pronunciation of his name, I cheekily said to him, "Your name is not Lorborti, but Robert." He was going to have no Westernizing of his name by a little brat who thought he knew better than his own *Keke*. "My name is not Robert. I am Lorborti. That's the way I have always been called and that is the way it is going to remain," he said bluntly. Put in my place that time, I never again tried to persuade him to call himself something else.

A part of my school holidays were also spent with Rev Jackson and his family wherever they were stationed in the country. The times were spent doing a few household chores. But some of the time my cousin Henry (one of teacher Yambasu's sons whose fees were being paid by Rev Jackson) and I spent going through primary school registers and checking them to see that they were properly marked and closed by teachers of the various schools Rev Jackson managed. Again, like the times spent in my village or elsewhere with relations, the times spent with the Jacksons were often very rewarding and fun-filled times. In those days we were the envy of most people as we spent some of our holidays with a white man and his family, eating white man's food, and travelling with the white man in his car. For most of our friends these were things they could only dream about.

The rest of my secondary school years were not much different from my first year. The work load in school got heavier and more difficult, of course, as I progressed; but being more and more familiar with the way of life in and out of school compensated for the demands of school work. The competition for first, second, and third positions in my class was fierce throughout those years. There was a girl called Florence who was extremely clever and did very well in all her exams. Some of us used to study whole days in the forest or under tree shades by a stream and with our feet in buckets filled with cold water at night times to prevent us from sleeping. We did all this with the hope of beating Florence at exams times.

Those times were not easy especially because we did not always have enough food or pocket money to sustain us. Ordinary Level exams time were the most difficult in this regard. But there was an older girl in my class who helped me greatly during my preparations for those exams. Hawa Ngaojia was a friend who got financial support from her boyfriend. She needed help with her studies. One day she came to me and asked if I would agree to study with her in her house. She would provide coffee, food and kerosene for study time, she promised, and I would study with her and discuss questions that she had on different subjects. This arrangement was a God-sent for me and it helped me in no small way as I prepared for my exams.

Reminded of a Promise

Having done reasonably well in the exams, I joined Rev Jackson who was at this time serving in Kenema, the third biggest city in the country. Since he was the school manager of one of the largest primary schools in the town, he employed my cousin Henry and I as pupil teachers in that school. While we were doing this, we were also expected to conduct Scripture Union classes in the school twice every week after school. We were also encouraged to study for and take lay preachers' exams to equip and qualify us to preach in Methodist Churches if and when we wanted to. It was after successfully doing all these exams that I one day made an appointment to see Rev Jackson.

I had gone to bed one night and for many hours was unable to sleep. What had happened was this. I had been reminded of the vow I took on the morning my mother and I were going to the farm, wondering whether I would be able to continue my schooling. It was now about seven years since I took that vow. Was I still willing to do what I promised God I'd do? Would I be able to do the job of a Reverend Minister? What would my family think? What about my friends? All those from my village who completed secondary school were by this time either school teachers or were training in college to become school teachers? Why should I do anything different? These and many questions going on in my mind that night was what prevented me from sleeping. I resolved there and then that night that I was going to honour my promise no matter what, and that I had to see Rev Jackson and tell him for the first time about the promise I had made and my desire to fulfill it. Incidentally I had been reading the story of Hannah in the Bible before I went to lie down that night.[11] Hannah vowed to offer her child to the service of God if God blessed her with a child. When she gave birth to a son she remembered to keep her promise and so offered Samuel, her only son, to serve God. "I should make good my promise", I said repeatedly to myself that night as if to convince myself of the need to do so.

[11]   I Samuel 1:9-11

SEVEN

KEEPING THE PROMISE

Becoming 'Property of the Methodist Church'

O n visiting Rev. Jackson and telling him of my decision, his response to me was frank and open-minded. "I don't want you to feel that you have to do this because my brother and his wife paid for your schooling. Ministry", he continued, "is a difficult vocation especially for somebody like you from a very large and poor family; the financial rewards are not great. In time to come, if you become a minister, you'd find that all of those you went to school with would be high up there on the social ladder and you'd be low down. I want you to think seriously about what I am saying to you. Besides, and more importantly, you need to be called by God to do this work."

That notwithstanding, I still felt that ministry in the church was the right thing for me to do. It is a promise I made, and

I was going to keep it. I felt a strong urge to proceed as I had planned. This was reinforced by a clear lack of interest in any other work. I took these two experiences as confirmation that it was the way God wanted me to go. Consequently, I reiterated my desire to Rev. Jackson in response to his comments. "All right then" he said to me. "Go home and think about what I have told you. If after that you still think this is what you want to do, come back to me and let me know."

So I left, returning a month later to tell him my mind was made up. "The proof of the pudding is in the eating," he said to me. It was the first time I heard that saying and I did not really understand what it meant. But it was no time for an English lesson, I reasoned. I was there for something I believed was more immediately important for me than that. Understanding what the saying meant could wait for another time. But what he proceeded to say to me gave me an idea of what the saying meant. "This is now July and schools will be closing for the summer in less than two weeks, right?" "Yes sir", I replied. "Next September", he continued, "you won't be going back to school to teach as you have been doing. I am going to employ you as a catechist in the church here in Kenema. You will stay here until you take your exams to qualify you for going to theological college for your training to become a minister." As I listened to him I nodded approvingly. "But I want you to know that the salary you will be getting as a catechist will be half of what you have been getting as a teacher." "No problem, sir", I responded confidently.

Thinking to myself as I walked home from Rev. Jackson's office that day, I reflected: "So this is what he meant by 'The proof of the pudding is in the eating?' Why did he not just say 'Your bowl of rice will get smaller as a catechist compared to what it is now working as a teacher; and we shall know then if you really want to be a minister?' That would have been a better and humorous Sierra Leonean way of making the same point." Thinking about this I smiled as I imagined the laughter with which a group of Sierra Leoneans would have received such a statement.

Opposition from my Family

That was that, anyway. The decision was made and came September, I left primary school teaching and became a catechist. My responsibilities included pastoral visits, setting up and leading Scripture Union groups in secondary schools in the town, helping in organizing church events, and taking services. I also spent some time preparing to take the exams the church required for all who wanted to train as ministers. In a year I was ready to go to theological college for training, and news of my decision had reached my village and parents.

That was in the summer of 1978. Before I proceeded to college, I went home to tell my parents what was happening and to say my formal goodbyes. I will never forget the reception I got on that visit. For the first time in my life *Nde* welcomed me in tears instead of with joy and laughter. I was baffled and deeply upset. What was the matter with her? *Keke*, I observed, was not happy either. He looked long-faced and downcast, and his reply to my greeting very cold and lifeless.

I discovered later that someone from the village had told them before I arrived that I had opted to become a minister and that it was a very badly paid job. This person went on to tell them that even white people who were ministers were supported by their own people, and not the church. Knowing that everyone else with an education in my village was either a teacher or wanted to be one, my parents did not understand why I had decidedly differently. Their concern was that as minister in the church I would not be in position to help them financially as other sons of the village who had become teachers were doing for their parents. All my explaining did not make any difference to how they thought and felt.

So I left home for theological college in Freetown that summer deeply troubled about my parents' refusal to accept my decision to become a minister. But perhaps what troubled me more was the fact that that summer I was not blessed by them in the normal and expected way. I recalled that when I first left home for secondary school, *Mama* Amie, *Keke*, and *Nde* made me kneel down in turns at their feet, and each spoke out aloud their wishes for me, asked my father not to forget me, and prayed that *Hala* would bless me and protect me from evil people and their machinations. At the end of what each had to say, each spat a little on their two hands, rubbed them together and placed them on my head. My uncle Nabieu Sovula did the same. That way they symbolically placed their wishes and prayers of blessing on me, their spittle representing the words that came out from their mouths.

Training at the Theological College

The Sierra Leone Theological Hall and Church Training Centre was owned and run by three main Protestant Churches— The Church of Sierra Leone (Anglican), the United Methodist Church (American), and the Sierra Leone Methodist Church (British). The three church bodies which were then already autonomous entities from their parent churches were a salient reminder of the Christian white man's scramble for and colonization of souls that Sierra Leone had experienced long before I was born. There were other forms of Christianity involved in this history of the battle for the souls of Sierra Leoneans. These included the Roman Catholics and Baptists. But like the now infamous transatlantic slave trade in which Africans sold their fellow Africans, I was to learn later that the foot soldiers in that spiritual battle were interestingly often black people themselves who had converted to Christianity.

The history books I read illustrated clearly the singularly important roles of African men and women in propagating the various Western brands of Christianity in Sierra Leone and elsewhere. The earliest agents in this respect were freed slaves who had been converted to one Western brand of Christianity or the other while living as slaves in the Americas and Britain. On being freed and returned to the 'Province of Freedom' as Freetown was known before it became a British colony, they organized themselves into effective thriving worshipping communities led by their own pastors and supported locally. Not infrequently, much of the initiative for encouraging missionary activity in the country lay with these local leaders.

I found out later while studying at the Theological Hall for example, that it was a Joseph Brown, a leading black Methodist preacher and one of the Settlers, who wrote to the English Wesleyan Methodist Conference asking for a missionary in 1806. Five years later the Rev. George Warren and three school teachers arrived in Freetown. Warren Memorial Methodist Church, one of the two churches I was assigned to in Freetown after my own college training and in which I was eventually ordained is named after this first Methodist missionary in Sierra Leone.

Many who know of The Amistad story may not know that some of the leaders of the revolt were Sierra Leoneans. When Sengbe Pieh, the main leader, and his other fellow Sierra Leoneans were eventually returned to Sierra Leone as free men from the United States, they were instrumental in starting Christian missions among their own peoples. It was the beginning of the United Brethren in Christ Church (USA) missions among Mende and Sherbro peoples, many of whose peoples later joined with the United Methodist Church of Sierra Leone.

So, walking into the protestant owned and managed Theological Hall and Church Training Centre on that first occasion as a student, I was truly walking into an institution which in many ways was representative of the complex political and religious history of my country as a whole. It was a history which was not too far removed from the stories of *Keke* Yambasu as agent and advocate for the white man's religion and ways of life.

In the Theological Hall, students lived a very sheltered life with two relatively comfortable students' hostels, three good meals a day, free medical care, and a very reasonable monthly allowance. Friends of ours who were students in government—managed colleges often envied the care we received from our churches. As a result, life in college was in this and many other respects totally different from the constant daily struggles for survival in my secondary school days. Instead of a mat spread on the floor to sleep on I had a room shared with another student, my own bed furnished with a comfortable mattress, plus a set of pillows, pillow cases and bed-sheets provided for by my student allowances. Instead of collecting water from a public tap (or water well when the public tap was not working), pipe borne water was always available in the hostel. Between the ten of us students living in our hostel we shared two indoor bathrooms and toilets. General public electricity replaced the kerosene shade lamp, and a college cook's expert cooking my own 'make-do' cooking. The use of Kissi and Mende languages was largely replaced by the use of Krio language which I had first encountered in Segbwema.

I still remember vividly that first encounter with Krio. It was in my first month in the town and at the end of the school day as I walked home. On that particular day, instead of staying on the main street as I usually did, I had decided to use an alley way through a cluster of houses which I believed was a short cut home. With a pile of text and exercise books on my head supported with one hand, I began to walk leisurely through what I was to later discover was a Creole lady's compound. As I was approaching the other end of the compound, I suddenly I heard an angry voice shouting at me from a corner of the compound saying in Krio "Waitin do you dae walka na me yard en you nor dae tell me adu?" (Why are you walking through my yard and not greeting me?") The truth is that I had not noticed there was someone there. Afraid and eager to explain to my interrogator that I meant no disrespect to her, I responded in bad Krio saying, "I not hear you ma". Probably further irritated by my bad Krio, she urged me to get on my way quickly remarking as I went, "Mende Korsor" meaning, 'Mende through and through'. I was later to learn that it was the Creole people's way of expressing their prejudice against Mende people as backward and inferior to them.

That was my first encounter with the Krio language and a Creole person, and I have never forgotten it. During the rest of my time in Segbwema I worked on my Krio and managed to reasonably master it. I especially learned that the proper way to have responded to that lady was to say, "A nor yeri you ma", the 'A' sounded like the 'a' in 'ma".

Reflecting on this incident later, I realized how prejudice can easily lead us into making simplistic assumptions about people. While I spoke Mende, what this lady did not know was that I was in fact a Kissi. And while she may have concluded that my Mende was what was responsible for my bad Krio, I have never been certain myself that that was the case. Both primary schools I attended forbade us from using any other language on the school grounds as a way of encouraging us to learn the English language. So by the time I arrived in Segbwema both my spoken and written English were, considering my background, reasonably good. That was what made it possible for me to even say what I managed to say to her on that day. Be that as it may, my limited encounter and experience with Krio in Segbwema had provided me with a working knowledge of the language for life in Creole Country—Freetown.

Reconciled to my Parents

For the whole of my first year in college I decided not to go back home to my parents. I stayed, instead, with friends in Freetown or Kenema during holidays. The following year when I summed up courage and decided to spend my Christmas holiday at home in Lalehun, however, I was warmly received by *Nde* and *Keke*. I never quite understood why they changed their minds and acted as though nothing had happened between them and me. On my part, however, their attitude towards me before I left for college and how I felt about it were still as fresh in my mind as though everything happened only the day before that Christmas holiday home-coming. As a result I had agonized for weeks over my plans to visit them and about how I may be received. Consequently, I was baffled, to say the least, about what seemed to me a complete change of disposition towards me on their part. But I guessed that after deciding to stay away from home for a year, they probably were concerned that unless they changed they might drive me away from home for a very long time. They had probably come to the conclusion that the lesser of the two evils was to make me feel welcomed at home regardless of what I chose to do with my life.

From then on, college years were great, with a lot of academically stimulating studies and simple fun. My studies for the local preachers' and college entrance exams had given me a very good grounding for the standard of work expected from us at college. Biblical Greek and Hebrew were the only two subjects that I had no idea about before I started. But the focused time of study allocated to them helped me greatly.

Students, Lecturers and Principals

The Rev. Hughes and Mrs. Joan Thomas were Methodist missionary tutors. They taught me and my colleagues how to speak and write English properly. Whatever weaknesses I have in this area today in no way suggests any inability or neglect on their parts in carrying out their task. The truth is that English is not an easy language to master for many of us Africans, especially those of us who were born and grew up in remote rural areas. Mrs. Margaret Baxter, a very intelligent Anglican missionary, inspired me to think creatively as I read and applied the Scriptures. Margaret, Hughes and Joan were natural teachers. It showed in the way they approached their lessons and in their concern to carry all the students along with them as they taught a class.

Margaret's husband Stewart was a chaplain to the Seamen's Club. He gave me one of my most memorable student placements visiting boats in the Freetown Queen Elizabeth II Quay and being available for any help asked of me. Once, a boat nearly left with me onboard talking to some of the staff. By the time the captain realized what had happened, the boat had already left shore. So he had to reverse the boat back to shore for me to disembark.

Moira Shaw and her husband Alan taught us how to think theologically and sociologically. They were a great and admirable pair: young, enthusiastic, and bright. Professor Canon Harry Sawyerr, a Creole world renowned Africanist and the oldest member of staff, taught us the art of not taking anyone's view on anything as gospel truth. "Ask questions of everything you read and everyone you listen to", he used to say to us emphasizing every word. "And look for ways to improve and/or add on to what others say or write", he often added. Critical thinking and scholarly honesty were what I learned from him above everything else. If he did not know, he said so directly and without any scholarly academic pretence. A brilliant New Testament Scholar, I remember once asking him something about Saint Paul. I cannot now quite remember what the question was but I still remember more or less the answer he gave me. "I don't know", he said, furiously smoking his pipe. "And Paul is too long dead for us to find out from him." The two things together—the matter-of-fact way he answered me and the way he smoked—made everyone in the class including myself laugh. All of these people and more made college life fun and rewarding.

Sometimes secondary school teachers came into college to do a course in chaplaincy studies. There were also those who were part time Theological Education by Extension (TEE) students. Their primary interest was to enhance the particular lay ministry they were involved with in their churches. In the space of two years we also had two foreign students from the

Methodist Church in the Gambia, both of whom were old enough to be the father of many of us full time ministerial students. With such a great mix of students and experiences, our college socials used to be wonderful occasions. Most of our tutors used to attend as well, although they never stayed for more than a couple of hours. Needless to say these social occasions never ended until the small hours of the morning. With plenty of good food to eat, lots of drinks, many friends present, and lots of good music, the nights were guaranteed to be just the sort of nights we wanted them to be.

In my first two years we had an English Anglican Priest as principal. He was quite a charming and funny, but hardworking man. Most of his time was given to administration except for an odd time standing in for a tutor who was absent for one reason or another. But Canon Ross sometimes had what we believed were peculiar ways of doing things. He would, for example, sometimes just decide not pay us our allowances on time even though the money was there. At one time the students decided to go on strike as a result. Since one of the student hostels was about a mile down the road from the college, the students in the other hostel which was adjoined to the college walked down to the other hostel. With all of the students together in one place, we barred the gates and decided to stay at home. The stand-off took about three days during which tutors went to college but there were no students to teach.

Afraid that he might be confronted by students, the principal decided to go to college at night time to do his work. Once we got to know this, some students decided one night to walk up to the college and lie in wait for him there. It was easy to do so in the African night with very little light in the corridors of the college. Suddenly they heard footsteps gingerly coming up the stairs as if the person was avoiding drawing attention to himself. It was not too long before the waiting students knew it was the principal's footsteps. "Take your positions everyone", one of them quietly told the other three students' union executives who had taken positions in different places around the door of his office. They listened to him quietly taking out his keys, putting one in the keyhole, and opening the door. As he was about to close the door behind him and lock it (as he used to do), all four of the students jumped out from their hiding places together shouting, "Where is our money?" He was so frightened that he threw the keys on the floor. When he realized who they were and why they were there, he wasted no time in apologizing, promising that he would pay students' allowances the following day. So they went away and left him in peace; but not before knowing exactly what time the moneys would be paid out.

More than half of our lecturers were missionaries either from England or America and most of them were in the country with their families. For most of the time, the only two subjects for which we had African tutors were African Traditional Religion and African Church History. Now and again we may have had an experienced African minister who would come into college to teach us about practical aspects of ministry in Sierra Leone. By the end of my second year, most of the missionary staff, including Principal Canon Ross, had left. Professor Harry Sawyerr took over as principal after Canon Ross and remained principal for the rest of my time in College. Rev. Canon Professor Harry Sawyerr. His name represented everything that most of us students dreamed of—a Christian minister, academic and an accomplished churchman. He had travelled the world as guest lecturer in many Universities, had had a stint as lecturer in a University in the West Indies, lectured in and become principal of the then world renowned University of Sierra Leone's Fourah Bay College (affiliated to Durham University in England), had published numerous articles and books, and influenced many white and black scholars. For us young aspiring African trainees for ministry in the Church he was our role model and inspiration. In addition to everything else I owe to this our African hero, he was the man who recommended to my head of Church at the time, Rev. Leslie Wallace (an Irish man), that if ever the opportunity arose to expose one of their ministers to further training they should consider me as a possible candidate.

So when in 1984 I was stopped from going to Fourah Bay College for further studies by the same church that had asked me to seek for admission there, I was the unhappiest man on earth. The church had decided, instead, to send me to Kailahun from the Freetown Wesley Circuit (to this day considered as the number one Circuit of Sierra Leone Methodism by many), where I was first stationed after I left college in 1982. Then, I had served for over a year on this Circuit under a very experienced and friendly Ghanaian missionary by the name of Justice Owusu Ansah. He was the one who taught me most of my first practical duties as a minister.

My First Appointment as a Minister

In Sierra Leone Methodism in those days, most Creoles in Freetown preferred Creole ministers to non-Creole Sierra Leonean ones. Ministers from other areas of the country were considered somehow lower in status to minister in their churches. I had known this before I left college. From my studies at college I had learnt that the history of that attitude went back to the very early days when the first freed black slaves were resettled in the 'Province of Freedom'. Exposed to English, Western education, and ways of living in the lands of their enslavement, they considered themselves civilized and better than the natives. Consequently, they looked down on the latter as unequal to them in every sense.

Yet they often took in their homes as wards the sons and daughters of the natives. While with them the wards were brought up as Creoles, educated in Western style schools, Christianized, and their native languages and names were silenced and replaced by the Krio language and names. In this regard Creole efforts at taming country peoples in Sierra Leone was arguably a much more successful and effective cultural colonization programme than that effected by Christian missionaries. When Creoles employed natives, it was only to do their menial jobs. In those days many non-Creoles who aspired to important positions in the civil service and elsewhere had to align themselves closely with Creoles. Sometimes they even had to consciously take on Creole lifestyles. Consequently, many who later became known as Creoles were in fact originally natives. The other side of this story, of course, is that this attempt at taming and domesticating 'natives' has also resulted in neutralizing Creole culture in no small way.

Given that history, I was not surprised to find, when I was posted to Wesley Circuit, that there were many there who were opposed to the idea. But there were also others who readily accepted me. Some even invited me to their homes and while with them expressed their disgust at those who opposed my being sent to their Circuit. I was to learn in those conversations that some of them, though they had Creole names and lived like Creoles, were country people. Those who were opposed to me were the diehard Creoles. They sometimes even pretended not to be able to pronounce my surname because it was so alien and different to surnames like Johnson, Clarkson, McCarthy, Coker, Peterson and so on which their own people carried. Sometimes one of them would come to the Circuit office wanting the services of a minister. But immediately they learned from the secretary that I was the one available, they would decide to wait for when my boss would be available.

That experience brought in sharp focus again my first encounter with a Creole in Segbwema. I was, however, better prepared to deal with the situation on that second occasion. "This time", I said to myself with all the conviction I could muster, "I am not going to take this condescending discriminating attitude lying down." One morning I arrived at the Circuit office with a special announcement to the secretary. "From now on", I said to her, "print my name in church notices and literature as Rev. Sahr J. Yambasu instead of Rev. John S. Yambasu." Asking me why, I explained to her saying, "Sahr was the name I was born with. It is the name of the first born son of any family among my people. Unlike John", I continued, "Sahr is not a given name. Among my people children are named according to where they come in the family and there is no choice about this on their or their parents' parts. Since Sahr is the name that my mother, father, sister, and grandmother call me at home, it means a lot more to me than John." That is how I concluded the conversation and proceeded to my desk.

While everything I said was of course true, my real reason for suggesting the change was to let those who opposed me because I was not a Creole know that I had no intention whatsoever of denying who I was. The secretary and I knew that my decision was going to anger the group opposed to my being on their Circuit. If they were not happy with Yambasu, we both reckoned they would not be happy with Sahr. "But", I reasoned, "it is their problem; let them deal with it whichever way they choose." And, as we had predicted, it indeed angered the group of people in question. One of them raised the issue with me at one of our church meetings and I replied by telling him exactly what I told the secretary on the morning I announced how she should print my name on church documents. What effect, if any, my explanation had on this man and others at the meeting I was unable to determine. But something profoundly important happened to me as a result of that incident. It occasioned, in a way I had never experienced before, an acute sense within me of who I was and the need to value and honour my roots and history. It was like a new birth experience. From then on, I resolved never to suffocate who I was because of the ignorance of others. "Never apologize for being who you are", I warned myself.

My Creole Confidant

By the time I was asked to leave for Kailahun, most of the people who had not initially accepted me as their minister began to appreciate my ministry. They were among the most outspoken protesters against the decision to move me. But in the end I had to go. In Methodism, then as now, one goes where he or she is sent; and refusing to go would be tantamount to resigning. When asked 'Will you go where we send you?' at the outset of the process of recruitment for ministry, one has already answered in the affirmative.

That notwithstanding, though, my decision to go was helped greatly by a senior member of one of the churches I served. By the end of my first year working in Wesley Circuit, I had independently come to the conclusion that I needed someone I could confide in. My choice was a Dr. Harris, a quiet and unassuming grey-haired Creole private medical consultant in whom I had sensed a loving and caring spirit. Since I could not understand why the church was going back on its promise to send me to college for further studies, I decided to go and share my frustrations with Dr. Harris. One morning I walked into the reception of his surgery which was only a stone's throw away from the church office to make an appointment to see him. The receptionist, a middle aged medium built and light skinned beautiful lady who knew me quite well asked, "Is it medical or business?" "Personal", I replied. "He is free at 4.30pm, Reverend. Can you come at that time?" I said I could and left.

Now and again for much of that day when I thought of the appointment, I worried about how I was going to put my request to Dr. Harris. That afternoon, as I walked into his surgery, I had only one thing in my mind: "Just simply make your request. If he asks for clarification then take the opportunity to explain yourself." That is exactly what I did and had a very satisfactory outcome.

By the time I did so, many people had already come to advise me to challenge the decision to move me. To be honest, what those people advised was my own first gut feeling. But I also knew very well and understood the church's expectations. After voicing my frustrations and dilemma, Dr. Harris sat me down and began by reminding me of the integrity of those who had decided that I do not proceed to college as had been decided earlier. "They must have a good reason", he said to me. "So I would advise that you go to the President and Secretary of Conference tomorrow, tell them you have accepted to go where they have sent you, and get ready to go." It was not the advice I expected, but it is exactly what I did. So in less than two months I left after well attended farewell services in both churches on the Circuit.

Ministry in Kailahun

The minister in charge of Kailahun Circuit at that time was the Rev. Christian Peacock. Christian was also a very senior minister in the Church and the Chairman of the Kailahun-Kono District of the Methodist Church Sierra Leonean. His wife, a secondary school teacher, had been awarded a government scholarship to study for a Masters degree in the University of Reading in England. As it happened, Christian was also supposed to go for further studies in the same University the year after his wife was expected back home after her studies. To prevent them being separated from each other for the duration of their studies the Church decided that Christian would take his study leave to coincide with the time his wife was going to be away. This was what triggered the need for an emergency stationing of someone who would take over the work Christian was doing. That was how my appointment to Kailahun came about.

On arrival I quickly realized that it was a valuable training ground for my future ministry. For, in Kailahun, I had eight primary schools and over twelve churches to manage. Sometimes I would be away from home for a whole week taking services, visiting schools and chairing church business meetings. Not surprisingly, work on this circuit was physically quite taxing. It would have been virtually impossible to accomplish much of value without the sacrificial commitment of some trusted and experienced lay leaders.

I have since wondered about the significant training and support roles of such lay people in the life of the Church and what importance the Church assigned it. While I valued the support I received from teachers, catechists, and others, my time in Kailahun opened my eyes to something I had not encountered in Freetown. With one ordained minister on a Circuit that large and the overwhelming amount of responsibilities he was expected to carry, it dawned on me that the real ministry and mission of the church existed at village level and was largely carried out in the absence of the minister. In the villages were praying communities, but they were Eucharistic communities only once every couple of months or so when the minister visited. In his absence, the day-to-day ministry and mission of the church was carried out by the catechists and elders of the church. They were in actual fact the real teachers and pastors of the people. Yet, in almost every case, they were biblically and theologically untrained lay men and women.

This state of affairs raised many worrying concerns in my mind with regard to the interpretation of the scriptures, the teaching of key Christian doctrines, and the handling of cultural matters especially where they contradicted Christian teaching and practice as handed down by the Methodist Church. In the Kailahun Circuit, I not only found profound ignorance in all these matters and more among those day-to-day teachers, evangelists, pastors and ministers of the people, it also seemed to me that they were neither aware nor bothered about them.

Despite that, church services and meetings were often very well attended. Even when the spiritual and moral life Christians lived was more or less the same as that of those who were not Christians, it did not seem to bother the former in any significant way whatsoever. Instead, they believed they were embarked on a new spiritual journey and were followers of Jesus. To be certain, I identified few but significant instances of movement towards a different and new way of living by some Christians. These had stopped consulting sorcerers about their problems or fortune tellers about their futures. But most had just added Jesus to their list of spiritual personalities and powers whose help they sought and appropriated in times of need. All had accepted as un-Christian certain behaviors they once engaged in without any qualms, even if they often failed to live up to the expectations of their faith in those respects. And the religious vocabulary of all reflected a new and additional religious perspective on their age-old journey of faith in *Hala*.

A Feeling of Inadequacy

Ministry in kailahun made me wonder about the whole notion of conversion in terms of theory and reality. Was going to church and participating in church rituals all that was needed for one to consider oneself a Christian? Did it matter how one lived one's life in relation to other people and the natural world? Of what value, if any, was the teaching and example of Jesus to one who confessed to be Christian? Were the different and new ways of living I witnessed a consequence of Christianity or modernization? It also made me wonder whether the Church was interested in addressing these issues. I knew, of course, that the Church was aware and concerned about these issues. But I was not so sure about whether or not it was interested in addressing them. But even if it was, was it equipped to deal with this problem? What human and other resources did the Church have and deploy in this direction?

I, like most other ministers, was trained in a Western style theological institution and sent out to work among people the vast majority of whom did not read or write even in their own languages. Their traditional religions were not missionary by nature. In other words, their practitioners did not have or feel any obligation to go out and convert other people. The only obligation they had and felt was to practice their religions. Theological arguments in defense of the object of one's worship were therefore uncommon. Priests, priestesses, and other mediators of the spiritual world hailed locally, were identified to be so by their communities, lived permanently with their people, and were compensated in kind or cash for their services by those who used them. The spiritual world was believed to be too mysterious for anyone person or religious system to claim a monopoly of knowledge, access, and power over. All mere mortals could do is to discern which best served their need at a time and utilize it.

While I had been taught African traditional religions during my college training, the time and effort allocated to it included no real attempt at seeking ways of using that information to aid me in the propagation of the gospel. Much of the theological education I received was almost exclusively based upon and informed by Western approaches to learning. Academic output was the predominant measure of the quality of students. Intellectual knowledge was more readily rewarded than practice. Rational logical thinking was the preferred approach to every human reality, even though there was much to human life that did not make logical sense, not least in the realm of belief and faith. Little or no consideration was given to studying actual experiences vis-à-vis the predominant notion of conversion as a simple straightforward event leading to change from one state of being (sinful) to another (sinless). With one exception, even my African tutors only regurgitated what they themselves had been fed by Western teachers, literature, and universities.

So in Kailahun, I was brought face to face with a situation that I was never equipped adequately to deal with. Although I did speak the two main languages of the area, I had not been sent there at the people's request. It was a decision made hundreds of miles away from them in Freetown and by people most of them did not know—not even the people in the churches I was assigned to. Yet those people were expected to pay me a monthly salary prescribed by an external body, and much more than the average monthly earnings of most of those who were expected to contribute towards that salary. The same people were also expected to pay me any additional work-related expenses, including the costs for travelling to serve them in their communities. Needless to say that this heavy burden placed on my clients for looking after their spiritual wellbeing presented a lot of problems.

Confronted with the realities of ministry and life in Kailahun I was at a loss as to where to begin. Yet there was one thing I was never in doubt about. I was convinced that ministers, catechists and lay leaders in the Church needed to be provided with space and time to reflect seriously on the historical content of the faith they professed, the contexts within which they were expected to disseminate and express that faith, and the experiences of living out that faith vis-à-vis the complex and often difficult realities of living.

I recalled that when I was in college one of the issues we discussed in our African traditional religions class was the religious tradition of pouring libation in the context of ancestral veneration. I can't remember now the exact reason, but one of the students wanted to know how the celebration of the Christian ritual of Holy Communion could be made more African. This question generated such an interest in the class that the following two classes were dedicated to discussing it and assessing various suggestions for their Christian and African merits. At the end of the sessions, we suggested to Prof. Sawyerr that we would like to hold an experimental service of Holy Communion in one of the local Methodist churches. We also suggested that we invite local Methodists to attend the same. For that service the Communion elements were going to be roasted cassava and palm wine which, unlike bread and wine, were easily accessible and affordable countrywide. While we could find no symbolic problems for the use of cassava to represent the body of Christ, we debated the difficulty of using palm wine to represent the blood of Christ since it was whitish. After a long time reflecting on this we came to the conclusion that one important element of blood is water and palm wine resembled water.

That experimental service not only attracted a lot of people, it also generated a lot of healthy debate. I have never forgotten the smile on the face of the Communion steward at that service as he walked back into the church after disposing appropriately of the left over elements. We had just finished singing a short chorus when he suddenly walked into the chapel belting out the chorus:

> "Jesus is passing this way, this way, this way;
> Jesus is passing this way.
> He's passing this way today."

Spontaneously, everyone joined him in singing the song.

Did this man just sing a song he liked singing, or was he making a statement about the relevance of the service to him, or was something else the reason? I have often wondered about this? When at the end of the service I spoke to a member of the church about that Communion steward and the lightness in his spirit at that service, he said to me: "I have been attending this church for over thirty years and have never seen him this happy in a church service."

That Communion event in college and the classes and discussions that led to it were a once off as far as I can remember. But it came to mind when I pondered the realities of ministry in Kailahun. "Would that process of thinking through issues relating to ministry and arriving at solutions that were both Christian, African, and reflected actual experiences of people involved in the faith journey serve as a way forward?" It certainly was my best experience of doing situational Christian theology and ministry for the entire duration of my training in college.

As I reflected on that experience, I resolved to employ the same method with my Circuit catechists and church leaders. One Saturday every month all the catechists, lay people who conducted worship services, and I would meet. The purpose of the meeting would be threefold: pray together, discuss issues of concern related to ministry and life that we may have encountered or experienced in the weeks before the meeting, and read and discuss a passage of scripture with a view to discerning its message for the contexts in which we were ministering. Some years later, I discovered from a

SAHR JOHN YAMBASU

conversation with Rev. Wallace that he had employed a similar method many years back when he served in Kailahun.

It was also in Kailahun that I discovered that a minister must deal very carefully and cautiously with parishioners who readily volunteer unsolicited information about fellow members. Unaware of the in-fighting and power struggles that had been going on in the Circuit before I arrived, I took to a teacher-catechist who befriended me immediately I arrived and told me the names of all the people he believed I should be careful with in my dealings. While what he did initially rang bells with me, I eventually ignored those concerns, trusting this man with a lot of things including harvest offerings of money, rice, cocoa, yams, palmoil, and so on for safe keeping until the meeting of Circuit officers where a report would be given and the offerings handed over to the Circuit Steward. To my dismay, a few days before the meeting, I found out that he had used some of the money and items. It was at the end of my third month on the Circuit and I had to refund the money and pay for the items he had sold. It was only after that incident that I was made aware of the real character of that man. "We did say that you will discover for yourself the true nature of the man and learn your lesson", one elderly man stood up and told me on the floor of the meeting.

An Offer to Study Abroad

Six months on in Kailahun, I was invited to head office in Freetown and told that a scholarship had been found for me to go for post ordination studies at Edgehill Methodist College and Queens University in Belfast. I was given application forms to complete and post to those institutions and asked to prepare to leave the following September. This was in February 1985. Part of my preparation included getting a passport and visa. Within a short while on that road, I quickly discovered I needed a birth certificate. Many years back, and for the purposes of completing school forms, I had fixed my birthday even though I had not gone on to get a birth certificate. I was born in a place where no births and deaths were recorded. This is still the case in many areas in my country. So when I was required to complete my Selective Entrance Exams forms about sixteen years earlier, I had to ask teacher Yambasu when he thought I was born. He made an informed guess of the year and time of year but did not know the exact day. So I had to choose both the month and day for myself. For those of my classmates who did not have any educated person in their family to make an informed guess, their parents had to count backwards the different places they had farmed since the sons and daughters in question were born. That way my mates too were able to fix their own birthdays.

The following April I was ordained at a service in Freetown at which Rev. Charles Eyre, preached. Mr. Eyre was the President of the Methodist Church in Ireland that year and had been attending our annual conference. One Mama Cole, an old Creole lady, and her family had adopted me as their son when I was ministering on Wesley Circuit. They were well known and respected members of the Warren Memorial Methodist Church where I also used to sing in the church choir. Since I had no family in Freetown when I was ordained,

Mama Cole and her family took it upon themselves to kindly organize a party for me and all my friends in their home. Among the many things I learned from this family is never to paint an entire people with the same brush.

That summer, after my ordination, I spent some time in my home village with my parents who had already paid me several visits in Kailahun. At that time, my younger brothers Fayia (*Keke* Yambasu's last son with *Nde* before he died), Fallah and Nyuma (the first two of *Keke's* sons with *Nde*) were living with me then. Being the oldest son of my family automatically conferred on me family responsibilities that I could not relegate to others. One of them was looking after my siblings and educating them. Having seen that I was taking those responsibilities seriously, including those of looking after their own needs, *Keke* and *Nde* had begun realizing that I did not have to be a teacher to care for my family. They had convinced themselves that all that mattered was that I was where God wanted me to be; and God would supply my needs and theirs in that place. A few years later I also had to send Halle, the last of my surviving brothers, to school.

"Sweet Mother, I will not forget you because of the way you have suffered for me." These were the lyrics of a piece of music being played as *Nde* and I danced at my farewell party in Kailahun. Just as well, it was not played early on in the party, as it inevitably brought the party to an end. For once my mother and I started dancing and everyone stood round us clapping, we both started to cry in each others arms, for what reason I could not exactly say. But this I knew. There were a lot of mixed emotions at work in us—unspoken joy and

162

thanksgiving on the one hand, and, on the other, deep sorrow and pain at the thought of parting. This time, it was a different kind of going away. I was going out of the country, far away to where she could not go even if she wanted to. And this was the last night we were going to be together before I finally leave for Freetown and then Belfast.

But that was not all. Someone had told my mother about the Belfast troubles. She was worried and wondered why the church decided to send me there. To be honest, I was worried too. Some of my non-Methodist friends even wondered whether the Church had not decided to send me to Belfast as a form of punishment for something I had done wrong. In their memory, all Methodist ministers who had gone out for further studies before went to Britain, Germany, or the United States of America. "Why this sudden change?" They wondered.

But there it was! Whatever my mother, others and I thought about Belfast, I had to go where I was sent. Besides, was it not what I had always dreamed about—going to the white man's land? If those who came from there were so tamed, religious, well educated, and materially well off, it must be a wonderful place to be, despite the fact that there may be fighting there. But even if it was not, could I now retreat having travelled so far upstream following the path my father and his contemporaries put me on so many years ago? The journey back might prove to be much more difficult and riskier than carrying on. So I left, believing that God was with me, and so things can only be better. "This, in fact, was a unique opportunity to be grateful for", I convinced myself.

EIGHT

OUT OF AFRICA

Journey to the West

It is believed that there are three stages of culture shock that those who find themselves in another culture go through. The first is seeing everything as totally different from their culture; the second is when they try to make sense of the culture in which they find themselves; and the final stage is when they seek to assess objectively their own and the other culture for the strengths and weaknesses each has. My experiences in Europe very much confirmed this staged approached to culture shock. To be certain, my colleague Stephen Boima (he was being sent to Cliff College in England) and I were given some mentoring by the Secretary of our Church Conference, Rev. Leslie Wallace before we left Freetown. Besides we had lived with, read and heard about, and watched Western films before. But when we arrived in Europe, we were visibly overwhelmed by the differences in attitude and approach we witnessed.

Our travel arrangements having been made and paid for by the Church, we had left Freetown at midnight on a KLM Dutch Airline plane and arrived in Holland's world famous Schipol Airport in Amsterdam in the early morning hours. Being my first flying experience, I found it to be a less than enjoyable one. I found take-off, the period before the plane stabilized, the times when we flew through turbulent weather conditions, and landing particularly uncomfortable. In those times I held firmly to my seat and all sorts of possible horrible scenarios of what could happen to us rushed through my mind in quick succession. Stephen told me he had flown before but only in small planes in Sierra Leone's once famous diamond mining area of Kono. That was Stephen's home area.

In the West

In Amsterdam, our first major problem was how to get on an escalator without falling off and breaking a limb or two. On approach to the moving staircase, we stopped, stood out of the way of others, and carefully watched what others were doing. We had a little consultation there on the side to be sure that both of us were happy enough to give it a go. So we did. But what happened next proved that we obviously had not fully grasped the technique. Stephen went first because he was the older one, and I followed. Before my two feet got steadied on the escalator, I saw Steven's suitcase threateningly tumbling downwards towards me. Attempting to catch it and prevent it from knocking me down, my own suitcase mistakenly slipped out of my hand and headed the same direction as Stephen's. Suddenly there were two suitcases travelling uncontrollably in the opposite direction to their owners and endangering fellow travellers. Thankfully, two young men who were just about to commence their ascent kindly caught the two suitcases and brought them up to us. Embarrassed and glaring sheepishly at each other, we received them, profusely thanking our helpers as they quickly disappeared in the crowd. "Phew! That was some deal eh, climbing up to this place?" As I said this to Stephen, I noticed a strip of sweat running down the side of his face. Conscious that I too was experiencing the same, I decided not to mention it to him. That was our first hurdle over in the white man's land; but not without the help of fellow travellers. When we most needed them, they were there to help us tame the alien jungle we had found ourselves in.

Then we had to find our departure gate. We needed to find it as soon as we could because we did not have a lot of time to get on to our connecting flight to London Heathrow Airport. We ran to and fro like a panicking child who has been accidentally separated from its parents in a big shopping mall. Fortunately, however, we did manage to locate our departure gate in time. A year later, I was in conversation with another colleague of mine who was on his way to Germany to study. His experience of trying to locate his departure gate in Schipol was not a positive one. He told me that as he ran to and fro looking for the direction of his departure gate, he saw a black man passing by. With great relief he thought to himself "here is one of my own. He will be able to tell me where this gate is." So he walked to him and accordingly asked for directions. To his great dismay and disappointment, the man answered him in Dutch. "How come you, a black man, speak to me your fellow black man, in Dutch?" he thought. Bemused and frustrated, he left him. While he did eventually find the gate, my colleague said he missed his flight and had to wait for another one.

On the flight bound for London I was amazed at the nearly treeless, lush green, well kept and clearly demarcated fields we flew over. It was completely different from the landscape of farmland in Sierra Leone. "What have they done to all the trees and forests of this placed?" I wondered. Lost in wonder at this strange phenomenon, I hardly noticed we had been in the air for nearly an hour. Then the pilot's voice announcing our approach to London Heathrow came through the Public Address System. Before long we landed, disembarked the flight, and dutifully followed our fellow passengers to the luggage reclaim area and out to the welcoming area.

There, waiting patiently to receive us was Susan Barr. Susan was the Methodist Scholarship Secretary in the London office. We were to learn later that her job was to look after our wellbeing while we were away from our home country. More immediately, however, her job was to arrange accommodation for us while in London and eventually arrange our passages to our respective colleges. Susan had been holding a placard mounted on a stick with our names written on it. "Welcome to Revs. Stephen Boima & and Sahr Yambasu" it read. The usual ritual of salutations over, Susan brought us to the Methodist International House in Bayswater where we stayed and were looked after for three days.

Embarrassing Experiences

Whilst there, we got lost at least twice, once on a wrong tube which brought us to the wrong place, and another time walking from a tube station to where we were staying. But those are long stories. Suffice it to say that on each occasion we managed through the help of others to get to where we were meant to be. The most shocking and embarrassing thing that happened to us in those few days in London, however, was an experience we had with a West Indian man. A bus that we were meant to be on had stopped at a bus stop. Just out of Sierra Leone where there was no culture of queuing, Stephen and I, without even noticing there was a queue, just walked on to the bus. A West Indian man walked from the back of the queue, up into the bus and headed straight towards us as we were trying to sit down. Before we knew it, he held both us by our collars, and more or less marched us out of the bus. As if that was not enough, he shouted out at us: "You Africans", he said "you have spoilt Africa and now you want to come here and spoil it for us."

I was too embarrassed to be angry. Standing there in the glaring public I just wished the ground under us would open up and hide us from view. There was nothing we could do about it though. We knew we were in the wrong, although we had not done so deliberately. So we heavy-footedly walked to the back of the queue, our heads bowed down low with shame. While Stephen and I later reflected on that incident, we did so largely at a logical level. I suspected, however, that there was much more going on inside us than we both let on. I was especially baffled—not about the facts that we did not notice the queue and that we had behaved badly—but at how this black man behaved towards us his fellow blacks. "Of all people", I quietly reflected, "was he not the one who should have displayed more tolerance and understanding towards us? And were there not many white people in that queue? Why was it that none of them decided to treat us the way this fellow black man did?" It was something I pondered for a long time. A welcome of sorts from unexpected quarters!

This experience in London and my colleague's experience in Amsterdam most certainly taught me that I was now in another place where things I had taken for granted before seemed to not apply necessarily. For better and for worse my cultural eyes began to be opened and my analytical mind began to be stretched in ways they had not been required to do before. On the morning of our third day in London, Stephen and I parted, he to Sheffield and I to Belfast. The two of us never met again until he returned to Sierra Leone at the end of his one year course. Needless to say, however, that we had many telephone conversations comparing our experiences.

Belfast

At Belfast International Airport, I was met by the Rev. Dr. Dennis Cooke. Dennis was the Principal of Edgehill Methodist College to which I was headed. "Thanks for coming to meet me Dr. Cooke", I said to him. "No problem", he said, "but please call me Dennis". "Dennis?" I pondered quietly. "How can I call you Dennis? You are not only older than me, but you are an academic doctor and the principal of the college in which I'll be studying. Do you understand what you are asking of me? It is like a visitor to the Queen of England being asked to address her as Lizzie. Besides, I have been brought up in my country to give honour where honour is due. And I know and I'm convinced that honour is due to you from me, sir". But that is how he wanted it, and I had to learn to do it his way. I knew, though, that it would take me quite a while before I could get used to it.

As we talked on our way into the city my eyes were focused intently on the streets and my ears tuned appropriately waiting to see and hear the chaos and noise of fighting and shooting. After all, I was in Belfast, the allegedly warring city someone had told my mother about. Catholics fighting Protestants! That is what I was told also. To my surprise, however, neither a sound of gunshot, nor a scene of fighting did I hear or find; only graffiti and images of hooded men and guns on walls and posters mounted on lamp posts. But for a man programmed to be fearful of the Catholic-Protestant war in Northern Ireland, that was still chilling enough.

Edgehill Methodist College

Once in the college Dennis took me up to my study bedroom. "This is your home for the next three years." He said to me. "The showers and toilet are just there opposite your bedroom. I will leave you for a while to unpack your bag. I will be back to bring you down for a meal in my house." With those words he left, walking through the corridor, turning right, walking down the stairs and disappearing. Soon after he disappeared,

I heard a door open and close again with a bang. "May be he does not live far away from here". I thought to myself. At this time college had not opened yet and it was pretty quiet.

On my own, I looked round the room. Suddenly, like a bolt from the blue, it hit me that I was now truly away from home. On realizing that, I fell on to the bed overcome with emotion and sobbing. "Why had I not felt that way in the last three days?" I asked myself after I had stopped crying. Maybe it was because I was with Stephen. With him a little bit of home was still with me. But with him gone away, I felt very much alone and lonely. Not wanting Dennis to know I was crying, I quickly went into the bathroom, washed my face with cold water, before I returned to unpack.

That afternoon, I had a meal with Dennis and his family. It was my first Irish meal—mashed potatoes, roasted chicken, some vegetables and gravy, followed by ice cream. In the Methodist International house I stayed in in London, the meals were very international. For all the time Stephen and I were there we had rice followed by fruit salad or cake and custard. After the meal Dennis took me to Ruth Beattie and introduced me to her. Ruth was a young research student who had been living in the college for a few years before I arrived. Even though most other students had gone to their homes for the summer holidays, Ruth had stayed behind to continue with her biochemistry research. I later found out that she was in her final year of research.

A tall and slim lady, Ruth looked so young to me that I could not believe she was already at that level of academic achievement. Coming from a part of the world where education was not easy to come by, I knew very well that in my own country people of Ruth's age, if they were lucky enough, would be beginning their undergraduate studies. Even I was older than Ruth, I reckoned, and I had not yet got my first degree. Dennis had brought me to Ruth because she had kindly agreed to show me round the college facilities—library, launderette, kitchen, food store and dining room. She had also undertaken to show me how to use the washing machine, dryer, cooker, and some other kitchen utensils. "Welcome to the white man's land". I said when I left Ruth and returned to my study-bedroom. "I have just arrived in this place and have not yet even spent a full day. But here am I, already expected to look after myself."

Discovering New Things

The weather was very cold for my liking even though it was still September. In my first few days in Belfast I honestly did wonder whether I would be able to survive it. Yet every time the weather got mentioned (and that was in almost every conversation), everyone was talking about how pleasant it was. Pleasant! That was how they described weather I believed was the worst I had ever experienced in my life. At first I honestly could not understand why the weather got so much mention and why everyone thought it was good. But when the winter set in a few months later I understood. It took me at least half an hour to dress up and another half an hour to undress. Through those months I felt like a walking onion, layered with thermal pants, a pair of long John's, warm trousers, a thermal vest, a warm shirt or two, one good wooly jumper, a good overcoat, scarf, wooly hat, a pair of hand gloves, a good thick pair of socks, and warm trainers. In addition to these I used to carry a hot water bottle under my coat to class every morning and refilled it in the early afternoon. Little wonder that on seeing my first pictures home everyone approvingly commented on how much weight I had put on. All they thought was that life in the white man's land was very good for me. "I wish they knew why I looked so bulky", I thought to myself.

There were obvious advantages, however, dressing up this way. It helped to keep me warm. So everyone also thought. But there was another advantage that was known only to me. It was this. It saved me possible moments of embarrassment in class. I remember several times, for example, when I was asked a question especially in our most dreaded Greek and Hebrew classes. By the time I undid my scarf which was tightly rapped several times round my neck and most of my mouth, I had managed to salvage enough time to think of the answer. This was all very interesting to the Irish students, especially the very long pauses after I had been asked a question. They could hardly keep their faces straight seeing this only African in the class taking so long to unveil his well padded mouth before answering a question. I did often wonder whether they knew the advantage that operation afforded me. While I initially did not dress the way I did for that purpose, I got to realize and utilize it well. And there was no hurry on my part to give up this advantage.

I never knew how black I was when I lived in Africa. Living with mostly black people around me, it was impossible to know this. Then one day in Belfast, surrounded with white people everywhere, I suddenly discovered that I was very black. Ireland in those days had very few non-white people and still fewer black people. I still remember one day when I was nearly knocked over by a car as I tried to cross University Road to meet the first black person I had seen since I arrived in Belfast. This was in the university area. On getting to this man, I vigorously embraced him as I greeted him. Visibly shocked and not knowing how to respond to what might have seemed to him strange and lunatic behaviour on my part, I released him from my smothering embrace and explained that he was the first black person I had met since I arrived in Belfast about six months earlier. I went on to tell him how lonely and alone I had been as a result. Listening to my story I could see him gradually recovering from his earlier shock. He told me he was from Zambia undertaking his doctoral studies in musicology at the University. He too had experienced a few years earlier something of what I was experiencing, he told me. That day I cancelled all my plans and went with him to the halls of residence for the rest of the day.

Dealing with New Realities

Food was another big cultural challenge I faced. I was almost always normally given potatoes. At college meals, in homes of people I visited, and in restaurants it was generally potatoes in different guises—peeled boiled, jacket boiled, mashed, chipped, and baked potatoes. Sometimes they were even made into salad. And yet when I told people we ate rice in my country all the time they could not understand how any one could eat the same food all the time. For the odd times when it was not potatoes for a meal, it was salad. "Grass", I called it—"goat food". To be certain there were other kinds of foods, but, like salad, they were all side plate affairs. Potatoes were the queen and king of meals.

Like I did with salad, I renamed all those side plate meals: green peas I called 'green pebbles', scotch eggs I called 'Moses in the basket', rice pudding I called 'sick man's food', strawberries I called 'scabies fruit', and brussel sprouts I called 'green tennis balls'. One day, though, I pondered what I was doing in my renaming exercise of these foods. Was I, perhaps, engaged in an unconscious power game in what I was doing with the white man's food? Years before I arrived in Europe, I recalled, the white man went to my country and renamed many of my people, replacing their African names with English forms of Greek and Hebrew names before they could be baptized and made members of the church. It was, for those missionaries, a way of letting my people know that they were now new people and must abandon their former pre-baptismal ways of life. But here was I engaged not in renaming white people but white people's food. What was it all about? I was not sure.

I too knew of missionaries my people had also renamed in their own local languages. So while the missionaries were busy renaming my people the latter were also busy renaming them. The only difference was that missionaries' renaming acts were formalized in public rituals during which my people were made to own their imposed new names. As I reflected on this, it occurred to me that the acts of both groups were acts of power—one hidden and silent, the other visible and audible; one local and its existence known only by the group that exercised it, the other transcending the boundaries of the group that exercised it as it sought to annex and assimilate the other.

Yet I knew from the history and impact of Christianity on my people that one act of power was certainly no more powerful than the other. They were just different ways of exercising power. Just as my renaming of the white man's food did not change necessarily the nature of the food from what it was to what I named it, I reasoned that the same was largely true for my people who were renamed by missionaries. Yes, renaming things and people for whatever reason may be a legitimate effort to represent them in our own image. But the story of my people's encounter with missionary Christianity had taught me that change and the form it takes cannot be dictated merely by renaming. It takes a lot more than that. In that sense I realized that my renaming of the white man's food was in essence a silly exercise whose only purpose was the satisfaction of my own need. What that need was, I could not figure out.

Throughout my years in Edgehill, however, I had one saving grace: the college cook, Joyce Robinson. Joyce was a very kind hearted and considerate person. Now and again she would go out of her way to prepare what she believed I would like: boiled rice and hot curry.

Etiquette

Talking about food, I remember being invited once to a home for Sunday lunch a few days after I had arrived in Belfast. Other people who attended church with me had also been invited. All the best cutlery, china, napkins, and table linens were out on that day. The food served was roasted steak, mashed potatoes, Yorkshire pudding, Brussels sprouts, and a very tasty gravy sauce. The table properly set with two different sizes of table knives, forks, spoons, and dinner and side plates, I knew I was in for a taxing challenge that day. First of all, I hadn't the foggiest idea which cutleries to use first. Careful not to betray my ignorance, I let others go first. As each took a turn to serve himself or herself, I closely watched what they were doing. When my turn came I followed suit. Then it was time to eat. To buy a little time during which I would be able to know which knife and fork to use first and how, I initiated a conversation with the host who was also the minister of the church I attended that day. "So when were you posted to this Circuit?" I asked. As I listened to his response I was also observing what was happening around the dining table. But as I came to realize, that was only the first hurdle.

Fork in left hand and knife in right hand, I began to cut a piece of the steak as I had seemingly carefully observed others do. Then I suddenly realized there was more to this than I had thought; for try as I did, the piece was not coming off. As I began to sense that I was been watched, I started to apply a reasonable amount of force to the knife and fork, as I hooked the steak and gave it another go. As I did so, the drinking glasses on the table began to shake. I noticed that the more I caused the table to shake, the louder the conversation of the other guests became. I guessed they were embarrassed for me and were trying to save me from the awkward moment. I began to feel a little hot under my arms and felt a little sweat dribble down from my arm pits down on my sides. With a sense of panic setting in and the need to hasten the end of my embarrassment, I decided to give the meat one final big go. I succeeded, but not in the way I expected. For as the piece of meat came off from the larger piece, it flew off the plate and landed about a foot away from the table on to the carpet. Embarrassed for me, the lady of the house started apologizing profusely. "I am sorry. It is my fault." She said. "I should have let the meat cook a little bit more." I knew she was just trying to be kind. But there was nothing I could do about it. I just accepted it as one of those things in life. And it was not the end.

Cultural Gaffs

Within a couple of weeks of my arrival in Belfast, Andrew Boucher came to bring me out to a family for what turned out to be a buffet evening meal. Andrew was a banker but had decided to leave banking and candidate for the Methodist ministry. He was to start his training late that September and would be in the same class with me. Several days before, he and his wife and children had come to see me at the college and introduced themselves. Before they left on that first day, Andrew offered to help me in any way he could while I stayed in Ireland. He had subsequently brought me out for a meal at their home and showed me round the city and other places.

On this particular night that he brought me out for a meal with a family, there were many other people there, most of whom knew each other very well. So, like the meal, the atmosphere was also great.

As the night wore on, Andrew came to me and informed me it was time to go home. Before leaving I went round with Andrew to thank our hostess who was in a different part of the room. As I said 'thank you' and 'goodbye' to the lady, she leaned forward towards my cheek to kiss me goodbye. I was so shocked and embarrassed that I felt my head involuntarily moving very gradually backwards away from her lips. But before I knew it, it was over. I could not believe it. For what she did to me was something that in my country happened only between a pair of the opposite sex going out together. Flustered, unnerved, and not knowing how to respond, I repeated my thanks to the lady for the very warm welcome and lovely meal. "Thanks for coming", she responded. Still wanting to hide my embarrassment, I said to this somewhat chubby, well rounded and beautiful lady, "You are lovely". She smiled. "You are beautiful!" She smiled even more. Looking back, I think this behavior was getting a little embarrassing for her, to say the least. But I had no way of knowing. I thought she was enjoying every moment of it. "You are fat." I continued. Then I saw what, clearly, was a sudden change in her countenance. Her faced dropped, her smiles faded away very quickly, and the colour of her face started to change into what looked like a ripe tomato. I also began to sense that my friend Andrew was very uncomfortable. "What wrong have I done now?" I asked myself. You know the sort of thing that happens when you sense something is wrong and you want to explain yourself! Everything I attempted to say to mend the situation made it worse instead.

As Andrew realized what was happening he could bear it no longer. He held my hand and literally dragged me out of the house before I caused any further hurt. As we walked out he said to the lady who was at this time a little distance away from us, "I am really sorry". "It's alright, thanks for coming anyway." She shouted back. But I knew something was drastically wrong. Walking to the car Andrew said to me, "Do you know you really insulted that lady?" "How?" I asked. "By telling her she is fat." "But I was only complementing her." I innocently replied. "If I had said what I said to her to a lady in my country, I would have made her night." I continued. "Well", said Andrew, "in this country you don't tell ladies that they are fat." Having found out what I had done to such a kind and warm hearted lady, I was mortified and angry with myself for spoiling what had been a good night for that lady, my friend, and even myself. Scared stiff to face the lady again, I told my friend to apologize to her on my behalf. But that was the first and last time I ever set my eyes on that lady, as I consciously avoided the area of the city where she lived.

That, however, did not save me from further cultural gaffs. My friend Andrew was the next victim. I felt so comfortable with Andrew that once in a Boots Chemists in Belfast City Centre I grabbed his hand to walk with me to a shelf of goods. I wanted him to advice me on an item I wanted to buy. After a few steps, I felt him drawing his hand from mine. What I had not noticed was that by that time quite a few eyes in the shop were fixed on us. Unable to free his hand at his first attempt, I surprisingly heard him shout out in a subdued but clearly audible voice, "Leave me", as he more forcefully and successfully dragged his hand out of mine. "Was he embarrassed that he was being seen in the company of a black person?" I wondered. "Or had I offended him in some way?" I could not tell. Not sure about why he behaved the way he did, I asked him what the problem was, but he pretended not to hear.

It was not until on our way back to the college that he answered my question. As we walked up the street Andrew turned to me and said, "You know why I dragged myself out of your hand in the Chemists?" "Tell me why?" I replied. "In this country", Andrew continued, "two men holding hands are regarded as 'queer'". Now, the way he pronounced that last word alerted me that he was on to something that I hadn't a clue about. And, honest to God, I did not even understand what he was talking about. "What do you mean by 'choir'?" I asked him to explain. "I mean 'queer', not 'choir'" spelling out each of the words. "Two men holding hands in this country means that they are gay." Before he finished, the penny dropped. "O-ho-o, is that why so many eyes were fixed on us in the Chemists?" "Yes", he said emphatically, "and that's why I withdrew my hand from yours as quickly as I could. "I am sorry, Andrew," I apologized.

Andrew knew of course that I didn't know what I was doing. "In my country", I went on to explain to him, "what would have invited people's disapproval is a man and a woman holding hands and walking in public. Neither would you see a man and a woman kissing in public. A public show of emotion

181

in that way by adults is considered a bad moral example for children in society. It is also seen as an indication of inability on the part of people who do such things to exercise self-control."

And then there was that conversation I had in the students' common room in my first year at Edgehill. It was in the evening after tea as we sat watching the news on television. Somebody mentioned the idea of marriage to one of the students whom many students believed, because of his cynicism about marriage, would never marry. As I listened to the conversation making no comments one way or the other, one of the students turned to me and asked: "What do you think John? Will you ever marry?" The question took me by surprise. I had been brought up to believe that marriage for a man or woman was a given. It was not about whether or not one wanted to get married. It was about whether or not one found someone who would agree to marry one. When I answered the question in the affirmative Ruth, a biochemistry research student asked why I wanted to get married. I thought for a while and then said, "Well, I want somebody to be cooking my meals, washing my clothes, cleaning the house . . ." Before I finished, Ruth impatiently interjected, exasperatedly saying to me in a rather sarcastic tone, "Well, John, I think what you need is a slave not a wife." All the students in the room, except me, laughed their heads off on hearing Ruth's comment. It was their way of saying, "We agree with you Ruth". Embarrassed, I said nothing. Quietly, however, I impatiently hoped that the conversation would move on to another subject. But Ruth's comment that night opened another cultural window on life for me. Through it she made me see flaws in my long held view of the role of a woman in marriage that my society and culture had taught me. Even her directness in the way she responded to me taught me something of the differences between her upbringing and mine.

This cross-cultural ignorance, though, was not just on my part. Had my hostess not kissed me, sparking off a whole lot of related complications for me? And about six months later I nearly fell out with the Scholarship Secretary, Susan Bar. Susan was unhappy about the fact that each month I was sending some of my student allowances home to support my family. She wrote me more than once telling me that it should not be so. On an official visit to Belfast to see how I was settling down, she brought up the same issue. At that point I had no choice but to let her know that it was my obligation to look after the welfare of my family no matter where I was. I had done it for years before coming to Belfast, I told her, and I had no intention of stopping it. Seeing how determined and forthright I was about the matter, she explained that it was for my own good since the money they were giving me was meant to be just enough for my needs. I thanked her for her concern but noted that in Belfast I had a place to sleep, my bed linen was supplied and washed for me, I had free washing powder to wash my clothes, free electricity, medical care, and food, and a monthly allowance provided. "My family at home", I continued "struggle daily to make ends meet. How could I not support them as best as I am able?" After that session that issue was never raised with me again. It died a natural death. I have often wondered whether it was because she saw the logic of my argument, or she realized no amount of rules or persuasion was going to stop me from sending money home to my family.

Whatever the reason, the issue let me discover a cultural mindset that I had not encountered before. Had she known the principle, "I am because we are and because we are I am", she most likely would never have queried me in the first place. For that was the principle by which I was brought up and which informed my perspective on life. The society in which I was born and brought up taught me that people and not money were the essence of life. People and good relationships with them, I was told, were more important than possessions. *Keke* starkly put this to me once when he said to me: "Sahr, your money alone cannot dig your grave and bury you no matter how rich you are; it is people who will do it." I was about ten years old when he told me this. I did not understand then what he meant. But about six years later I did. A man in our village died. By the standards of most people in our village then, he was a very rich man. But this man's most important interest in life was to make money. He did not allow anything else to stand in the way of that, not even relationships. When he died, it took a very long time for the elders and chiefs of the village to get people to run errands for his funeral arrangements, to dig his grave, and to bury him. Then I recalled what my father had told me six years earlier. People, not possessions, matter more. They were a better resource to have than material wealth. As I once overheard an elderly man in my village say, "You know who your real family and friends are when you are poor not when you are rich".

The Challenges of Life in College

I found studies much easier than other aspects of life in Northern Ireland. Having gone successfully through my ministerial training in Sierra Leone, I was very well placed for the degree course at Queen's University. I had learnt in my previous school and college life the art of disciplining myself for studies. During my time at Queen's I, in keeping with what I was used to in Sierra Leone, often had a little sleep in the afternoons after lectures. Fortunately for me I had found and bought myself a door sign. It told intending visitors what I was doing: sleeping, studying, busy, out, or in. This meant that I could sleep in the afternoons for a couple of hours or so undisturbed. I would then go downstairs for tea at 6pm with the rest of the students. Immediately after tea and catching up with the news of the day, I settled down to study and would go on until one or two in the morning before going to bed again. I more or less adhered religiously to that routine especially on week days.

Any initial problems I had were to do with my acceptance by some students. Edgehill Methodist, Union Presbyterian, and Belfast Baptist Colleges formed the Department of Theology at Queen's. The first two shared lectures. I never visited nor met any of the students of the Baptist College. Quite a few of the Presbyterian students were not as accepting, tolerant, and open-minded as I had expected. To be certain, there were also a few Methodist students who displayed mild forms of narrow-mindedness, especially with regard to other forms of cultural expression and ways of being Christian. But the latter were not only more diplomatic and sophisticated in how they did that, they also seemed to have a much better capacity to listen with respect than their counterparts. Being the only African in an otherwise all-Irish class, I became very conscious of this quite quickly. As time went on, I discovered that some Presbyterian students did not even believe that an African was capable of becoming a Christian by their own definition. Some of the same group of students did not even take part in Holy Communion services held in the Methodist College because they did not believe Methodists were reformed enough Christians.

Having endured living in that situation for a month or so with, in the main, only Methodist students talking to me, I decided to find a way of dealing with the problem. My tactic was this. I resolved that during break times, I would go round and take the note books and biros of all those who were avoiding to speak to me and hide them. I reckoned that on their return to class and finding out that I had them, they might have no choice but talk to me, even if only to ask for their belongings back. As a way of introducing the joke to the rest of the class, it was my friend Andrew I chose to start with. One lunch time he left me alone in the lecture room and went to the gents. I quickly got his notebook and hid it under my bag. It was not too long after his return that the afternoon lecture began. Looking frantically for his notebook as the lecture started, I waited until others in the class became aware of his predicament before I produced it. My tactic proved to be the magic wand. All to whom I did this without exception started talking to me, and by the end of the first term I was on reasonably good speaking terms with everyone in my year and class.

I still remember being really sorry for a Sudanese Anglican priest called Francis Paul Elatie who came for a year of studies with us. It was in my third and final year. On the first day of the first term, one of the lecturers decided that each of us should introduce ourselves to the rest of class. Most students just stood up, said their name, the Church they belonged to, and sat down again. Francis was present. When it came to his turn, he stood up and started introducing himself in typical African fashion. "I bring you greetings from my family, the people in my village and the members of my parish in Sudan." Guessing how some of the students might be feeling about this, I looked round just to confirm or otherwise what I was thinking. I had guessed rightly; impatience was written all over the faces of some of the students.

As Francis continued introducing himself, the impatience gradually turned into intense anger bordering on hostility. "My name is Francis Paul Elatie", he announced. "If you like, you can call me Francis, because that is my name; if you like you can call me Paul, because that is my father's name; or if you like you can call me Elatie, because that is my family name." Before he could finish and sit down, one of the students who, by that time had become very fed-up with Francis and visibly fuming shouted out from the back of the classroom, "I will call you sir." And the others who were in the same frame of mind and attitude laughed aloud. Sorry and embarrassed for the way he had been treated, I could only bow my head in shame. But for me that incident was a very clear confirmation of my assessment of some of those students. Here was a man who was representing another world and way of life to them. How come they did not consider his presence among them as an opportunity to learn something about the world he represented? But no! Because he did not see or do things their way, they were not prepared to listen to him.

That incident also made me wonder about much of the Northern Irish Protestant mentality I had experienced since I arrived in the country. For the short time I had lived there I had encountered through the media and personal experience a mentality which, roughly expressed, believed: "You are only as Christian as I define Christianity; and if you do not fit my definition, I am not ready to tolerate you, nor listen to you." Coming from a country where Muslims and Christians lived amicably together and supported each other, and where Catholics were believed to be as Christian as Protestants, I found this mentality a very bizarre and arrogant one. And when I got to learn later that mixed marriages between Roman Catholics and Protestants were, to say the least, often frowned upon, I was even more baffled. Perhaps it was because my people had taught me that one married either from among one's own people and group to underline the already strong ties of relationship one has with them, or from another group and people in order to form alliances and increase one's circle of relationships. Yet, here was I living in a society where parents, if they had a choice, would rather give their daughters in marriage to anyone else but an Irish person who did not belong to their particular brand of Christianity. Their views on whom their sons married were no different. While I sympathized with their views and attitudes, I was unable to understand the mindset that informed them. When, after speaking at a church meeting one evening about life in my country, a gentleman asked me whether the Muslims in my country were Catholic or Protestant, I realized how deeply the Catholic-Protestant divide informed the worldview of many people in Northern Ireland. "Here are a people who are indeed prisoners of their history and culture". I thought. "But what people are not?" I pondered. As those thoughts occupied my mind I was struck again by the singular importance of the teachings of Christ that all peoples should be equally valued and loved.

Examples of Generosity in Northern Ireland

Yet, it was during my time in Northern Ireland that I came across some of the most loving and generous people I have ever met. It was, for example, in Belfast city centre that I first met a shop owner who was more interested in being honest than in making more money at any cost. One afternoon I walked into a shoe shop looking for trainers. After finding out that I needed them for wearing to lectures, the shop owner brought me out of her shop to another shop where she said they sold better quality trainers and cheaper than the ones in her shop. Such a thing had never happened to me before and not even in my own country. For as long as I used those trainers I never forgot that lady.

Another example was the sheer kindness and generosity I experienced from the Methodist people in Antrim. By the end of my first year in Northern Ireland a vacancy occurred in the Methodist Church in Antrim, about twenty miles outside Belfast on the east coast. I was approached and asked by the Church to fill the vacancy temporarily. It involved spending my weekends in Antrim and returning to college for lectures during the week. A fully furnished manse was made available to me, and my duty was to make pastoral visits and conduct Sunday worship services. The people of the church provided me with everything I needed to make my work easier, including a motorbike and accessories. A very well experienced Irish Methodist minister in the adjacent Ballymena Circuit (in the famous Ian Paisley's constituency at the time) supervised my work. Bertie Amstrong and his wife had previously served as missionaries on one of the Caribbean Islands. Sometimes we exchanged pulpits. Through that I also came to know a lot of the people in the Ballymena Methodist church.

I will never forget the preparations for my first visit back home from Belfast. The Antrim Methodists and their colleagues in Ballymena arranged a special shopping day for me. They wanted to make sure that when I went back home my family and friends would know I had been in good hands. On their chosen day they brought me out with them into a shopping centre in Ballymena where they bought me clothes, shoes, socks, ties, gifts for my family and friends, you name it, plus a big suitcase for me to carry the things. Before I left they also wrote a special letter to my family and Church thanking them for me. Some of the friendships I formed during my time in Antrim still continue today, a testimony, I reckon, of the sincere good heartedness of the people there. And wherever I went in Northern Ireland during my three years there I experienced an immense amount of love and generosity. My sense of things at that time was that

Irish people, generally speaking, were very welcoming and friendly people. And that was what I told people back home in Sierra Leone.

Breaking the Mould

I discovered a problem in the church in Antrim which I had not encountered in any significant way in my home country. In the first few months of my ministry there I discovered that at least half of the congregation would normally leave the church immediately before the Lord's Supper (Holy Communion) was administered. After doing a little research I found out that one of the main reasons was because people thought they were not good enough to receive the sacrament. Paul's First Letter to the Corinthians Chapter 11 verses 17-34 was cited to back up this view. The passage begins by pointing out that the meetings of the Christians in the church in Corinth to observe Holy Communion did more harm than good. "In the first place, I hear that when you come together as a church, there are divisions among you . . . No doubt there have to be differences among you to show which of you have God's approval . . ." Paul then goes on to list some of the wrong things they were doing: ". . . each of you goes ahead without waiting for anybody else . . . One remains hungry, another gets drunk." He asks them, ". . . do you despise the church of God and humiliate those who have nothing?" After telling them the history of when and how celebrating the Lord's Supper became a part of the life of the church of God, Paul concludes, "Therefore, whoever eats the bread or drinks the cup of the Lord in an unworthy manner will be guilty of sinning against the body and blood of the Lord. A man ought to examine himself before he eats of the bread and drinks of the cup. For anyone who eats and drinks without recognizing the body of the Lord eats and drinks judgment on himself. That is why many among you are weak and sick, and a number of you have fallen asleep. But if we judge ourselves, we would not come under judgment . . . . So then, my brothers, when you come together to eat, wait for each other. If anyone is hungry, he should eat at home, so that when you meet together it may not result in judgment."

Prayerfully studying this passage, I decided to preach on it one Sunday. I first drew people's attention to the fact that the Lord's Supper in Paul's time was celebrated within the context of a church meal. Secondly, I highlighted the specific set of problems Paul was seeking to address in the passage and how they would have been possible, given the fact that the Lord's Supper was part and parcel of a meal. Thirdly, I noted the differences between that context and ours. Fourthly, I talked to them about the sinful nature of all men and women, including ministers who preside over the Lord's Supper, and reminded them of God's forgiving grace freely offered to us in Christ. I also reminded them that the founder of the Methodist Church, John Wesley, regarded Holy Communion as both sanctifying and converting grace. Finally, I encouraged everyone to take seriously the Word of God which promises that if anyone sincerely confesses their sins, God is faithful and just and He would forgive them and accept them completely.

It was the first Sunday in the month when the Lord's Supper was celebrated. That Sunday, not one person left before the

Lord's Supper was celebrated. The communion stewards ran out of communion glasses and had to rewash and refill them at least once in order that everyone who wanted to partake was able to do so. This continued for the rest of the time I ministered in that church. That experience made me wonder whether ministers of Christ have not sometimes turned Christ's gospel of grace into a gospel of laws and, by doing so, denied people Christ's free offer of possibilities to live as forgiven children of God.

Northern Irish Sayings

In college, Antrim, and Ballymena I also learnt many uniquely Northern Irish sayings. They were called 'Ulsterisms' after the Province of Ulster. They were popularized by a man called John Pepper. On first hearing them as a stranger in Northern Ireland, they made no sense to me whatsoever. Before long, however, I began to show people the nonsensical side of the sayings from the perspective of an outsider. One such occasion was when the young people of the church in Antrim and I organized a big youth rally to which we invited many youth groups from the churches in the area. It was to begin at 7pm. On the afternoon of the day it was scheduled to take place, a group of worriedly—looking ladies came to me at the manse. Their problem, they told me, was that they did not have enough cups to serve the tea and coffee at the end of the event. Before that time, I had often heard people talk about 'a wee drop in the hand' when they offered someone tea or coffee. "Listen ladies", I told them, "there is no problem to worry about. Each person coming tonight will bring a pair of hands. When the time comes for serving tea and coffee", I continued, "just give them a wee drop in the hand." Their response was just as I had predicted: laugh at the stranger's perspective on their saying.

Another time I was invited by a couple to their house for Sunday lunch in Ballymena. As we ate she got up from her seat and walked towards me and asked, "Would you like a wee warmer?" I knew of course that she wanted to know whether I needed a bit more hot tea added to my cup. But I blandly looked at her with a touch of surprise and shock on my face, knowing that one of the things a lot of Northern Protestants prided themselves on was total abstinence from alcohol. Seeing the surprised look on my face, she suddenly rephrased her question, "I mean would you like a wee drop of tea?"

One of the things I learned earlier in my school days was the saying, "Self praise is no recommendation". You would therefore understand why I was not amused when, the first time I offered a cup of coffee to an Irish man who came to visit me, he replied, "I'm lovely, thank you." In reply to him I said jestingly, "I know you are lovely, but would you like a cup of coffee?" On another occasion when a student meeting was going on in college, I found it really hilarious when the chairman of meeting asked me to 'stick my head through the door and see if Alan was coming'. Alan was one of the students. As the words came out of his mouth I just imagined my head stuck through the door while the rest of my body was in the room. "Colin", I said to him, "What you are asking me to do is totally impossible." Knowing what I was driving at, the rest of the students in the room started laughing.

Jokes are Culture-bound

Such were Northern Irish sayings. Yet they made perfect sense to those who used them. But, like 'Ulterisms', I discovered in those days that even humour was related to culture. In college, one student would say something and everybody will laugh except me. At other times I would say something that I thought was really funny and nobody would laugh. On reflecting on that reality for a while I came to the conclusion that part of the reason is because when people tell jokes there is a lot they take as read. That 'lot' would normally be known by 'insiders' of the culture of the jokes teller. The former, as they listen to the latter, effortlessly insert the missing links. So while the insider may be readily able to see the funny side of the joke, the same may not be the case for an 'outsider'. People need to know something of what is taken-for-granted in a culture to be able to fully appreciate the thrust of a joke.

My Secondary School ID Photograph—
taken in 1ˢᵗ Year (1970)

These men are my mother's brothers in Bokodu Village. The three
women are the wives of the one with glasses. He was my mother's
closest brother and was very helpful to her and her children.

Teacher Yambasu, my father's nephew, in whose charge
he left us before he died

My dearly missed sister, Messie—the eldest child of
our family—who died giving birth to Fayia

R-L: *Keke, Nde* & I

L-R: Rev. Dr. Dennis Cooke (Principal of Edgehill
Methodist College, Belfast) & I

At the main entrance of Edgehill Methodist College,
Belfast, in the autumn of 1985

Playing in the snow in Ireland: it was my first time of seeing snow

Back Row—L-R: Rev. James MacCormack & Rev. Ivan
McIlhinney. Front Row—L-R: Mrs. Joan McCormack,
Clodagh, Sahr & Rev. Tom Johnston. James, Joan & Ivan
were very kind to me during my time in Ireland.

On our Wedding Day 14th July 1988

L-R: Peter, Ruth, Gill, Paul & Derek Jackson; Sahr & Clodagh Yambasu; Richard & Steven Jackson. Derek & Gill (my adopted English parents) sponsored my Secondary School Education. Richard introduced me to them. He was a missionary in Sierra Leone.

At our Wedding Reception in the Shamrock Lodge Hotel, Athlone. Rev. Leslie Wallace looks up. He is the man who negotiated my scholarship to study at Queen's University, Belfast. His wife, Agnes sits on his left. Leslie served for about 38 years as a missionary in Sierra Leone.

L-R: Our Three Children—Fayia, Sahr & Abbie at home in Freetown

R-L: Clodagh, Fayia, Sahr (Jnr.) & I in the Victoria Park in the Centre of Freetown, Sierra Leone

R-L: Fayia, Abbie, Clodagh, Sahr (Snr.) & Sahr (Jnr.)
on holiday in Ireland from Sierra Leone

R-L: Abbie (our daughter), Nde (my Mother), Clodagh (my wife)
& Fayia (19 Feb. 1991)

My parents-in-law: Edwin & Nancy McCormack
at the award ceremony when chosen as the
Longford Town People of the Year (2000)

At my Installation Service in Galway, July 2001 with Church
Representatives and Major of City

NINE

FOR BETTER AND FOR WORSE

Prospects for Further Study

'The struggle continues' are words that were engraved on my mind by Samuel Doe who in 1987 overthrew the government of the Republic of Liberia to become that country's first rebel Head of State. In those heady days in Liberia, Doe ended every State broadcast with the words, "In the interest of the people, the struggle continues." After hearing those words so many times huddled round a radio with others, they stuck with me. Since then I had made it a habit to repeat quietly or audibly the same words to myself in times of my own struggle to survive different challenges I faced in life. "The struggle continues!" I often responded when people asked how I was.

By the end of my second year in Belfast the principal started talking to me about the possibility of undertaking research in the University of Cambridge in England before returning home. The money to do so, he told me, should not concern me; nor should the permission from my home Church. But I needed to produce a good result in my final exams to be able to utilize that opportunity. Before he could go ahead to make necessary contacts, however, Dennis said he wanted to know if I was interested in his offer? As our conversations continued, it became very clear to him that what he was suggesting was what I wanted to do exactly. Promptly taking action on the basis of the feedback he got from me, he initiated contacts with Fitzwilliams College, through Wesley Methodist House in Cambridge. In addition to that he also contacted the head of my home Church, Rev. Leslie Wallace and the Methodist Overseas Division Scholarship Secretary in London to share his suggestions with them. All the indications from the people contacted soon made it clear that the only thing that would stop me from going on was death or my own inability to do well in my final year exams.

I still remember the first night when my conversation with Dennis on this issue started. Skipping up the stairs back to my study bedroom after the meeting, I shut the door after me, punched the air several times with great gusto and excitement, and danced round the room. For a while I shouted repeatedly, "Thank you God" as I realised that a door was being opened to me that would finally get me to what I had always dreamed about. That is what Dennis did not know, and that is why he thought he needed to ask for my consent before he could start exploring the possibilities for me to go on for further studies. I had, long before arriving in Northern Ireland, made up my mind that it was the way I wanted to go. And this was the reason why.

Among my people, a deceased man's possessions are inherited automatically by his brothers if his sons are not old enough to look after themselves. His wives and children were considered as part of his possessions. The oldest brother would preside over the distribution of the possessions of the deceased man. In my father's case none of his sons were old enough to look after themselves and none of his brothers were alive when he died. Therefore, his nephews had to step in and play the role which his brothers, if alive, would have played. While there were enough wives of my father for each of his nephews to have one, my father left only two farms of coffee. It was decided that one went to *Mama* Amie his first wife and the other to *Keke* Joseph the oldest of my father's nephews living at home. Consequently, *Keke* and *Nde* who were the youngest of my father's nephews and wives respectively did not benefit from the only source of financial income that my father left. In fact the only thing they inherited from my father was the children he had with *Nde*. *Keke*, of course, also inherited *Nde*. While *Nde* was allowed by tradition to leave and marry another man other than any of my father's nephews, that decision would have made her lose her rights even over her own children. So, deprived of a share in my father's plantation and convinced that were he alive he would have used the income from it to pay for my education, *Nde* was bitterly disappointed. Tearfully telling me about how she felt about the whole affair, I decided foolhardily to call a family meeting at which I strongly voiced my dissatisfaction with the inheritance arrangements.

As N*de*, *Keke* and I had expected, there was an almighty row especially over the fact that I was challenging tradition and the authority it gave to my elders to decide how to disburse what my father left. While the row itself lasted for only an hour or so, for several years afterwards the older relations of my father treated me with suspicion and always read too much into every move I made.

After that family feud over inheritance, I had resolved single-mindedly that I was going to forge my own future in the best direction possible and away from reliance on any possessions of my deceased father. The best education possible in Western ways, I believed, would be the way to proceed. "That", I reasoned, "was the inheritance my father left for me before he died: education. That is why he sent me to school", I convinced myself.

Since then, that had become my ambition. And my trust in God to help me fulfil it was an invaluable encouragement towards that end. On my part what Dennis was suggesting I do was simply an answer to many years of prayerful yearning. "It was for the best education I left home for Ireland; and I was not now going to turn down an invitation that promised an even better deal, was I?" I asked myself. So the beginning of the academic year following my discussions with Dennis saw me settle down quickly to serious study in a way I had never done in the previous two years. I was determined not to let anything on my part hinder the wonderful chance that was being offered to me.

Proposing to Clodagh

In a way, the year that Dennis suggested I could enroll for a new programme of studies turned out to be a year of make-or-break decisions for me, for it was also at the beginning of that academic year that I proposed to Clodagh who is now my wife. In the previous year when she had just commenced her training for ministry in the Methodist Church in Ireland, she and I had started going out. "Those who think that students for ministry do nothing in college but study, fast and pray must think again". I often say to people. Ministerial students at Edgehill Methodist College were, thank God, no different.

The first time I met Clodagh was in Belfast after she had left primary school teaching to work on the Youth Evangelism Team (YET) of the Methodist Church in Ireland. The following Christmas (my first in Ireland) I travelled with a Rev. Tom Johnston who had worked as a missionary in my country to spend Christmas in Longford, her hometown. Tom's family also lived there and he was going there, as he always did, for Christmas. On that Christmas Day I preached in the Methodist Church there. It was at that service that I met Clodagh again, her mother and father Nancy and Edwin, her sister Gillian, and her brothers Niall and Brian. Gillian, I found out, was a midwife preparing to go to the Gambia as a Methodist missionary. Because she wanted to find out a little more about the region, she asked if she, her sister and brothers could come over to where I was staying one evening shortly after Christmas for a chat. When they came as arranged, we spent a couple of hours or so playing Connect Four and talking about West Africa and Gillian's appointment there.

Asking Clodagh to go out with me was not an easy thing for me. It took me several agonizing months to sum up courage to tell her how I felt towards her. Much of the reason had to do with my own thinking that she may not accept me because I was black. "How would I handle the shame of living in the same college community with her if she turned my request down? Besides, I had already had a couple of bitter disappointments with girls I had gone out with in my home country. Would I be able to handle another rejection and far away from the support of family and friends?" With these questions and more going round in my head, I decided to pray and fast for a whole month, asking for God's direction. A month later I started to feel more confident and at peace about the situation. This was followed by invitations to her to a meal outside college and to the cinema. Suspecting, after a while, that she might have some idea about why I was inviting her out, I eventually took the chance to share blushingly with her my feelings towards her. I can't remember exactly what I said to her, but whatever it was and however it sounded, it must have made sense to her. I am not sure, however, that she noticed my blushing for, unlike white people, black people's blushing is not noticeable by the change of the colour of their faces.

"A great achievement eh", I told myself back in college in my study bedroom. But my sense of excitement quickly dissipated when it dawned on me that our relationship may not result in marriage necessarily. From the first day I started developing feelings for her my intention was to marry her eventually. Now that I had received her consent to go out with me, thoughts about the ultimate step immediately possessed me. It suddenly occurred to me that like the first step, the next steps would come replete with their own very real worries: proposing to Clodagh and getting her consent to marry me; then winning her parents' consent.

When it came to it, there was nothing grandly romantic about it. It was on a Saturday evening when most students in college were away home with their families for the weekend. Clodagh and I were the only students in college that weekend. We had gone earlier in the day to an Asian Market to buy okra, smoked fish, palmoil and red kidney beans. On returning to college she helped me prepare spicy okra stew, which we had with boiled rice. In the early evening we watched Cilla Black's once famous Blind Date programme on television. It was at the end of the programme that I casually asked Clodagh to marry me. Needless to say she consented. And beginning from that time until early Sunday morning she and I sat in the television room and talked about almost everything as we shared various concerns on our mind. Although she reassured me that night and on several other occasions that her parents would not oppose my proposal, I still had my fears.

Getting Engaged

Hoping to get engaged formally immediately after Christmas that year at her parents in Longford, this was the plan we put in place. I would go to spend Christmas in Darlington, England, with my adopted family (Derek, Gill, David,

Steven, Paul and Ruth). Clodagh would do the same with her family in Longford. On the 27th December I would travel to Belfast by boat and train, and onward to Dublin by another train, where Clodagh will meet me at Connolly Station. She was then to drive me to her home. She would have the engagement ring with her and on arrival at her parents she would hand it over to me. Whenever I was ready, I would call her parents, and ask them for the hand of their daughter in marriage, presenting the ring along with the request. The ring was bought in Belfast and presented to Clodagh before I went to England.

As planned, Clodagh was at the train station in Dublin waiting for me when I arrived on the night of the 27th. What I was going to do that night when I arrived at her home was rehearsed several times on our way to Longford, and each time it seemed I was doing it for the very first time. As you might guess, it was probably the most tortuous thing I had ever done in my life—facing her parents. At home in Sierra Leone, it would have been my parents' responsibility. But I was not at home. I was in fact thousands of miles away from home. The only support available to me apart from Clodagh was myself. I had therefore to get on with it. "But what if, contrary to what she told me, her parents turned down my request? What if they asked me to leave?" I reflected. That is what would happen among my people if a man went without his parents asking to marry someone's daughter.

On arrival at Edwin and Nancy's, after exchanging a few niceties, I was shown my room. I then proceeded to have a quick bath, dressed, and I went out to sit in the family room where Clodagh and her parents were sitting. Niall and Brian were in the kitchen. Clodagh's sister, Gillian, was at that time away in the Gambia. After a short while Clodagh gave me a look which was our pre-agreed cue for me to begin the long awaited deliberation. If you have ever run a race and experienced the anxiety and adrenaline flow of an athlete as she took her marks, got ready, and waited for the order to go, then you know something of how I felt at that moment. In this case Clodagh was the umpire and I was the athlete. I was so nervous that for a moment my mind went blank. It seemed all the rehearsals were in vain. I took a very deep and long breath, and started off. "Mr. and Mrs. McCormack", I called their attention. "You probably know that your daughter and I have been going out for some time now." As I was about to finish that first sentence my voice began to break and my words fade. But I had to press on. "The main reason for this my first visit to your home is to kindly ask you for your daughter's hand in marriage. "This", I continued, "might be coming to you as a surprise . . . but that is what I have proposed to do." With those words I was definitely finished. I had no more strength or courage in me to carry on. As I finished saying those words, I immediately took out of my pocket the encased engagement ring, handed it over Mr. McCormack and kindly asked if he would bless it before I give it to Clodagh.

There was a moment of silence which to me seemed like a year long silence. Then Edwin started to speak. "Nancy and I and the boys thank you for visiting our home and for your kind words. However much we may want to respond to your proposal we can't do so without hearing first from our daughter. Clodagh, you obviously know this man better than we do and you are the one who has brought him to us. What do you say to his proposal?" After a positive response from Clodagh, he referred the matter to Nancy who said the decision was Clodagh's and that she could count on their support for whatever she decided. Both Nancy and Edwin then gave their blessing to us. Edwin, vice principal of the Longford Technical College and a lay Methodist preacher, then prayed over the ring, and passed it on to me. I in turn gave it to Clodagh who there and then wore it. Then Niall and Brian were called into the family room and informed about what had happened. That night we told them when we intended to get married. That information set the stage for the engagement to be announced in the newspapers and the search for a hotel for the wedding reception to begin. Only then was I able to eat and relax.

So ended the day when I carried out one of the most important decisions in my life. I had left England at 6 o'clock in the morning of that day, travelled hundreds of miles by boat, train and car, and arrived in Longford at about 8.30pm. But it was all worth it for the lady of my dreams. The only important and necessary thing that was not done by the end of that day was that neither my family at home, nor my adopted family in England were informed of my move. That had to wait until the following day.

Covert but Real Opposition

News does not walk. It flies. By the time we were back in college in January, everyone knew about our engagement.

Reactions ranged from very happy to hostile. In between were those who were diplomatically happy and others who were clearly unhappy, to say the least. My greatest surprise was that almost all who were in the 'unhappy' and 'hostile' groups were ministers of the Church. I discovered that the concerns of some of the people in those two groups had to do largely with how our decision might impact on their Church. One of them even went as far as accusing me of stealing Clodagh from the Church in Ireland. Others were doubtful that an inter-racial marriage relationship would work. Still others were simply opposed to a black man marrying a white woman. That stance was informed by views of the racial superiority of white people to black people, sharply distinctive cultural differences between the two, and the conviction that it is impossible for a white person to live permanently in disease-riddled and poverty-stricken Africa with a black man who had meager financial means.

For those people, the love that brought us together did not figure in their reasoning, even though they preached love as the basis of all good relationships, especially marriage. If it did, I never sensed or discerned it. Instead their primary concern was colour, culture, and money. To be sure I had listened to a lot of them before talk about love as being the key prerequisite for marriage. That was, of course, with regard to the marriage of white Irish couples. In our own case the requirement of love simply got dwarfed if not buried by other concerns which were effortlessly given priority of place.

That experience combined with the one I had earlier had with some Creole people in my country led me to conclude that prejudice was a general human problem. It taught me that principles we proclaim and advocate, however lofty they may be, may sometimes be relegated to the back seat when we discover that living by them may threaten our status, privilege, or sense of value and security. "And yet", I reflected, "until a Christian lives out the gospel especially when it hurts his or her social, cultural, racial, and other preferences, he or she has no gospel to proclaim."

White Prejudice

In Ireland I was brought face to face with white people's prejudice against black people. It showed itself largely in the images of black people and society presented through the media. It took a little boy to drive home that reality for me. It was on a Sunday morning when I had gone to take a service in Donaghadee Methodist Church outside Belfast. As I walked from the vestry into the church to start the service, I saw and heard a little boy in a front pew asking his mum, "Mum does he have food to eat? Has he got clothes to wear? Does he . . . ?" As the questions uninhibitedly poured from his mouth, his mother was frantically but unsuccessfully trying to stop him. "Sh-sh-sh", she attempted. The boy got louder and louder until I walked quietly towards them, told her to leave the boy alone because, I told her, "the boy is only voicing what he had been seeing and hearing on television." It was the time of the famine in Ethiopia and the decontextualized pictures of many naked, sick, starving and emaciated Africans were been paraded on Western television screens. Seeing an African coming into the church, the boy could not help but equate him with the Africans he had been seeing on his television screen over many weeks.

The brutal, naked, hungry, sick, poor, dying and dead African! This was the most recurring image of Africa and the African that I remember of the Western media in the time I had stayed in Ireland. Yet I knew those realities represented only a part of the life of my people. I also knew that brutishness, poverty, hunger, suffering, and death were not exclusive experiences of Africans. But that was not what I was being told by the images and topics of discussion carried in the Western media. Sometimes those images of my people and I gave rise to self-hate and low self-esteem. At other times they gave rise to bitterness towards those who represented me and my people in such negative, decontextualized, unrealistic, even racist ways. "Did they have a hidden agenda for this kind of behaviour?" I sometimes asked myself. My history lessons at home had taught me that it was one of the weapons European colonial intellectuals used to argue their need to colonize us. It was also one way they sought to break our wills into subjection to theirs. It was the white man's way of making himself feel better and more powerful than the black man. Didn't a German priest say that if you want to put a people down the first thing you do is to mock and ridicule them? How true the saying, "My problem is not how I look; it is how you see me!"

It was this experience of prejudice and discrimination against my person and people that made me decide that if I did succeed in going to Cambridge I would formally change my name from John S. Yambasu (which my official records still carried) to Sahr J. Yambasu. It was for me a practical way of owning up to being an African and a vowing to remain so. It was a way of officially enshrining a decision I took long before I ever knew I would live in the West. I saw doing so as a tangible way of revolting against black and white people in and out of my country who would not accept and value me for who I am. It was my way of telling them that despite all their efforts to make me and my people feel somehow less human than they, I was not going to apologize to anyone for being who I am; and I was going to live my own life and not another person's.

Looking back now I can see that this was where my somewhat ambiguous relationship with the West first started. Before then my experiences of the West were largely ones of acts of benevolence towards me and my people. Yes, the history of the colonization of my people, its accompanying violence, dehumanization, pain and anger was never lost on me. I had, before visiting and experiencing life in the West, however, resolved to categorize that experience as a history that was behind us. But my experiences of how my people were represented in the Western media and how my own love relationship with a white woman was responded to by white people taught me that I was wrong.

That realization also made me think a little more critically even about those who seemed happy about my relationship with Clodagh. "Would they have been that happy", I asked myself, "if their daughter or sister or granddaughter, or niece was the one I fell in love with and had decided to marry? Did my being a minister and the fact of being reasonably educated in Western ways influence their reaction to the news of my getting engaged to Clodagh? Or were they simply genuinely happy?" I resolved that I might never know the answers to those questions. I also reminded myself that I could have experienced the same amount of opposition had I decided to marry a Creole girl in Freetown. Yet, I also knew from experience that not all Creoles or Irish, nor all black or white people, discriminated against people on the basis of their race and background. As I reflected on those issues and experiences, it helped end my naivety about human relationships across races, gender, social status, and culture. My experiences with both black and white people had taught me never to generalize about any people.

Two Examples of Open-mindedness

During the time of mixed responses towards my relationship with Clodagh, for example, we were especially blessed by a couple of far-sighted and open-minded ex-missionaries to Africa. Leslie Wallace and Jim McCormack (of blessed memory) had served in Sierra Leone and Zambia respectively for many years before returning home. One of the things that struck me most about those two people was that they grabbed even the most insignificant opportunity they had to talk about Africa and their experiences there. And whenever they did so it was with great love and admiration for the people they worked with. Unlike most other people I had met who visited or worked on the continent of Africa, Leslie and Jim hardly ever said anything negative about their experiences on the continent. Instead they always talked about the creativity, hard work, helpfulness, fun, and wisdom of the African people they encountered in their work there. I often wondered why? Was it that they never had any negative experiences in Africa? As I got to know them better in Ireland I came to realize that they too had their own share of the problems of living in Africa. But, as Jim once told me, there were enough problems to talk about living in Ireland and that he did not have go to Africa to experience problems.

Clodagh and I benefitted greatly from the counselling we received from Leslie and Jim especially from our period of courtship up to and after we were married. Leslie, whom I knew in Sierra Leone and who negotiated my scholarship to Ireland counselled us for our wedding. He was best placed to do so not only because he was a trusted mentor, but also because he knew and understood Irish and Sierra Leonean ways very well. Jim was probably one of the most open-minded of my lecturers at Queen's and Edgehill. His office was always open to us to see him whenever we needed to. His broadmindedness came through his lectures in the philosophy of religion and ethics. I often wondered how many of us students really understood the change of mindset on our parts that his lectures demanded.

A Graduation and Wedding

While all this was going on, I gave the best I could to my studies, with a lot of encouragement from Clodagh. The month of May of that year proved to be one of the most difficult. It was the month of exams. By mid-June the results were published and I found out thankfully that I made the grade I needed to proceed to Cambridge. I also learnt that the graduation ceremony was going to be held on July 7, 1988, exactly a week before our wedding.

So July was a month of celebrations. There was the graduation ceremony with some friends who had helped me along the way during my three years of study. They included the Irish administrators of my scholarship, some of my Antrim friends, and Clodagh. Then there was the wedding ceremony celebrated with friends and family from near and far away, white and black, Sierra Leoneans and Sudanese, English and Irish, Protestants and Catholics. My adopted parents Derek and Gill, their son Stephen, Rev. Jackson and his wife Carol, and their son Peter came from England to represent my family in Sierra Leone who were unable to attend. My parents were not able to attend purely because of financial and immigration problems.

It was perhaps the first Longford-African wedding. That, in any case, is what the local Longford Leader newspaper claimed. With about a hundred guests present, the Rev. Wallace addressed us using Ruth's words to Naomi as she swore to her: "Don't urge me to leave you or to turn back from you. Where you go I will go, and where you stay I will stay. Your people will be my people and your God my God. Where you die I will die, and there I will be buried. May the LORD deal with me, be it ever so severely, if anything but death separates you and me."[12] Very appropriate words indeed, for our situation.

---

[12]   Ruth 1:16-17

True to form, the African guests from England and Ireland, to the delight of all present, gathered in the churchyard at the end of the service, sang a Creole song, and threw grains of rice on both Clodagh and me as a prayer for blessing, especially with children. It was a very good and appropriate conclusion to the church ceremony, which was followed by a reception in the Shamrock Lodge Hotel in Athlone. After the reception, there was a dance organized for the very many other friends of ours.

The first indication that life often does not proceed the way we plan it came when at Dublin airport the following morning I was refused permission to fly to Paris for our honey moon because I did not have a visa. Long before our wedding, I had taken my passport to the Students' Union Office at Queen's asking for information about getting a visa. But I was told, for whatever reason, that I did not need one as long as I had my Students' Union card. At the airport, I was told something else. But for a friend of ours who knew somebody at the Belgian Embassy and arranged for us to have a visa to fly that day to Belgium, we would probably not have gone away for a honeymoon. "For better, and for worse!" I sighed asking what a world we are living in where the letter of the law often seems more important than the needs of human beings.

Back to Ireland after a lovely time away in Brussels and Bruges, my friend Tom Johnston (of blessed memory) provided us a place in his home in Belfast where my wife and I stayed until I left for Cambridge. Tom was another saintly man who helped me enjoy my stay while working in the Cregagh and Glengormley churches. Many a weekend away from college was spent with him in his home. I remember him once introducing me to a neighbour who was busy working hard in her flower garden. This lady showed me her flowers with great pride and satisfaction and asked me if we had flowers like those in my country. "We have", I honestly replied, "but most people consider them as weeds. They would rather grow food crops than flowers". She was not a bit impressed with my comments, Tom later told me. But it was the truth.

TEN

CAMBRIDGE

A Unique Experience

Off to Cambridge I went in September 1988, leaving Clodagh behind to complete her final year at Queen's. I have often felt that it may have been the year British Telecoms made its highest profits since Clodagh and I were on the phone every day and night and for long periods.

At first I found Cambridge to be a very intimidating place. One first visit to the University Library told me this was not just like any other University. The facilities, the people, the place itself overwhelmed me. Even though I was with a friend who knew the library, I got lost in it several times before we left it that day. I was later to find out that each one of the twenty-seven or so colleges that constituted the University also had their own well equipped libraries and manifold facilities.

Wesley Methodist House where I stayed had so many facilities that Edgehill College could only dream of then. The student population there was a lot bigger and student accommodation a lot more comfortable. The kitchen had huge modern electrical appliances and the dining room was very large. Each corridor of students' study/bedrooms was equipped with its own small kitchen and there were flats for married students with families. As in Edgehill College in Belfast, the college employed cleaning staff who also supplied, changed and washed bed linen. The previous year, Clodagh had visited this college on a student exchange visit and told me all about it. But it was another thing to see it for myself.

In Cambridge I often sensed my life as touching history in a very real way. Going into my department building (the Divinity School) there was the big, heavy, and short black door which reminded me of hundred of years of history. As I touched and pushed that seemingly eternal door to go into the building, I always sensed that I was also touching the time worn hand prints of thousands of people down the ages who had walked through it. Then there was in the building itself the smell of the past from the bricks and wood curiously blending in with the smell of modern manufactured cleaning products. Picking out books from library shelves I could not but be reminded that many of those books had been read by many people before me. In short I often experienced an awesome sense of being surrounded by a great cloud of witnesses in the Divinity School—an experience which I found to be both inspiring and awesome.

Then, of course, there were world famous colleges like King's, Trinity, St John's, Darwin, Jesus, and Christ's which seemed to compete for attention with the narrow quaint streets in the University area, the meticulously well-kept lawns, the willows hanging over the river Cam, Professors riding to lectures on bicycles with their academic gowns on, and thousands of students and tourists milling around in the college courtyards. Those scenes never ceased to amaze me, even though the eccentricity of some academics and students sometimes made me laugh.

Amidst all of that entertainment, however, I found my life in Cambridge to be quite lonely. In the midst of many people, I often felt I might as well be in the forest on my own. Everyone was often so busy that little time was available for socializing. Then there was the fact that I knew less than a handful of students outside of Wesley House where I lived. Being a research student did not help either because I spent most of my time doing my own work. Most of the other students at Wesley House with whom I lived were undergraduates and so attended different programmes of lectures.

An Experience of London

This experience of feeling alone and lonely in the midst of crowds of people was epitomized for me during my research visits to the School of African and Oriental Studies (SOAS) at London University. Surrounded by hundreds of people on underground train platforms I observed something I had never before experienced. It was the sight of healthy and strong people in very close proximity to each other who never spoke to each other. Like cattle being led to the slaughter making no noise, so we hurriedly edged our ways down station stairs and along station platforms towards approaching trains, only to disappear hurriedly again into other crowded trains or buses, or workplaces at the end of our journeys.

The first time I found myself in that situation, I found it so strange and amusing that I decided to stand on the side and observe what was happening. The sea of people I observed looked like a huge jungle of old, middle age, and young trees walking. On the train it was no different. Each person looked somewhat suspicious of the others and pretended not to know they were there. And yet, on closer observation, everyone was sneakily trying to look at the persons next to or across from them.

"Welcome to London", I said to myself quietly when I left the train and walked out of the underground. "This is the headquarters of the society and civilization that has always sought to humanize your people. This is the much envied example of development which has inspired you all your life. These are the products of it—virtual strangers, eternally suspicious of each other, tree-like beings, alone in the midst of many, constantly yearning, restless, running, chasing . . . after who, what?" I stood still for a while. I looked at large and tall tower blocks, the complex network of roads, different makes of cars, vans and trucks, and the mix of people from different racial backgrounds. "This truly is another jungle, only a different one from the one that shaped my life," I said to myself. Yet, confronted with the magic of the underground trains, the convenience of the network of public transport, the ease of life that economic wealth offered in a city like London, I could only stare with admiration.

My Tutor at Cambridge

But what overwhelmed me most in my first year in Cambridge was an encounter I had with my tutor in my first few weeks after commencing my study. Rev. Stephen Sykes was an Anglican priest, a Professor of the Divinity School and Dean of St. John's College. On my first visit to him he asked me and an English Methodist student Steven Curleys to write him an essay on the Methodist doctrine of the afterlife. We were instructed to get back to him with our essays in a couple of weeks. A week after we did so he invited us to go back to him for feedback.

As we left Wesley House on the morning he had arranged to see us, some students who had gone through the process before waved us goodbye and good luck. We left not a little worried about how our first tutorial would go. How right we were! The feedback we got was just simply unbelievable. He did not just tell us that we had not a clue what we were doing, but he warned us that if we thought Cambridge was a place for just any anybody, then we were to think again. He told us what was wrong with our essays and asked that we do the assignment again. For the whole of that day and evening I was in a state of shock, disbelief, and very low spirits.

One of the things that I first realized about Cambridge professors is that they were always so busy studying and writing that one would think they had the most important exam of their life coming up the next day. Under the tutorship of those people, I was convinced that they did not expect me to take my work less seriously. As a postgraduate student, I did not have scheduled lectures as such. Instead, I attended what advertised seminars and public department or university lectures I was interested in. Other than that, the only obligation I had was to attend tutorials recommended by my supervisor.

Academic Cruelty

It was especially at departmental lectures that I discovered how cruel academics could be to each other. Lecturers in the Divinity School were no different. Responding to papers presented by their colleagues, they were often so brutally scathing in their criticisms that I left feeling very sorry and embarrassed for the presenter in question. At Cambridge, I witnessed and experienced everything that Prof. Harry Sawyerr taught us about critical thinking and having an independent mind. There we were taught and encouraged to think our own thoughts and formulate our own views as long as we could back them up with reasonable and logical arguments. It was not too long when I began to find my footing in that environment as I resolved I was going to give whatever it took to pursue successfully my course of studies there. But this was not without costs.

In Cambridge I often felt, and for the first time, that my faith in God—what had always helped weather many storms and sustain me—was under threat. Overly academic approaches to the study of theology and spirituality left me with little, if anything, to believe in. I would not be telling the truth if I said that I was entirely happy with all the lectures I had at Queen's. I was particularly unhappy, for example, with lectures in biblical studies, modern church history and theology because it often seemed to me that some lecturers saw their task as one of arming us with arguments against Roman Catholic beliefs and practices. It was as if they wanted to make sure that in our biblical and theological understandings and practices we do not sell out to Rome. At Queen's, however, I at least generally knew where the lecturers stood on certain theological matters and in terms of their faith. I was never in any doubt, for example, that they believed in God as revealed by Jesus Christ and the Holy Spirit and in the authority of the Bible as the inerrant word of God for guiding belief and practice. That was not the case at Cambridge. There I never knew where a lot of the lecturers stood in terms of their faith in God. Once I protested to one of my tutors on this particular point commenting that I found most lecturers, as it were, 'sat on the fence' in matters of faith. "What do you think they should do?" He asked me. "Come down on the one side of the fence or the other", I replied. There and then he told me emphatically that an academic's job was to raise questions and not to provide answers or take sides. He went on to also tell me that the lecture theatre was not the place for talking about faith matters which he told me were private and individual matters. I went away that day questioning whether or not he was right. Was there any difference between a Christian academic theologian and a non-Christian one? If so what was it? While I did not agree entirely with him, however, I appreciated the fact that his forthrightness with me that day set me off thinking seriously about what the proper role of an academic Christian theologian might be.

Developing a Proposal for a PhD

By the middle of the second term of the first year of my two years' Masters' programme, I decided to start working on developing a proposal for a doctoral research programme. My intention in doing so was to upgrade my registration by the end of my first year. This idea came to me as the thought hit me one day that once I returned home at the end of my course, I might never be given another chance for further studies again. I knew there were many others of my colleagues who dearly wanted a chance to study overseas. I also knew that the Methodist Scholarship Committee had awarded me only a two year scholarship for the study programme in Cambridge. But I also reckoned that if I got my department to upgrade my registration by the end of my first year, I might be able to persuade them to extend the scholarship to cover the rest of my intended course of study. While I was aware that this might never happen, I decided to take a gamble.

Alongside my normal work I began to do extra research to help me develop a proposal by the end of that first year. Eventually, I was able to put together a proposal I believed, would be accepted. It was to critically examine missionary encounters and interactions with my people up to 1967 when the Methodist Church in Sierra Leone became independent and autonomous from the Methodist Church in Britain. My interest was in how, if they did in anyway, my people influenced missionaries, the message they preached and the Book from which they got that message. To find this out, I needed to study missionary letters, magazines, and minutes of meetings. I also needed to interview those missionaries still alive who served among my people and some of my people who worked with and served missionary interests and theirs. The study of the background histories, cultures, beliefs and spiritualities of both my people and the missionaries was to be a significant part of this research programme.

By the middle of the third and final term of that first year, I submitted my proposal to the Degree Committee of my department. And, as God would have it, it was accepted. I was accordingly registered as a doctoral student and the Degree Committee decided that my first Master's year would count as my first year of research. In that case, instead of me writing to the committee that offered me the scholarship to ask them to extend the scholarship, it was the secretary of the Degree Committee that did so on my behalf. Consequently, my scholarship was extended by another couple of years, but with a very strong warning that even if I did not finish my research at the end of those extra years I would have to return to my home country and church. The ball was then totally in my court. But that incident taught me an important lesson I practice to this day: to listen to and honour my inner convictions.

"Three further years of study and research in England and Sierra Leone and, then, producing an acceptable dissertation at the end?" I sighed. While it might have seemed an unenviable position, I was convinced, nonetheless, that it was worth it. By that time, Prof. Stephen Sykes, my initial tutor and supervisor had been appointed Bishop of Ely and was preparing to leave. Consequently, two supervisors—a historian, Dr. John Lonsdale of Trinity College, and a theologian, Dr. Nicholas Sagovsky of Clare College were assigned to me by the Degree Committee.

The Birth of Our First Child

By that time, my wife Clodagh had completed her course at Queen's in Belfast and joined me. She was about seven months pregnant. We shared two adjacent rooms while waiting for a flat to be made available to us by another family that was leaving college that year for Zimbabwe. Two months later in early September 1989, Abbie, our first child, was born in Addenbrookes University Hospital after nearly eight hours of labour. It was my first time to be with a woman in labour. In my country I would not have been allowed that. I recalled that even in my secondary school days at Segbwema men were not allowed to go into the labour and maternity wards in the Nixon Memorial Methodist Hospital. This was not a written sanction imposed by the white administrators of the hospital or the Church. It was, instead, an unspoken, taken-for-granted, norm of Sierra Leonean society as a whole. It was that taboo that I had broken.

A man having to play any prominent role during the birth of a child was anathema, especially among Kissi people. In fact some of my colleagues who had thought about going into nursing after secondary school were immediately scolded and discouraged from doing so by their parents. The reason was this straightforward: it would involve them in dealing with childbirth and women's matters in general. This was considered inappropriate for men, and it was even believed that it would harm their health in some mysterious and inexplicable way. Influenced by those traditional beliefs in no small way, I was very reticent about going into the labour room with my wife that day. I wondered if the nurses there understood my reluctance to do so. It was not, for me, simply a question of love; instead it was singularly a question of culture, history, obedience, and loyalty to tradition, even if questioningly so. I have never even had the courage to tell *Nde* or *Keke* about this. Is this an indication of a continuing strong hold of tradition over me or is it simply just a desire on my part to protect my parent's views? I don't know. But I do sometimes feel that it is probably both. I have often wondered, though, what their response might be if I were to tell them. But would it matter? I can't tell?

Be that as it may, what mattered most for me at that time was that our first child had been born, and I was proud to be a father. "Welcome to the world Sia Abbie Ann Yambasu", I said to myself. "You are a lady of many parts even before you know it. You are Sia, for you are the first daughter of your Kissi father. You are Abbie, for by you I want to honour my mother who gave me life and never relented in helping me to live it to the fullest possible. You are Ann, a name you will bear as my 'thank you' note to your mother's mother—a courageous woman of faith who graciously let me, a total stranger, marry your mother. Your arrival does not only announce the beginning of another life, but you also signal the completion of my journey from childhood to manhood. 'You rightly come'. This is a Kissy way of saying 'welcome!'"

Research Findings

In Cambridge I received great help from professors in the University who were neither in the Divinity School nor staff of Wesley House or Fitzwilliam College. The world renowned sociologist and Fellow of Christ's College, Prof. Anthony Giddens, was one such person. Warmed to his ideas, I had decided to use their main thrust as a tool to help me interpret my research data. Anxious that I understood and represented his ideas correctly, I requested that he read a paper I had written detailing those ideas and suggesting the potential they had for understanding the nature of relationships that pertained in non-Western societies between modern missionaries and the objects of their missions. The session with him launched me in my research with a lot greater confidence than I had before. During the three years that followed, that quest led me to several libraries in Cambridge, London and Swindon, to different people who were relevant to my work, to my home country, and through many agonizing days and sleepless nights. It was, however, a pretty rewarding exercise as I came across information that gave me invaluable insight into a history of my people that I knew nothing about before I commenced by studies. And the hope of learning something new every day gave me much inspiration to continue with my quest.

Of much interest and significance to me was my discovery of how much missionaries depended on my people's help and resources to be able to live among them and carry out their missions. That was a mind-blowing revelation to me since the picture of missionaries I had in my mind was one that represented them as valiant soldiers of Christ who, against myriads of odds, single-handedly championed the cause of the gospel of Christ among my people. While I had discovered beforehand that that was not the case for Christian missions in the Freetown area, up until then I had thought that it was different for missions among Up Country peoples. It was probably because all I heard from my Kissi and Mende people, for example, were stories of the good works of different missionaries who had worked among them and little or nothing about the crucial roles their own people played in that task. But I think the other reason was my assumption that because they were illiterate in English and their own native languages they had no education to influence the processes and outcomes of missions among them in any significant way.

To my delight, however, I discovered from archival records and interviews that my people made Trojan contributions to Christian missions among them. That discovery gave me a new sense of respect for my people. They served as translators of the scriptures, evangelists and preachers of the gospel, pastors and healers of their people, cooks, gardeners, informants, researchers, messengers, servants, and interpreters of missionaries, and builders of schools, churches and clinics for their communities. That was not all. I also discovered for the first time my people's courage to stand their ground when they believed what missionaries required of them in the name of conversion was unreasonable. "How can I leave this religion for yours when this one works?" one of my people asked. The man who asked that question of a missionary never became a Christian because his question was never answered. Instead, he was just simply dismissed as a heathen and savage who was too depraved, ignorant, and backward to see Christ's liberating and saving light.

Yet this man's response to missionary Christianity deserved much more serious attention than he received. He was asking the messengers of the gospel to give reason for the faith they professed and propagated. But thinking the gospel of Christ to be self-evident, this man's request for them to convince him fell on deaf ears. Like many of my people who decided to convert but not become carbon-copies of missionary Christians, this man's question challenged profoundly missionaries who dealt with spiritual matters simply in terms of right and wrong belief and practice. Instead of seeking to dialogue unpatronizingly with them, many missionaries evaded dealing with such awkward and yet basic human spiritual issues that begged for attention. They engaged in ridiculing my people's beliefs and practices using Western scientific and philosophical rationalizations to deal with basic commonsense human dilemmas that were purely of a spiritual nature. Such rationalizations were meant to shame my people into conversion from what those missionaries believed were primitive, ignorant, childish, and senseless pagan religious practices.

It seemed to me, reflecting on what I discovered, that missionary language, approach, enthusiasm, and conviction left them incapable of understanding or even accepting that spiritual matters are essentially open-ended matters, unable to be completely grasped or possessed, and more at home with questions than with answers. Moreover, their cocksureness about what and how to believe and live made it impossible for them to grasp the obvious fact that everything in the world can be imitated except truth. For, truth that is imitated—including spiritual truth—can no longer be truth. People learn truth more from their own successes and failures, and their own tragedies and triumphs than from those of others. That way, they avoid mistaking the spiritual map for the spiritual territory in which they live daily, as they try to handle the often difficult and awkward dilemmas of living with varying degrees of success and failure.

Probably because they lived constantly with such complex and demanding situations, my people never capitulated to the missionary language of derision, ridicule, demonstration, orthodoxy, and conformity designed to shame them into imitating Christianity. They probably knew that matters of faith and practice had to do with working out one's own salvation and not living by pre-defined, well argued and rehearsed answers of others, however 'sensible' those answers might seem. Consequently, they settled for believing and practicing in the way that best reflected their experience of divinity and the world in which they lived. As a result, often reluctantly, missionaries had to accept the reality of what was.

As I thought through those realities, I was reminded of the experiences I had in Kailahun a few years earlier which led me to think of creating space and time for Christian leaders there to reflect on their faith journeys and callings. I was also aware, of course, that the religious life is a journey which involved an agonizing process of searching, stumbling, falling down, and getting up again. That journey involves us in a process through which we discover that we are only mere mortals carrying within us hints of divinity. It is a process in which we recognize that it is not how far one has travelled that is important, but how far one has yet to go in order to reach one's destination. I knew that much of my own spiritual life could be characterized in this way. "But why did I fail to see the tendencies and behaviour of my sheep in Kailahun in this light?" I pondered. "Why did I characterize them simplistically as unconverted?" Was I too unconsciously practicing 'power religion'? Was I denying them a fundamental human reality of spirituality? In doing so was I, like my missionary mentors, justifying, enforcing and facilitating the exercise of both my power and the power of the church that put me in that position and place.?"

Perhaps most instructive of all for me was that I had to travel all the way to England before I could learn of these heroic strides of my people towards shaping their own destinies. Why did my primary, secondary, and theological schools' text books not pay tribute to the talents, skills, commitments, and stout-heartedness of my people in responding to and shaping the Christian presence among them that we took so much for granted? The answer, as I discovered, was simple: my people were not the ones who wrote those books. I think it was Chinua Achebe who said that "Until the lions produce their own historian, the story of the hunt will glorify only the hunter."[13]

The Might of the Mighty Challenged

That aside, my discovery raised for me a further question. It was a question which was influenced by words of a Catholic theologian I had read. "Never did the might of the mighty bring them solely what they planned"[14], Karl Rahner once wrote. If he was right as I thought he was, how could the missionaries have ever hoped to achieve even half of their intentions in their bid to convert my people when my people were the main agents through whom they had hoped to achieve their goals? In my research I discovered that the truth of Rahner's statement was, as the following rather long complaint shows, written all over missionary endeavours to Christianize my people. It was written in 1958, about sixty-two years after Methodist missionaries started working Up Country. It was written by a missionary called W. T. Harris to the Methodist Missionary Society office in London. In his letter he admitted that my people's resistance to live as missionaries expected them to live gave only:

> . . . faint expression of a very real topic which was
> raised in the first case at the Mende Area Council.
> Stanley Brown, who was the Chairman of that
> Council spoke very sweepingly in condemnation

[13]   Achebe, Chinua (2000:73), Home and Exile. Oxford: Oxford University Press
[14]   Theological Investigations, vol.4 (1957:407) Translated by Kevin Smith. J. London: Darton, Longman & Todd

of Poro and Sande and to my surprise there was a strong adverse reaction from our Mende Leaders who refused to discuss the matter but insisted that they were leading members of Poro and Sande and resented the white man's attempt to say anything about them . . . I came away deeply distressed and feeling that we had put our finger on one cause of the weakness of our Mende Church, that is, that our Leaders have divided minds. They belong to the Christian Church and they belong to Secret Societies and at the moment there is no obvious clash between the two . . . What will happen when that clash comes . . . we cannot say now, but judging by the fervour with which some of these Mende Leaders spoke, it will be Poro and Sande that will retain their loyalty. A committee was formed which we are quite sure will never meet as it consisted of those same Mende Leaders. When the matter was raised at Synod very little progress was made and the final resolution was this weak one, that our Mende Ministers should discuss the topic and then bring their findings to the members of the missionary staff. This leaves the really concerned people safely out of the discussion where they want to be. There will be no trouble. I am not at all sure that there ought not to be trouble.[15]

---

[15] An archival letter to the General Secretary of MMS at the time, Rev. T. A. Beetham [see Yambasu, Sahr (2002:156-7) Dialectics of Evangelization. Accra: Asempa Publishers

When I first read those words I could not but think that the essential question was not whether or not there should have been trouble. Instead, it was what the outcome of such trouble would have been? In the end the matter seemed to die a natural death for fear of undoing all the good work missionaries had already done. Missionaries settled for what change my people embraced, not what change they wanted to see them embrace. After all we are not saved by the form of Christianity that we practice but by the saving work of God through Christ. Paul could not make this more clear: "If you confess with your mouth that Jesus is Lord and believe in your heart that God raised him from the dead, you will be saved. For it is by believing in your heart that you are made right with God, and it is by confessing with your mouth that you are saved." As the Scriptures tell us, "Anyone who trusts in him will never be disgraced." Jew and Gentile are the same in this respect. They have the same Lord, who gives generously to all who call on him. For, "Everyone who calls on the name of the LORD will be saved."[16]

Benefits from Missionaries

Despite Harris' skepticism, there is overwhelming evidence documented by missionaries themselves that missionary teaching, preaching and life aided an unstoppable change among my people. Among other things, it is to the missionaries, I discovered, my people owed the privilege of having their language and other forms of their culture

---

[16] Romans 10:9-13, New Living Translation

preserved in written form. The building of schools, churches, and clinics also introduced the English language and Western forms of education and health care among them. All these and more discoveries made what was a difficult time of research also quite enjoyable.

The Stress of Time Limitations

Extreme pressure to finish my work in time caused me to live a somewhat dazed sort of life in those three years. Often intensely focused on studying and writing, there were times when conversations I had with my wife never registered with me. We would, for example, decide to visit someone or place, but when the time came and she had got herself ready to leave, it was then she discovered that I had not taken in what we had discussed. To her request for us to leave, I would ask, "Leave for where?" It was only when she patiently reminded me that I recalled we had talked about it. Wherever I went during those three years—to church, market, park, friend and so on—I always carried a note pad and biro with me to record any thoughts that I believed were relevant for my work. Consequently, even though I was sometimes away from my study, I was really never away from work. I carried my work with me always.

By April of my fourth and final year, I managed to complete writing up my dissertation. I will never forget the weeks before that when I had to read through and edit it so that it would adhere to the word limit prescribed by my department. It was a process I found to be much more difficult than the actual writing of the dissertation. Not until then did I realize that every word, sentence, and paragraph of the dissertation was where it was for a good reason. In a tightly argued work, as was expected of work of that nature, taking out a word or sentence or paragraph could easily turn what seemed a logical argument into a pear-shaped one. At one point while engaged in that very tedious, unexciting, and uninspiring work, I became so sick of the exercise that I felt like throwing the whole thing out through the window and forgetting about it. But the understanding and encouragement of my two very helpful supervisors was able to carry me through those very trying times. When eventually the dissertation was bound, one of them held it in his hands, looked at me and said, "This is what you have been pregnant with for the last three years. Now your baby has been born. Congratulations!" What a beautiful way to put it, I thought; for I had never thought of the exercise in those terms. The title of the dissertation was, Dialectics of Evangelization: A Critical Examination of Methodist Evangelization of Mende People in Sierra Leone. This was later published as one of the Legon Theological Studies Series.

The Viva and Result

The viva, though, was still to come. As was the practice, the two external examiners were to read independently and write their reports on the dissertation. On the day of the viva, the two of them were also expected to write a joint report on the work and on my performance. Then the independently written reports and the joint report would be sent to the Degree Committee who would then decide whether or not to award the degree.

The viva consisted of two hours of gruelling questioning by two examiners, one from Cambridge and the other from Edinburgh Universities. All I can say is that it was a tortuous experience, although it should not have been had I not been so nervous that I failed to hear them congratulate me as I entered the room in which they were waiting for me. Truth to be spoken, they put my work through the mill. The whole thing lasted for about two hours, as both of them questioned me on issues that needed to be clarified or elaborated upon. By the time they released me, I felt physically and emotionally flattened. My two supervisors were also waiting anxiously to hear how it went. I do not need to say that my feedback to them was not very reassuring. But from what I shared with them of the experience they were in no way as pessimistic as I was about it. Instead, as they often did, they encouraged me to look on the bright side while waiting for the result. So I went home, unable to eat anything that afternoon. I just went to bed to rest.

Three long and anxious weeks passed when one afternoon I went into the students' common room in Wesley House and surprisingly found a letter from the Degree Committee in my letter box. I had checked my letter box earlier that morning as I had done many mornings before that day. There were other letters there but not THE letter I had been anxiously waiting for. But that letter had arrived sometime later with the internal university postal services. On seeing that it came from the graduate studies' office of the University, my heart started pounding and my hands shaking as I attempted to open it. "Should I open it in that public place? What if someone walked in and wanted to know? Maybe I should go into the toilet where I am sure no one else will see me. I want to be alone when I open it just in case I have not made it." I thought to myself. Straight to the toilet I went and closed the door firmly. The essentially one paragraph letter discreetly opened, it congratulated me on successfully completing my doctoral research and giving me a date for the graduation ceremony. On reading it, I flew out of the toilet upstairs to our flat to share the good news with my wife. What a relief I felt that day! It seemed as if an unbearable weight had been lifted off my shoulders. I went immediately to the telephone to share the good news with my supervisors first, my sponsors, and then my friends in and outside Wesley House. Clodagh took care of informing her family.

Graduation and the Birth of another Son

For a couple of months that summer I worked at Kentucky Fried Chicken and English Churches Housing Association to raise some money to buy my graduation gown and hood. And on the graduation day—the day that officially concluded my time at Cambridge—my adopted parents from Darlington, my supervisors, my former supervisor, the principal of Wesley House, Rev. Dr. Ivor Jones, my wife Clodagh, a cousin of mine Patrick, and a fellow countryman Joseph Jabbie and his friend joined me at the ceremony. We then had refreshments for all at our flat. It was on that day that Professor Sykes let me into the secret of how he dealt with new students he tutored in Cambridge. He, in his own words, ". . . humbled them at the first session they had with me so that they would work as hard as possible." That was why he treated Steven and

I the way he did on that awful day when we met with him for our first tutorial.

In September 1992, exactly four years after I first went to Cambridge, we left for Edinburgh where my external examiner had invited me as a visiting scholar to participate in a few lectures and seminars at New College Edinburgh and the University of Sterling. By this time Clodagh was heavily pregnant with Sahr Junior; or should I say she was ready to give me another opportunity to break the taboo? That time my experience was worse than the first. At the Eastern General Hospital in Edinburgh where she went to be delivered, I did not only stay in the labour ward for the time of labour but also for the actual birth. I was so traumatized that night that the nurses found me a bed in the hospital to stay for the night because, according to them, I was not fit to go home.

My name sake was born, Sahr the first son of a Kissi father. "You have made it possible for me to contribute towards the continuation of the Yambasu family line", I said to myself as I lay in my hospital bed that night. "Therefore you will be also called Yaniwah in honour of my father the dreamer par excellence who never stood still in life but took risks in the bid to fulfil himself. Born after the completion of my studies, you remind me of the unmerited grace of God that I have enjoyed in so many different ways since I came to the white man's land. So you will also be called Derek, the man who first made me understand the unmerited grace of God in action by sponsoring my secondary education. May God's name be praised forever", I concluded my conversation with myself.

ELEVEN

BACK TO AFRICA

We are All the Same

I t was in November 1992 that my family and I left to live and work in Sierra Leone after my studies. But that was not the first time I returned home since I proceeded to Cambridge. Part of my research was done in Sierra Leone, and Clodagh and Abbie were with me on that trip. One of the people who come to mind when I think of that journey is a man called Abraham Tagoe.

Abraham was a Methodist minister in Wesley House who was also studying with me. A Ghanaian and an older and more experienced man, Abraham became a very close friend of mine during most of my time in Cambridge. He and I went to Wesley House in the same year, registered with the same college (Fitzwilliam), and for the same course. He was a strong support to me always. Abraham and I used to shop together and cook our meals together when we wanted to eat something African.

Whenever I remember those days with Abraham there are some incidents that still put a smile on my face. Abraham, for example, loved bananas a lot. Fridays were always market days in Cambridge. It was the day when traders brought good and cheap fruit, vegetables and other products and wares to sell. Abraham never missed market day. He would remind me early in the morning that it was market day and that I should accompany him when he was ready to go and buy a supply of bananas. It was not the buying of the bananas that I found hilarious. It was where he kept his money and the length of time it took him to get it out and pay for his bananas.

Abraham always kept his money wrapped up in several pieces of cloth which were old enough to be classified as rags. On being served his bananas and told how much they cost, he would begin the long process of openly unwrapping his money. While he did so a queue of other customers waited impatiently, wondering when he would conclude the transaction and move out of the way. From the look on the faces of some (including the trader), I often thought they were wondering where he may have come from not to know that he should keep his money in a more easily accessible and culturally acceptable place. As all that was happening, I stood by the side of Abraham quietly urging him, while trying hard not to laugh, to speed up and give way to other customers. It was only after months of encouraging him to buy a wallet for his money that he decided to do so.

The other incident happened in the final year of Abraham's Master's Course. His wife, Fidelia had come from Ghana to join him in Cambridge for six months. This was a policy of the Methodist Scholarship Committee so that spouses would have a taste of the culture in which their partners were living. During the time his wife was with him in college, I remember looking out of our flat window and seeing Abraham early one morning picking the college flowers. Horrified, I ran downstairs to him and asked him what he was doing. "It's my wife's birthday today and I am picking some flowers for her", he replied. By the time I finished telling him that he was not allowed to pick the college garden flowers the caretaker came out of his house to challenge him. My friend obviously did not know he was breaking a rule. But he reminded me again of the fact that in Africa if people pick flowers they pick them wherever they find them, and that would often be in the bush or in the backyard where they grow by themselves without any direct and planned human input.

But one of the things I remember Abraham for most is that he was the one who taught me something I have never forgotten. It is the saying, "We are all the same." Once I asked Abraham why he used this saying so often. In response he told me that he had, before coming to England, always thought that white people, unlike black people, were only capable of good. On coming to England, however, he had discovered to his shock that his conclusions were wrong. "Like Africans" he continued, "I have discovered that white people also steal, lie, commit adultery and fornication, cheat, get drunk, are poor, beg, and so on."

Assumptions

As Abraham shared with me what he had discovered, I could see he was genuinely shocked. I also understood why he would feel the way he felt. Stephen and I went through a similar experience when we first arrived in London and attended our first church service there. Thinking of the very key role white people played in the propagation of Christianity in our country and aware that much we had ever read, listened to and seen in movies about Christianity was written, preached, sung, and acted by white people, we had assumed that the church we decided to attend would be full to overflowing by worshipers. After all, we talked about it the day before, were we not in London, the capital city of England, Britain and the United Kingdom? Was it not the city in which most of the world renowned overseas missionary societies existed and from which many of the missionaries who evangelized the world were given their marching orders to go out and conquer the world for Christ as valiant soldiers of Cross? As we thought about those things we became more and more buoyed up with excitement and expectation. We got out our best Sunday clothes and ironed them, polished our shoes, and went to bed early that night so that we would be up and ready on time to be picked up and go to church.

It was a huge and magnificently built church. In our reckoning, no resource was spared in erecting such a building. Looking at it we could only conclude that the building was a symbol of the power and wealth of those who own it. As we walked in we were struck by how clean and meticulously ordered everything was. The pews were made of solid brilliantly polished mahogany wood comfortably cushioned. The hymn and service books were neatly stacked away on shelves made to fit. As we continued to cast our eyes round the building we noticed the tastefully carpeted long aisles and the altar and pulpit areas which were likewise furnished appropriately. Looking at the altar and pulpit areas one was left in no doubt which part of the church was considered more important and sacred. And then behind the altar table there were the long stained glass windows right behind the altar table across one of which was carved the words, "God is in His Holy Temple, let all the world fall silent at his feet."

Even as we were seated we constantly looked around with admiration at the building and different things in it. Suddenly we realized it was about 9.20am and there were hardly twenty people in the church. "The service will be starting in ten minutes time but there are very few people here", Stephen worriedly told me. "I know." I said to him. "I wonder why the people have not yet come!" Ten minutes later, at 9.30am on the dot, the minister with his entourage of choir and stewards walked into the church from the vestry to begin the service. By that time about another thirty people had joined us, and that was all—about fifty people excluding a choir of eight people. At the end of the service we could not believe that so few people were in church on Sunday, in London, and in a very big and expensively built cathedral-like church. What we had expected to be a wonderful and exciting experience turned out to be a total disappointment. Like Abraham was with his own discovery, we too were very shocked by that experience.

So, as Abraham shared his story with me, I knew where he was coming from. Having lived for all his life until then under the illusion that white people were only capable of good, he was shocked when he discovered how wrong he was in his assumption. Like a revelatory experience, Abraham had come to discover that the few white people he had ever known and associated with in Africa were mostly Christian missionaries or some kind of expatriates and, so, were not necessarily representative of all white people. Because he had also not lived close enough to the few white people in his country, he had no way of testing the truth of his assumption. In England, living with and associating closely with white people, he was able to see, hear, and experience what was impossible for him to do in Ghana. As a result he discovered a basic truth about humanity which years of ignorance, indoctrination, manipulation, oppression, and exploitation had hidden from him.

Listening to Abraham, I realized how he was not alone in the assumptions he had made. I knew that what he believed about white people was what most people in Africa also believed. When I went to bed that night, I asked what might be the reason for this. I reckoned that one of the reasons, like in the case of Abraham, was that they have not experienced living in the West. I wondered whether it also had anything to do with many Africans' perception of colonial vis-à-vis post-colonial times in their countries. From conversations with people in my own country, for example, I knew that many of them equated the colonial period with prosperity, plenty of food, well paid jobs, good market prices for their commodities, good roads, reliable transport systems, good health services, quality and less expensive education, honesty in the public sector, the rule of law, and quality goods. They compared that time when the white man ruled their country to the time since the country became independent and was governed by black politicians, and most of them concluding that the white man was only capable of good.

As I continued to reflect, I was also reminded of what might have been my father's first attraction to Christianity. It very likely was the phenomenon of a white man who had come all the way from his country to help educate people he was not related to in anyway whatsoever and in very difficult circumstances. White people's seemingly selfless charitable work, it appeared to me, was also responsible for the assumptions of many Africans that they are only capable of good. And, finally, I recalled the almost divine ability that many of my people would associate with white people because of their creative and daring skills in inventing aeroplanes, ships, motor cars, other machines and valued commodities. As I lay down that night considering these various reasons, I began to understand how many Africans, unaware perhaps of the downside of those taken-for-granted virtues of white people, could easily make the kind of assumption that Abraham made.

Introduced to Christianity by white missionaries and to ideas and programmes of development and progress by their secular counterparts, Abraham, like many of us Africans, mistakenly equated their talking about the values they taught us as inhering in them and the peoples they represented. We had also, like children, often accepted unquestioningly all those values as both reflecting the best of humanity and so something to aspire to. Abraham was the one who made me especially conscious of this. And for the two years we were together, there was hardly a day when Abraham did not find reason to remind me that, "We are all the same". By that he meant that all human beings were capable of and did wrong regardless of the colour of their skin. So, as Clodagh and I prepared to go to Sierra Leone for my fieldwork, Abraham made one request of me: "My brother", he said (for that is the way we often referred to each other) "when you go back to Africa, tell them we are all the same." "I will indeed, my brother", I replied.

Arriving Home

It was for me quite an anxious time of preparation to go home. I had been home to Sierra Leone at least twice since I first left for Europe. So my anxiety had little or nothing to do with my returning home. Instead, it was partly because of the work I was expected to accomplish there, and partly because it was going to be my wife and our fifteen months old daughter's first visit there. I was aware it has often being said that first impressions lasted very long. In addition to the cultural differences, I was also very much aware of some of the comforts my wife and daughter were going to forgo while they were with me in Sierra Leone. To be sure, I sent word home to my Church and family that we were planning to visit. So they were preparing to receive us. But that did not get rid of the anxiety. To avoid taking any risks, I made sure we brought everything we could possibly bring that they would need for the time we were going to be away.

On landing at Freetown International Airport, I had mixed feelings of excitement and worry. Off the aircraft, through immigration and baggage collection, we got in to the car sent by my Church to collect us. In ten to fifteen minutes we were at the ferry port waiting to be ferried across into the city. The airport is situated on an island and it takes about three quarters of an hour to travel from the airport side of the ferry port to the Freetown side. True to form, the ferry was on the Freetown side when we arrived at the port that night. Consequently, we were not in Freetown until about 11.00pm. That was about four hours after we had touched down at the Freetown International Airport, exhausted and hungry. As we got out of the ferry and drove into the city, it was pitch black. There was an almost total black out in the city. So, try as I did to point out landmarks of the city to Clodagh, it did not work. Humbled and annoyed that we found the city in the state in which it was, I quietly accepted the reality as we made our way slowly from the eastside of the city to the home of a Methodist missionary couple who lived on the west side. They had kindly agreed to put us up for a few days before we moved into the place that the Church had promised to accommodate us.

Visiting my Village

In Sierra Leone I had a lot of work to do collecting primary data in the form of interviews and Church archival information. I also had to look at secondary material in the library of Fourah Bay College, University of Sierra Leone. Before that, though, I had to bring my wife and daughter to my home village to meet my parents and extended family for the first time and to also spend Christmas with them. So we left Freetown for Segbwema, the town where I had my secondary school education. In Segbwema we stayed with a Methodist missionary medical doctor working in the Methodist Nixon Memorial hospital there. Dr. Jennifer Gibson was a Cambridge graduate. She warmly welcomed us in her home for a few days and later made her four wheel drive vehicle and driver available to us to convey us to my home village.

Leaving at about 5 o'clock on Christmas Eve, Clodagh, Abbie, a few other people and I headed for my beloved Lalehun. What a night it proved to be! About half way through the journey we got a puncture in one of our tyres. Fortunately it was in a town called Manowa, about twenty-five miles from our destination. The driver suggested wisely that we stay in the town while he went back to Bunumbu to repair the damaged tyre. He knew that the rest of the road we had to travel was a lot worse than the one we had travelled and so keenly recognized the need for a spare tyre. So we waited on the veranda of a house whose occupants had still not returned from the farm. It was about 7.30pm. Half an hour later, they appeared to find their home invaded by strange looking people. Their surprise over, they invited us to sit inside since it was already dark. By 9.00pm Clodagh and Abbie were so tired and sleepy that the three of us were offered a bed in the house while we waited for the driver to return. The people also offered all of us some food to eat. There were about seven of us travelling excluding the driver.

It was not until about 10.30pm that the driver returned. Up and ready, we left after thanking our very generous hosts. About six miles into the journey Clodagh was so tired and fearful of the condition of the road that she started to throw up. A little break and a few words of encouragement helped her to board the vehicle again. We arrived in Sandaru at about one o'clock in the morning. As custom required us to do, we briefly called with the Paramount Chief, greeted him and told him our mission in the area. Before we left him, teacher Yambasu, who had been woken up by the sound of the vehicle, joined us. Contrary to what the Chief told us, he warned us that on our approach to the main bridge between Sandaru and my village we should stop and check if it was good enough to hold the vehicle. According to him it was nearly a year since any vehicle had travelled the road.

How right he was! At the bridge, I asked the driver to stop the vehicle. I invited two other men to join me in walking to the middle of the bridge which was made of logs and planks. As we jumped up and down it to see if it was safe to hold the vehicle, I observed a spring in the bridge that led me to ask that everyone in the vehicle disembarked except the driver. We all left the vehicle, walked across the bridge, climbed to the top of the hill on the other side, and waited there to see how the driver would fare. The driver, who had many years of experience driving on rugged, hilly and extremely bad roads, got out of the vehicle onto the bridge to check it out for himself before he attempted the journey across. Slowly he drove the front wheels on to the bridge first, carefully trying to crawl across. As the front section of the vehicle passed the middle of the bridge safely, we began to hope that he might make it. But as the rear portion of vehicle got to the middle of the bridge, we heard a big cracking sound. It came from logs and planks under it snapping. Quickly and dexterously, the driver put the vehicle into auxiliary gear and drove it through the broken bridge and up to the top of the hill without stopping. That was how he escaped dumping that vehicle into the rocky river about twenty metres below.

As I realized what we had escaped from had we not been advised by teacher Yambasu, my legs shook and my knees knocked. "Thank you God for saving us from this moment", I prayed aloud, repeating the prayer several times. With five or so miles still to go, I advised the driver to take his time and to worry more about our safety than about when we get to the village. It was about 3 o'clock on the morning of Christmas Day 1990 that we eventually arrived in my village. By that time everyone was extremely worn out, especially Clodagh and Abbie. As the vehicle drove into the village, many who heard it approaching got up from their beds and out of their houses. And so did my parents. We had disturbed the calm of the dark and sleepy village. As we drove on through the village, I directed the driver to my parent's house. There was no telling that we had reached my parents house. All the family just came out rushing with excitement towards the vehicle as it stopped. "La cha hunor"[17], *Nde* and *Keke* repeatedly said in Kissy, as they hugged Clodagh, Abbie and me. Tired out and sleepy we begged leave to go to bed after the ritual of greetings and introductions was over.

---

[17]   It literally means "You rightly come" (that is to say, "You are welcome").

The following morning our house was full of frenetic activity with people coming to greet us and food being prepared for Christmas. The Christmas Day Church service to which Clodagh and I were expected started at 8am. Still tired and sleepy we managed to drag ourselves out of bed and attend—Clodagh for about an hour. I, however, had to stay till the end. The whole village had been blessed with very special visitors that Christmas and it was a time to rejoice.

People could not get over the way Clodagh was dressed. She had decided to dress in traditional cotton blouse and rapper costume. Commenting on her appearance they noted that she was as beautiful as an African woman. I could only smile at the implication of their comment. Abbie also commanded a lot of the attention. At that time she was quite able to walk by herself. Much of the attention that would have normally being mine on such a visit was that time focused on them. But I did not mind. To be honest, I was proud to come with my wife and daughter. "Yambasu's son has not only schooled in the white man's ways and land", some people announced aloud, "he has also married one of them." In the eyes of most of my people, that was the greatest achievement imaginable for a boy they witnessed growing in their midst.

Trip Down Memory Lane

The five days we were home were spent visiting and/or receiving relations from far and near and eating much missed African cuisine and fruit. Gifts of chickens, goats, rice, fruit, and so on were abundant. I also took the opportunity to bring Clodagh round to see interesting places in the village. Among them were the different sites on which the village primary school had existed. The first call was at a spot in the centre of the village which was at the time marked by a few large granite stones. It was there that the first school existed, in a large thatched wall-less hut which belonged to the then section Chief Fayia Nyorpowahun. Barely a hundred yards from our house it is to this place that Mama Amie used to bring me sometimes more than once in the day. Then I brought her to the outskirts of the village. This was about a thousand metres on the western side and on the road to Sandaru. There on the left hand side of the road was an overgrown piece of land where the school moved to from the centre of the village. At that time there were enough children in the school to warrant a large building. Finally we walked to a crooked twin classroom building which then housed the three classes of the school. Unlike the first two, this one was built of mud bricks and roofed with corrugated iron sheets. As I told her that I had attended school at all three sites, I could see the look of disbelief on her face that anyone could have progressed from such a place to Cambridge University. Beyond that, however, I could not tell what else went through her mind. For me, though, the journey to those sites brought back so many valued and cherished memories.

At the original site of the school, memories of my father calling me out from the round thatched house one early morning to join him in the barrie next to his house came flooding back. I remembered walking to him that morning and seeing a large group of boisterous village elders, chiefs, and parents with their shy and confused children not quite knowing what was happening. Suddenly, the supposed village teacher walked into the barrie, whispered a while to the town and section chiefs, called everybody to attention, and told everyone why he was there. It was, he said, to see how many more children were old enough to be enrolled for the school. Every household in the village was expected by the chiefs and elders to contribute at least one child to the school so as to ensure that the school remained open. "The white man who had allowed the school to start", he continued, had sent word to the chiefs and elders to ensure that enough children were enrolled to make the school viable." He then asked parents who had brought their children to present them for the process of recruitment to start. This process started with determining whether or not a child was old enough to start school. Unsure of the actual ages of the kids, each of us, one after the other, were asked to put our right hand across our head from the right ear to the left ear. All those who were able to touch their left ear were deemed old enough to begin school. The rest were asked to wait for the following year or when ever their hands were long enough to touch their left ear. It was that morning that my sister Amie and I were enrolled for school.

At the site where the school existed when we visited, I was reminded of the singularly embarrassing incident of two school girls fighting over me. I recalled the head teacher stopping all the three classes, bringing the whole school out on the rugged football pitch to watch the fight, sitting me right in front to watch them. He told the girls that whoever got beaten by the other would lose me. The fight took place inside the school's sand—filled long jump pit which was built right in the middle of the football pitch. Every time each of the girls was in danger of being thrown down she landed back on her feet. This resulted in loud applause from all the pupils and their two teachers. For obvious reasons, I was the only one who never applauded once. The applause of others was always accompanied by jesting comments directed at me and the girls. I have never forgotten that mortifying experience. While I was thinking about that incident, my mind strayed away to wondering why the long jump pit was located where it was. Then, in quick succession, I recalled the sack, egg and spoon, and needle threading and running races we used to do on that football pitch.

Morning devotions before school was another incident that came to mind. Every school morning the first bell reminding us about school rang at 7.30am. Twenty minutes later the second bell rang summoning all pupils to school for assembly. Prior to assembly, there was a pupils' inspection parade. This was done by a teacher who went round each of the assembled pupils looking at their faces, feet, head, teeth, and behind their ears to find out if they had washed them clean, oiled their bodies, combed or platted their hair, and cleaned their teeth. This was followed by the inspection of their uniforms to see that they were spotlessly clean, properly ironed, and in good shape. In those days we had no shoes and were not expected to wear any. In actual fact I got my first ever pair of shoes the year I started secondary school. This session of assembly was followed by a school march to the beating of the school band which had been supplied by the mission. Assembly ended with the singing of a Christian song, followed by a teacher saying a prayer and all the children and teachers praying the Lord's Prayer.

The two things that we worried about most on those mornings were being in school on time and in acceptable form. I recalled parents standing round at assembly time when the school was in the centre of the village to witness the inspection, marching, singing, and the praying of their children. It was a time of both great pride and anxiety. For, while it was their children that were being inspected, it was never lost on the parents that if their children failed the inspection, they too shared in that failure. At such times parents felt it more so than their kids because they knew it was their responsibility to make sure their kids presented themselves in the best form possible. Parents often sought to avoid such embarrassing public pronouncements on their hygienic standards. And any pupil who failed on any of the areas of the inspection was caned. Teacher *Tallu* (nine) is the name we gave one of our teachers in those days because he always gave us nine lashes when we did anything that he believed we deserved to be caned for. And he would announce how many strokes he was going to give before going on to do so. In addition to the caning, any child who failed the inspection was also sent back home with the parents to make good his or her lapses. Addressing lapses related to the state of the body took only a matter of minutes running to the river a few hundred yards away from the village to have a proper wash, or to the house to oil the body and or comb or plait the hair. It was however not so straightforward or even cheap with lapses that had to do with the state of one's uniform. It could cost the whole day of school, even days, plus money and a possible loss of face if it required parents to replace their child's uniform. Consequently, while the school's regimented disciplined approach to keeping the time and observing prescribed rules and scruples of hygiene were supposedly meant to be of benefit to the children in the long run, it nevertheless also became an instrument by which the entire village community was roped surreptitiously into the agenda of the school system and those who devised it.

Then there were those times we spent working on the farms of our teachers after school. This often involved ploughing. We were also sometimes made to fetch water from the river and wood from the forest for our teachers. In those days no one questioned why it was deemed our duty to engage in any such activities, nor did any one feel the need to ask. It was taken as a given. School pupils should work for their teacher and children should serve their elders. That was the norm. Later, I also understood that it was the only compensation teachers who agreed to work in very remote areas of the country like ours received for the myriad of inconveniences they suffered for choosing to work in those areas.

On the afternoons when we were not engaged in working for our teachers after school, we would walk to our own farms to help with any work our parents assigned us. As we did so, we often sang songs and repeated rhymes we had been taught in school. These included 'London Bridge is Falling Down', 'It's a Long Way to Tipperary', 'Peter Piper Picked a Peck of Pickled Peppers', 'Betty Butter Bought Some Butter', 'Three Blind Mice', 'Hickory, Dickory, Duck', 'My Grandfather's Clock', and so on. When we did not go to our farms we passed the time playing in the village or forest, making our own toys from local material, and hunting. Sometimes we did so in defiance of instructions from our parents to join them on the farm, or help clean around the house, or fetch wood for the use of the family.

As Clodagh and I walked back to my parents' house from our tour of the school sites we arrived at a place where I once fell and broke my arm. It happened one afternoon after school when I was meant to go and join my parents on the farm. *Mama* Amie had given me some food and encouraged me to make the journey to the farm. Instead, on leaving the house, I joined my friends on the other side of the village. All afternoon we played high jumping. Just before nightfall when I was taking a turn at the jump I slipped, fell on my arm, and broke it. Scared when they found out I had seriously hurt myself, some of my friends in a great fright ran home to tell *Mama* Amie. It was only then that she found out I never went to the farm as promised. For about a fortnight or so I had to suffer the pain of visiting a village traditional healer who sought to set my bone in place. Unlike other occasions, my parents considered my predicament as enough punishment for my truancy.

I was telling the story of that incident to Clodagh when we arrived at my parents' house. Standing on the veranda I could see right across the way a place where there once stood a large mango tree. In season it often bore hundreds of mango fruit and invited many visitors. These included butterflies, birds, flies, and human beings. All of these vied for access to the succulent juice of this blessed tree. I remembered how as children we used to gather round it during lunch breaks and after school with dozens of stones piled beside us to stone down its sumptuous fruit. That mango tree was no longer there. But I could see it in my mind's eye, with all of us gathered around it, aiming stones and sticks at its fruit, walking underneath its far flung and heavily laden and out of reach branches to gather more stones and sticks. Once, I was gathering stones and sticks under it when a stone fell on my head leaving behind a mighty gash. A friend of mind had thrown a stone at the fruit, missed it, and the stone ended where it did. Standing on the veranda there and recalling that incident, I could still see my *Mama* Amie and *Keke* Yambasu rushing me away from the scene. My head was immediately shaved clean and some iodine drops from the school's first aid kit brought by the teacher administered.

Visiting and seeing those sites in the village was for me like visiting some of the holiest sites of my upbringing and formation. Standing at each site felt like standing on sacred ground, imbued with power which moved me in a way akin to a profound spiritual experience. That experience taught me in an unforgettable way that memory is what gives time and physical spaces the importance they have for, and the power they exert over, individuals, groups and communities. On that visit and tour around the sites I wondered if Clodagh saw more than just ordinary sites. For me, though, those seemingly ordinary spaces were imbued with a history and emotions that made them electrically alive and full of energy. I felt truly at home, with past and present uniting in an inseparable thread to remind me singularly of the eternal reality that is me.

The sight of a Sahr Mambu, a teacher of the school then, whom I met on the visit led me to think of the long chain of teachers going back to the first time the school started. As I did so I became curiously aware of the often unnoticed and unspoken connectedness of history and human activity and how each of us become, for better and for worse, absorbed into other people's dreams, visions and histories. "How many of those in that long chain of teachers", I pondered, "ever knew that they were furthering a course which was identified long ago by a Yambasu Yaniwah and other elders of our village who were no longer alive? Did teacher Mambu know the history of how it all started and why? Would that fragment of history make any difference to the way he saw and approached his work if he did? Did it really matter anyway?"

One of the somewhat bizarre things I remember about that visit to my village with Clodagh and Abbie was the behaviour of some of the villagers. When they came to visit they were not satisfied with staying in the parlour when I told them that Clodagh was resting in the bedroom. Instead, they insisted on going into the bedroom to see the white woman sleeping. This is something they had never seen and they were not going to miss the opportunity. So they would walk into our bedroom and with a broad smile on their faces walk out again saying something like, "So they sleep just like we do?"

Leaving the Village

At the end of our stay, we left for Segbwema where we were going to stay for a couple of months in the Methodist Training Centre four miles from the town. We had planned to stay there so that I could travel from there to go round and conduct interviews with a few catechists, nurses, teachers and ministers who had served under the authority of missionaries before our Church became autonomous. Before we left the village, we asked my sister Sia Messie who was pregnant to travel to us a couple or so weeks later so that she could have her baby in the Nixon hospital where we believed she would receive better care.

On the morning we were leaving the village everyone who had reason to travel wanted to join us with some farm produce, or goat, or chickens to sell or bring to a relation they wanted to visit. When Clodagh saw how full the vehicle was with people and things, she refused to board it, calling it a death trap. She preferred to walk for the worst seven miles of the journey before boarding the vehicle. After convincing some of the people to stay, however, she agreed to travel, and we bade goodbye. As we left the village, I saw on the right hand side the path leading to the clearing in the forest where boys went through the traditional rite of passage into adulthood. Popularly designated 'secret society' by Western commentators, the programme of training normally lasted between six weeks to six months. I am told that long before Western influence it lasted for at least one year. *Keke* once told me that when his own father was initiated a banana socket was planted on the day, and the candidates were not released from their place of seclusion into the community until the day when its fruit was harvested.

Reflecting On Two Different
Systems of Education

I pointed towards the path that led to the place in the forest where the rite of passage into adulthood took place, and I told Clodagh where it led. For a while after that I was lost in reflection as it occurred to me that we were passing by a site where I was given perhaps the most important education in the history, values, thoughts, customs and practices of my people. A few days earlier I had taken the time to bring my wife round the different sites on which the village Western-style school had existed and I had experienced a profoundly moving sense of being reunited with that far removed past. Passing by the place of my education into the ways of my people, I began to explore the connections between the two schools where I was given my initial education for life.

To be sure, each of the schools was quite different from the other. That notwithstanding, they also had broad similarities. While, for example, the Western school system was different in the content of the education it gave to us, it was very much like the indigenous education system in its insistence on rules and instilling discipline and order in social and moral practices. In the traditional school, however, the duty to enforce social and moral discipline was first and foremost reckoned to be that of the family. It was to begin from the cradle. The community as a whole also had a duty in this respect. Much of that socialization process was, however, non-formal. The rite of passage into adulthood was the level at which much of that non-formal schooling was formalized. Its primary role was to equip the children of the community with knowledge of its values, norms, and beliefs. It also taught them its history, skills, and practices.

I was ten years old when I went through that rite of passage. At that time I had left the primary school in my home village for that one in Sandaru seven miles away. When the ritual for that year started it was during school session and so I was not in my village. Unable to leave school for it like the rest of my age mates did, I decided with the encouragement of teacher Yambasu to wait until the end of the Christmas term before joining the rest. I still recall vividly the night before I did so. On arriving home I could see that worry was written all over *Nde's* face. *Keke*, on his part, hardly looked straight in my eyes when he spoke to me. It was as if by looking at me he would communicate something of what awaited me in the weeks that lay ahead. Something told me they were both very anxious especially *Nde* who, according to tradition, was not even allowed to talk about her fears in relation to such men's matters.

Keke called me aside that night and told me to take off the fairly new shirt and shorts I was wearing and put on older ones. Having read the atmosphere at home, I did not ask him why. I rightly suspected that he was preparing me for the following day when I would be taken away to be initiated. That night *Nde* did not sleep in *Keke*'s house. Instead, *Keke* asked that I pass the night with him. For an hour or so before I went to sleep he spoke to me. But much of what he said was in parables to do with bravery as though he did not want to spell out in plain language the nature of the ordeal I was about to face in a matter of hours. Just before dawn I heard

271

a deafening shout of men all around *Keke's* house; and in a whisker of time the door was opened and I was snatched by a crowd of at least twenty men who ran me off my feet and out of the village into the belly of the dark forest. There the operator whose job it was to mark me up in an hour-long session was ready and waiting to inflict his terror on another young and unsuspecting victim. As I was being led into the clearing all my age-mates who were already initiates lined my route to the operator, knowing exactly the ordeal that awaited me. Together they all sang, "A chaa hunor" ('You are welcome'). All of them scantily clad and in ragged clothing, the sight of them scared me in no small way.

One of the things that struck me most about my time in the forest was the purposeful detachment of *Keke* from anything that had to do with me. While he often visited, he was not allowed to interfere with any matter of discipline, training, and duty that involved me. He had had his opportunity in those respects since I was born and it was believed to be the duty of the men of the village to make their own contribution without any input from him. Among the things we were taught were music-making, dancing, hunting, farming techniques, reading signs and symbols, war-games, strict observance and respect of hierarchy, respect for elders, and obedience to authority. In each of these areas those who excelled were rewarded by exemptions from some tasks and by a treatment of deference from colleagues. Like in the Western school system, needless to say this encouraged competition and rivalry. "Perhaps", I thought to myself just as we were approaching a very bad spot in the road, "the most significant difference between the education I received from my people and the one I was given in the Western-style school was that the former was seen as the duty of all of the community.

My Sister Dies Leaving Us a Gift

"Stop here driver and let everyone get down from the vehicle", I said. From the time we left the village, this was the first time I had done this. But on several other occasions subsequently, I made everyone disembark from the vehicle and walk when we approached very steep and perilously rugged spots in the road. At the bridge that broke on our way to the village, a diversion had been built through the water with stones. This had been done the day before. The town chief had instructed the men folks of the village to go and do that work. To make sure we had no problems crossing the river on the day, some of those men had also gone ahead of us and waited at the river in case we needed any help crossing. Fortunately, however, we managed without help from them.

About six weeks after we arrived in Segbwema from my village, my sister had a womb rupture in the process of giving birth to her son and died of bleeding a couple of days later. This was on the 9th of February, 1991. But my wife and I did not get to know about it until three days later when someone walked from the village to reach us with the awful news. On receiving the news my heart bled. "My sister, the one I was closest to in the family, the one who confided in me and I in her, is dead and in such traumatic conditions?" I asked. "How could this happen? I only wish she had come to us as she promised she would." But it was too late to do anything. She was dead.

As I left for the funeral, Clodagh advised that I buy some baby milk to bring with me. She also asked that we inquire from my family about the possibility of adopting my nephew so as to prevent him from dying of malnutrition in the village. That is what I did. After the funeral ceremonies, I was allowed to take with me my week old baby nephew Fayia. As I had no other means of transport back to Segbwema, *Nde*, *Keke* and I decided to travel on foot through the Republic of Guinea and back into Sierra Leone at the Moa river crossing into Kailahun. On the morning we had decided to leave, *Nde* woke up early and prepared us some food. After we had our meal, we put Fayia in a big white enamel basin with lots of pieces of cloth in it to cushion him and, then, started off on our journey. I carried him on my head while *Nde* and *Keke* followed us. That day we journeyed for nearly eighteen miles on foot into our District headquarters and administrative town, Kailahun. There, in the Manse where I used to live several years back, we spent the night with the incumbent minister, Rev. Francis Nabieu. The following morning we brought Fayia to be checked at the government hospital before we continued our journey to Segbwema by public transport.

In Segbwema, Dr Gibson did a thorough job examining Fayia. As she did so, I recall looking at him and saying to myself, "You are the third son of my sister, so your name Fayia will always remind you of your Kissi roots. I am going to give you a name that I hope will always remind you that you were born and are alive because God intends to do wonderful things through you in life. You will be called 'Monemelekah'. This name is Kissi simply saying you are a miracle—a wonder of God. To me you are God's miracle child, saved in conditions which for many spelt death. I pray that you never forget that God loves you. You are destined as a child of the wider world outside of the village in which you were born. It is the world that I your uncle and my wife are already a part of. To remind you of the gracious generosity that lies at the heart of that world we will also be naming you Edwin, to honour my wife's father who has graciously dealt with me since I knew him. May you live to know and appreciate God's boundless love for you, Fayia. You are the parting gift that my dear sister gave me and my wife until we meet again."

That was how eventful my wife and daughter's first visit to my home country and village was. On reflection, it was good we visited my village the time we did. Otherwise we would never have been able to do so for years. And even if we did, my wife would not have been able to see my village much as it was when I was born and grew up there. For, barely three months after we visited my village the now world famous civil war broke out in Sierra Leone. My village was totally destroyed during it and its inhabitants took refuge in neighbouring Guinea for ten years.

That war was started by disgruntled young Sierra Leoneans who had emigrated to neighbouring Liberia in search of work. While there, they were recruited by Charles Taylor to help him fight and oust the Head of State of Liberia, Samuel Doe, and his government. In return, he promised to help them fight and oust the government of Sierra Leone. So when in 1991 rebels invaded Sierra Leone from Liberia, it was in fulfilment of this promise. They systematically launched attacks on Sierra Leone beginning in the east of the country.

That was how my village was attacked. One night, early in 1992, rebels entered my village while everyone was in bed. Woken from their sleep by the sound of gunshots, the inhabitants of the village who could, including members of my own family, ran out of their homes and escaped under the cover of darkness into the bushes from where they crossed over into Guinea the following day. In the time following all the houses were unroofed, the tin-sheets and household goods sold off and the sheep, goats and hens killed and eaten. Gradually, all the houses collapsed and the village got overgrown with vegetation and trees.

I was also thankful to God, however, that we were in my country when my sister had her baby and died. "What", I have often wondered, "would have happened to Fayia had we not been there and taken him?"

Back Home to Sierra Leone after my Studies

About a year and a half after leaving Sierra Leone in November 1992, we returned to the country again. This time we reckoned it was for good. My studies in England had come to an end and I had to return home to serve my Church and country. But I went home blessed with a loving wife, three wonderful children, and a couple of well earned degrees. I also went back home with a few grey hairs, weakened eyesight, a pair of glasses, and a new outlook on life. I went back home, as I confidently declared on arrival at the Sierra Leone International Airport, "to stay". A neighbour who had overheard me say so at the airport paid us a visit about a couple of weeks later to introduce himself and welcome us back home. Before he left he told me of his admiration of what he characterized, even though in not so many words, as my 'exuberant, perhaps even naïve, confidence' about returning home to stay. Asked why a simple statement I made caught his attention, he told me about the harsh realities of living in Sierra Leone which made many yearn to leave for greener fields abroad. "Well", I responded, "there is no place like home", adding that "God can bless us anywhere in this world He chooses to do so, including Sierra Leone."

My Church and people who proudly and eagerly awaited my return to serve them had made all necessary arrangements to receive me and my family back. This included finding us suitable accommodation. Earmarked for the position of principal of the theological college that I was trained in for ministry, I was assigned to superintend one of the main Circuits in Freetown. With two large congregations of about six hundred, one medium size congregation of about a hundred and fifty, and two small congregations of about fifty each, Ebenezer Circuit had three other ministers, about a dozen lay preachers, and a full time pastoral assistant. There was also a Circuit secretary, finance officer, and messenger. My duty as Circuit Superintendent included managing the Circuit office and staff, preparing a three-monthly preaching plans, arranging a pastoral visiting rota, chairing the official meetings of the Circuit, and reporting to the annual Methodist Conference. In addition to that I taught part time in the department of theology at Fourah Bay College and in the

Sierra Leone Theological Hall, preached almost every Sunday, and attended District and Connexional Church meetings.

Life soon became very busy for me; in fact too busy at times to do anything very well. For Clodagh, it was no different. As a result of the war a number of my family had come to live with us in Freetown. So she was landed with looking after three very young children, a husband, *Nde*, *Keke*, two of my brothers, and a nephew. In addition to this, she was trying to learn a new language, understand life and living in a new culture, get on with different people, honour preaching appointments, and lecture part-time at the theological college.

Panic at the End of an Outing

It is a tradition in Freetown for churches, other groups, and individuals to organize an outing to one of the many sparkling white sandy beaches around Freetown at festive times. Consequently, on our first new year's day in Sierra Leone one of the churches on my Circuit decided to go out to Lakka Beach. They kindly invited my family and me to join the outing party. A lot of food and drinks prepared and a couple of buses and a music set hired, we left Freetown about 8am in real African party mood. Men and women, young and old, boys and girls were dressed in Africana and singing all the way to the beach. What a day it was! Among friends, with lots of food, drinks, games, and music, the day almost slipped away without us noticing it. As night fell the organizers began to inform everyone to get ready in preparation for departing. As bags were being packed and children rounded up, we suddenly discovered that our son Fayia was no where to be found.

Panic struck the whole group. Where could he be? Could he have wandered into the bush and lost his way? Could he have been carried away by the water? This was the main question on everyone's mind but no one dared voice it. Everyone knew that children and adults sometimes get drowned on these outings. In a matter of minutes two search groups were organized—one to search the surrounding bushes and the other to walk up and down the beach by the water. One of the organizers decided to walk across a stream to a beach house where some children of the party had spent much of the day playing together. But everyone thought Fayia was quite young to have crossed that stream and join that group. He would check anyway, he decided. As the clock ticked and time passed without any sign of him, Clodagh and I began to fear for the worst. Night was already falling and the buses were waiting to carry people home. Tension and a sense of urgency and desperation built up unbearably as we looked everywhere and found no trace of our son.

Suddenly, a shout came from a distance. It was from the organizer who had gone to search at the beach house. "I have found him" he shouted ecstatically, running towards the rest of the group with Fayia firmly clasped in his arms. Fayia had indeed managed to cross the little stream with the other children and had been playing with three other children from another outing group. Clodagh and I sprinted towards him. On meeting him, we hugged him and our son tightly. "Praise the Lord!" many began to give thanks, as the search was called off and everyone asked to get on to the buses as night had already fallen. Greatly relieved that the day had ended so well for us, we joined the others on the bus and left for the city.

Some Results of the Civil War

Life in Sierra Leone was not altogether as easy as I had expected it. The civil war had displaced several millions of people and many had come to live in Freetown. Thousands had been killed and thousands more maimed. There was hardly a day when I did not have people coming to me to ask for some financial help. I had known most of these people during my ministry prior to the war and my leaving to study in Europe. At that time they all had their own homes, took care of their own needs the best way they could, and managed their own affairs reasonably well. Displaced and with much of what they had possessed destroyed or lost, these people suddenly became dependent on the good will of others in order to survive. Previously well to do people were turned into beggars overnight. Many had arrived into the city barely escaping from the bullets and machetes of the vicious marauding child and adult soldiers. Many had lost loved ones. Not surprisingly, many who found it impossible to accommodate the drastic changes to their lives died.

In this desperate situation people like myself were seen as been in a position to give the needed help. At home, college, and church there were always people waiting to see me and ask for support of one kind or another. On a wage that only fed my family and me, it was often very difficult to convince people that I too did not have enough resources. Being married to a white person did not help the situation. In my country white people have always been seen as wealthy beyond all measure. The logic is easy to see. Did they not colonize us? Are they not the ones that always provide money to build schools, hospitals, and roads? Do they not still continue to give aid to African peoples and their governments? Are they not the ones who often head international aid agencies, drive big and new cars, source and control aid resources, live in good and air conditioned houses, hire servants, and so on?

I remember many times when people I had never seen with my eyes came to me asking to borrow money. Others came to ask me to buy food for them in the market. I remember a cousin of mine who always told me that the greatest crime I committed was to return home at the time I did. But all that notwithstanding, my wife and I often tried to help in any way we could, sometimes even sharing food that we had bought for the use of our family. My people say that one does not give food away because one is full, but because there is another who needs to eat. Thus the saying: "The source of food is also the source of hunger." Yet in many ways we were relatively better off than most of those people who came to us for help. We had a comfortable home to live in, healthy children, work to do, a monthly salary, savings in Europe, a car, enough clothes to wear, and so on. How then could we turn our backs on those who had little or none of these things? It was in those hard and difficult days that I suddenly realized that charity is different from aid. While the former need not involve sacrifice the latter demanded it. I had my own experience of helping others from my own meagre resources as a testimony to that discovery.

Life in the Church was not easy either. Manoeuvring and manipulating of charity for power on the part of both ministers and the laity were shamelessly blatant. I was often amused by lay leaders who set standards for ministers that they themselves could not meet, had no intention to meet, and so never attempted to meet. Yet they were the most vociferous and influential in the Church and wider community, influencing the formulation of policies and rules to guide the Church of Christ. 'Concerned Laity'! So they called themselves. In addition to influencing Church policy, they also somewhat indirectly dictated what many ministers preached. Poorly paid, often poorly educated, and with little or no confidence in themselves, many ministers often spent their week days doing the rounds of the offices and homes of those socially and financially influential people for handouts of money. The result of this was that some of those ministers never preached anything that they knew would offend their benefactors. Nor did they feel able to vote against any policies advocated by them, even if they were questionable, unchristian and divisive. It came to a time when some of those lay people literally held the Church to ransom.

TWELVE

THE SECOND COMING

My Life as Principal of the Theological Hall

My time as principal in the Theological Hall started in the summer after we returned to Sierra Leone at the end of my studies. Two other candidates, one from each of the other two sponsoring Churches, had been short-listed with me for interviewing by the special committee set up by the Board of the college to oversee this process. They were Messrs. Taylor Pearce and Alfred Tommy of the Church of Sierra Leone and the United Methodist Church respectively. So in August 1992 I left my appointment at Ebenezer Circuit to work full-time at the Sierra Leone Theological Hall and Church Training Centre.

As principal, I spent my first year looking at mundane non-theological issues of fund-raising from our international donors to keep the college open, organizing the acquisition and moving of furniture from one room to another so that staff and students would be reasonably comfortable in their work and study environment, and running up and down from one Church office to another getting partner Church heads to pay allowances they had promised to their students and salaries they had agreed to pay the staff they employed to run the college for them.

Other things I managed to find time to do during my two years of tenure included recruiting a few more necessary teaching staff. Among these were Clodagh who agreed to help us out with the teaching New Testament Greek. In addition to administrative duties, I took on teaching responsibilities for day and evening students, continued teaching modern theology at Fourah Bay College, and commenced teaching Christian Missions at the Sierra Leone Bible College. My aim in taking on the latter was to create and nurture a strong relationship between the two institutions hoping to upgrade eventually the relationship to cooperation in theological education and training. The main reason for pursuing this path was that I had already prepared and forwarded the first formal proposal and request for the Hall to be affiliated to Fourah Bay College, and I knew one of the requirements we had to fulfill to succeed in this bid was to have at least five post-graduate degree holders on our list of teaching staff. To further strengthen the co-operation between the colleges, I speared-headed the organization of an academic conference for which speakers were drawn from all three colleges. Finally, many a weekend during my time as principal was also spent away at the United Methodist Church guest house at

Hamilton Beach helping to revise Theological Education by Extension (TEE) manuals for use in Sierra Leone.

Perhaps the single most important thing to do with me and my experience in the Hall is what I call, for lack of a more appropriate term, 'presence'. Educated in the Hall myself and returning to it, especially as principal and at a comparatively very young age, gave, I believe, a huge boost of morale and confidence to both the students and staff of the Hall. From what many told me in those days and how they aired their views, I sensed a very strong and deep yearning for more and better intellectual development on the part of an increasing number of those who enrolled on the courses offered by the Hall. It was what partly encouraged me to invest a lot of valuable time in pursuing our affiliation with Fourah Bay College.

While this response, especially of the students, to my leadership of the Hall gave me a great sense of achievement and fulfillment, it was also a very humbling experience in so far as it made me more appreciative of the help I had received from so many people along the way of my life journey to that point. The result was that I often found myself readily giving guidance and encouragement to everyone who wanted to do a bit more with their lives and abilities.

The largely positive response to my leadership at the Hall reminded me again of what I had discovered about leadership during my own time at the Hall as a student. It was that people generally reflect the values of their leaders. For my part, a constant reflection on that discovery even long after

I left the Hall resulted in me questioning and challenging the often authoritarian approach to leadership which I knew was at the heart of much leadership in Sierra Leone and on the wider continent of Africa. So when I returned to the Hall as principal eleven years after my student days there, I had not realized how profoundly different my attitude to leadership and the use of power had become. I got to know this only when I got rebuked on several occasions by some members of my teaching staff that as principal I should be telling them what to do rather than consulting with them on possible ways forward. 'That is what dictators do, you know,' I once retorted to one of my accusers. 'That is what we need in Africa,' he responded in a matter-of-fact way, concluding, 'Remember, you are no longer in England'. Coupled with this was the initial resistance I had from some teaching and administrative staff concerning my suggestion that students and staff eat college provided meals together.

These two experiences made me think deeply about the immense challenges facing the Church in Sierra Leone and elsewhere with regard to the right attitude to power and modelling equality and humility in Christian leadership. What concerned me most was that the ministerial, spiritual, and theological formation programmes of our ministers in training lacked any consideration of these matters. It made me come to the conclusion that the dignity of another human being and the respectful, loving and just treatment of that person cannot just be read off the pages of a book nor merely taught in a lecture room. It has to be modelled in day-to-day interactions with people we meet, teach and live. There is such a thing as an 'unwritten curriculum'. It is our attitudes and behaviour.

And, sadly, this is what, I have come to believe, tells people more loudly how they too should live their lives than the written curriculum (what we teach or make them read) does. That attitude was sadly not an issue that concerned many at the Hall. Yet we expected ministers to start automatically living out the values of Christ immediately they step out of college to serve their people. The result was that we produced ministers with great intellectual ability but who lived as though they have never heard the name of Christ. Had I stayed longer in the college, addressing the 'unwritten curriculum' would have continued to feature largely in my approach to equipping ministers for the church of Christ in Sierra Leone.

A Telephone Call that Changed Everything

But, alas, it was not to be. One day I left the house at eight o'clock in the morning as I normally did for college. By mid-morning I had a call from London while I was seated at my desk. It was from our Methodist Church Overseas Division office. A voice came from the other end, "Is that Sahr?" "Yes", I responded. "I am terribly sorry, but I want you to go home now and get ready to leave the country with your family this evening. We have already booked your tickets and you are to collect them at the KLM desk at the airport. I don't know if you know this, but the last international flight out of Sierra Leone will leave tonight. So go home and tell Clodagh and the children to get ready to leave tonight." By the time the telephone conversation had ended I was on my feet in total disbelief of what I was hearing. As I stood there with the phone in my hands my whole body went numb. Here was I living in the country and knew nothing of what I was being told about flights to and from my country.

I walked into the administrative secretary's office to tell her the news before taking leave to go home. By that time the head of my Church had been notified about the arrangements that had been made. On my way home I went to collect the children from their school. We had no mobile phones at that time so I was unable to let Clodagh know what I was doing. On arriving home unexpectedly with the children at that time of day, Clodagh knew something was wrong. "I have received a call from our office in London that we should leave the country tonight. The last international flight out of this country leaves tonight, and the Methodist Church Overseas Division wants you, the children and I out on that flight."

What had happened was that the rebels had got to within twenty miles of Freetown. Most who knew this and could afford to get their families out of the city were preparing to do so. We were to learn later on that even the family of the Head of State at the time, Valentine Strasser, was on that last flight. Clodagh and I started packing frantically. We decided to pack only what she and the children could not do without. We knew that it was not the first time she and the children had had to suddenly leave the country. News of the rebel advance about a year earlier had resulted in them leaving and returning when the situation improved. So we hoped that this time round the same would happen. For my part I had decided that I was not going to leave the college without proper alternative arrangements. So I was going to stay. This was in February 1995. Clodagh understandingly helped me pack all my important documents and passport in one small suit case which I kept close by after they left in case I needed to flee the house at anytime in the night. She also reminded me about an Allied Irish Bank visa card in my possession which I could use in an emergency to get a flight booked. "Be very careful", she finally said to me at the airport before I let them go through to the aircraft.

For all the time I stayed behind I continued my work in the college, going to bed every night with my packed suitcase beside me. In those heady days everyone listened with both their ears and eyes, so to speak; and because one never knew who enemies and friends were, walls had ears and, so, one said very little.

Returning to Ireland

Six and a half months later in August, I had to leave to join my family again in Longford, Ireland. I have come to refer to this as 'the second coming'—my return to Ireland. Our son Fayia had been diagnosed with a serious health problem. Meanwhile, the political, social, and military situation in Sierra Leone had badly deteriorated, leaving several millions displaced, thousands dead, and thousands more maimed. Nearly three fourths of the country had been overrun by rebels and pro-government militia. Freetown teemed with people its infrastructure could not cope with, and thousands had become refugees in neighbouring countries and beyond.

Back in Ireland I felt safe and secure, and enjoyed the warmth and support of my family, friends and colleagues. There was no shortage of kind words of encouragement. But once in Ireland I became unemployed immediately. From being a principal of a theological college and all that meant in terms of work, responsibility and social status, I became suddenly, in many ways, a nonentity in my new found home, dependent on social welfare, and eventually offering my services as a kitchen porter in a hotel and later as a factory worker in a meat-processing plant in Longford town.

A Refugee Life in Ireland

In the Methodist Church, once accepted as a minister, it is generally one's home Church's obligation to station one. Clodagh and I were members of the Methodist Church in Sierra Leone when we escaped back to Ireland. It meant that the Methodist Church in Ireland technically had no obligation to employ us. Besides, there was no vacancy for them to do so. Fortunately, however, a vacancy occurred in Wicklow by the end of that year and we were approached about the possibility of filling it. Before that, though, we were both unemployed Sierra Leonean Methodist ministers in Ireland.

I still remember waking up one morning and saying to my wife that I needed a job. "Where are you going to get a job in Longford?" She asked. Insisting that it did not matter what kind of job it was, she decided that we take a walk into town that morning and call into the Longford Arms hotel. There she requested to see the manager of the hotel and we both went in to speak to him. That morning he offered me a hotel room to paint. Off we returned home for me to get ready for work. By nightfall the next day, I had completed painting the room after five hours of hard work. It was my first time painting anything, and my first time in a very long time to do anything that involved that amount of physical exertion. As I walked home that night I could feel all the bones and muscles in my body aching. And once I sat down on the sofa to eat, I could not get up from there until the following morning. That was how exhausted I was. But it was because of that job that I got the position of kitchen porter in the same hotel a couple of days later.

That experience led me eventually to the job in the meat factory almost next door to the hotel. My job? Trimming the tails of bullocks that were slaughtered and separating the fat from the head meat. Every Saturday, and for a day and a half wage, the tails were packed and exported to Italy. The fat was sent to a soap making factory and the head meat turned into minced meat.

Dressed in white overalls on my first morning in the factory, Wellington boots on, a belt holding different sizes of sharp knives tied round my waist, and a helmet put on my head, my wife who had accompanied me there could not keep her face straight. There standing in the midst of about a hundred all white Irish factory workers was her one black man in very alien uniform and in unfamiliar territory. The manager led me into the factory and briefed me on the jobs of everyone and on health and safety precautions. Then he took me to my table along the chain of other tables. "I will work with you for the first couple of hours until you are sure what to do. You watch me and do what I do. Is that okay?" "Yes, of course." I replied.

Within a very short time the factory floor became very busy, some whistling tunes, others singing aloud, others shouting instructions across the factory floor, and everyone pretty focused on what they were doing. By mid-morning the manager had left me; and now and again when I was holding up others along the chain someone would come and help me clear my backlog of work. I found many of those men very helpful, friendly and very down to earth people. Within a few days of working there I began to feel very much at home with them, although I sometimes felt I spent more time answering questions about Africa than doing the work for which I was employed. "Africa is a very big country, isn't it? Why did you choose to come to Ireland? Where did you learn how to speak in English? What do you eat in Africa? How long do you plan to stay here? When . . . . ?" On and on the questioning went during every break time especially for my first week there.

How Are the Mighty Fallen!

"How are the mighty fallen!"[18] David's searching sigh in his lament over Saul's death kept ringing in my ears in those early years of my return to Ireland. While I had considerable capacity in Sierra Leone to locate and acquire valued human and material resources for my life and work, in Ireland I had

---

[18] 2 Samuel 1:19b from **The Amplified Bible** (1987) Basingstoke: Marshall Morgan & Scott, p. 362

to depend on the knowledge and guidance of others to do so. Rather than being at the very centre of society as I was in Sierra Leone, in Ireland I hovered precariously at the margin, identified largely by the colour of my skin and my race instead of by name, often presumed by many as an economic migrant, and expected to speak in a certain way and always in English in order to be understood. I was not here too long when I found out that I would always have to live with the reality of covert and overt racist attitudes and cope with the difficulties of living in the different cultural sphere. "Its happening all over again", I would often say to myself.

Consequently, I felt like a straw in the threatening wind of displacement and change I was experiencing, lost, and often out of place, with most of the certainties in my life in Sierra Leone gone. This overwhelming feeling and sense of my world falling apart readily reminded me of W.B Yeats' words in *The Second Coming*:

> "Turning and turning in the widening gyre
> The falcon cannot bear the falconer;
> Things fall apart; the centre cannot hold;
> Mere anarchy is loosed upon the world."[19]

Until this time, I had lived believing that a successful life is one in which one always climbed towards the top. My experience until that time had taught me nothing different. For, had I not climbed up from being a peasant village boy

---

[19]   *The Second Coming* in Timothy Webb [Ed.] (1991) **W. B. Yeats Selected Poetry**. London: Penguin, p.124

to acquiring primary, secondary and theological college education in my country? Had I not gone on to become a minister of religion, gain access to a European university education, and eventually acquired a post-graduate research degree? And back in my own country, did I not go on to become a superintendent minister in charge of five congregations and four junior ministers in the city? Did I not go on to become principal of the theological college in which I was trained? Was I not one of the most senior leaders in my church hierarchy? In Ireland, displaced and a refugee of sorts, I hit rock bottom. So I believed anyway. Little had prepared me for the experiences I was now going through. The past was still very much present with me.

A Revelation that Gave Me Purpose for Living

Then, like a revelatory experience, it suddenly occurred to me one day as I was reflecting on my situation that perhaps success in life is not necessarily about a constant upward climb in good fortune. Instead, it could be about how successfully one manages both the upward and downward trends, and also the curves. It was the dawn of a new way of seeing and being. While I had experienced physical border crossing more than once, I was now on the verge of crossing another border. For, that revealing thought was like a conversion experience for me. It ushered in a profound rethink on my circumstances in Ireland that led to the decision to engage in positive action with the hope of re-building my capacity for the society I was now living in.

The jobs in a hotel and meat-processing plant referred to above were my starting point. My experiences there were an education in itself that no university college could have given me. For it was in those jobs that I first realised that having been brought up and trained in church-related circles and institutions, I had, in many ways, lived a very sheltered and protected life. That life had prevented me from having contact with real people who hide behind no masks, but speak their mind and in plain unpolished language. As much as it was a shock to my received wisdom, it felt refreshing and liberating to be with people like that. Not only that, the people I worked with in those places gave me a wider and more realistic insight into Irish society than all my previous education in Ireland did. It was also in those jobs that I was able to live as a Christian without any labels and words proclaiming me as one.

Church Ministry and Study

Four months on, we got a job with the Methodist Church in rural Ireland close to the city of Dublin. The Methodist Churches in Ireland and Sierra Leone had considered the situation of my wife and me and decided to put us on the Methodist World Mission in Britain and Ireland Programme as missionaries in Ireland. The invitation came to us after getting the consent of the local congregations of Wicklow, Arklow and Avoca. So in January 1996 we were on the move again from Longford.

With thoughts of eventually returning to my home country when the political and family conditions were right, I decided to equip myself for that future possibility. To do so, I chose to undertake training that would on the one hand enable me to contribute in some way to the rebuilding of my broken country and on the other equip me for living in Ireland. Being close as I was to higher educational institutions in Dublin, I enrolled for a Master's course in development education at the Centre for Development Studies in Kimmage Manor.

My re-education was greatly enhanced by the academic and social interactions I experienced there. By the time I had completed my course there, I had not only acquired skills in adult education and information on world development issues that I did not have before, I had also learnt a lot about Irish people and society in the context of world development, and about the legacy of development and its role in the continued displacement of millions around the world, including myself. The discoveries I made there also meant I had to unlearn ideas, information, attitudes and ways of thinking and being in the world that I no longer believed were right.

The experiences, skills, and knowledge enumerated above played no small role in helping reshape my identity in Ireland. They informed and influenced my private and public 'performances'—preaching, teaching, leadership, academic presentations, pastoral relations, and interpersonal interactions—in profound ways. This, in turn, created opportunities for me to attend different seminars, workshops, conferences, and social events at which I met different people. Some of the people I met at those events introduced me eventually to other people, thus widening my social network and also opening for me avenues of occasional lecturing in academic institutions, making presentations at conferences, becoming a member of different organisations, and being appointed to committees and boards in and outside the Church. Consequently, I could begin to sense that the acute state of between and betwixt which I experienced in the first two years of arriving back in Ireland was finally being replaced by a confident sense of moving forward, belonging and being at home in Ireland.

Challenges that Remained

There were, however, some things that would not go away, try as I did: the overwhelming sense of guilt for leaving my parents, brothers, cousins, nieces, nephews, staff, students, friends, church, and people when they needed me most; the continuing worry about their safety in a steadily worsening situation, the constant feeling of helplessness and depression in the face of a situation that I could do nothing to change; and my own deeply overwhelming inability to accept living away from my home country. Then on the 6th January, 1999 our worst fears were realized. The rebels entered Freetown as they had been promising for years. Within a few days they managed to disrupt most public services including the communications systems; and by the end of their first week in the city they had managed to kill at least seven thousand people.

With the telephone system cut-off, I was unable to reach *Keke*, *Nde*, my brothers, a nephew and cousins by phone in Freetown to find out how they were. The following couple of weeks were among the worst weeks I have ever experienced. All the news about the events unfolding in Freetown were coming to us through international reporters beaming images of marauding gun-toting killers, wantonly damaged properties, stiffly frightened civilians, and dead bodies to our television sets. Preparing for and taking Sunday services in those days was simply a nightmare. Here was a desperately needy man seeking to minister to the needs of others! That is how I saw myself. And it had been the case since I started ministering in Ireland. But the few weeks after the rebels got into Freetown brought it to a climax. Expected by my role to visit and provide pastoral care for my parishioners, it became clearly patent to me that I was the one who needed it more than them. I was the broken messenger of the gospel of wholeness. I do now wonder how my wife ever managed to cope with the emotional wreck I was during that period.

All this manifested itself very clearly on two occasions. The first was on a Sunday morning during worship when, as I talked about what was happening in my country, I broke down. As I was later to discover, that experience led to some people in my congregation allowing me into the secret hurting places in their lives. As one of them said to me later, 'I knew I could talk to you because you would understand the nature of debilitating helplessness that life can throw across our paths.' The second time was when we were driving back from my in-laws in Longford to Wicklow one late afternoon. Unable to hold down the swollen raw emotions within me any longer, they burst their banks involuntarily as I pulled the car to the side of the road and wept my eyes out uncontrollably. My wife knew what was happening. I am not sure if our children did.

But from that day onwards, I resolved to hand over control of whatever happens to my country, people, and myself to God.

Gradually, I began to experience a growing peace. By that time many Africans south of the Sahara had started coming to Ireland seeking asylum. That reality suddenly focused the media's attention on Africa and began to generate a lot of negative publicity. Concerned about this emerging and growing problem, I and five others (Rwandan, Sudanese, Moroccan, and Scottish friends) decided to found an organization that would help educate Irish people about Africa, promote positive perspectives of the continent and her peoples, provide informational support for them, and promote their empowerment in Ireland. Many months of meeting and sharing ideas around this issue resulted in the successful launching of the Africa Solidarity Centre (now Africa Centre) Ireland in 2001 by the then newly appointed South African Ambassador to Ireland, Melanie Verwoerd.

That same year our appointment on the Methodist World Mission in Britain and Ireland Programme came to an end. Our Church in Sierra Leone then officially transferred us to the Methodist Church in Ireland. This meant that we effectively became ministers of the Methodist Church in Ireland, and that Church assumed total and complete responsibility for our personal wellbeing and employment from then on. So we were transferred to Galway from Wicklow.

THIRTEEN

LESSONS IN THE CITY OF TRIBES

Ministry in Galway

'The City of Tribes.' That is the other name of the westernmost city of Ireland, Galway. The reason for this, according to historians, is that there were fourteen merchant families who dominated the political, commercial, and social life of the city between the mid—thirteenth and late nineteenth centuries. They were of variously Norman, Hiberno-Norman, Gaelic-Irish, French, Welsh, and English descent or some combination of these.

By the time my wife and I were posted to this city in 2001, it had added Latin American, Asian, African and Eastern-European tribes to its already famous variegated historical list. While some of the representatives of these new tribes were students or professionals, the vast majority of them were either migrant workers or asylum seekers. Most Africans in the city and beyond belonged to the latter. With the new tribal additions also came new religious practices among which were Islam and Buddhism and also new expressions of the Christian religion. Before long almost one-fifth of the city's population would be classified 'non-Irish'.

It was into that very culturally mixed society that we were sent in July 2001. Within a very short time my wife and I became heavily involved with organizations in and outside church life that were concerned about the wellbeing of the new residents of the city. These included The Friendship Club of our church, the Galway One World Centre, the Asylum Seekers' Group, the City Council Development Forum, and, a few years later, the Migrant Taxi Drivers' Association, all of which sought to address issues of social inclusion, integration, justice and equality.

Different African churches were set up to serve the spiritual, language, and cultural needs of their clients. I became closely involved with these as I started organizing city-wide ecumenical worship services with them. Other Irish churches and all civic authorities were also invited. These often proved very successful in bringing people from different Christian persuasions together to share in worship, food and conversation, in creating opportunities for understanding different approaches to worship, and in helping ease understandable tensions between and within these different groups.

More often than not, involvement in these activities attracted media attention and so helped in highlighting the issues that new residents were facing and how they could be addressed by individuals, groups, and public servants. I visited asylum seekers in their hostels frequently and was often invited into the homes of refugees. As a result, many confided in me in ways I had never thought would be possible. "Irish people ask too many questions the very first day you meet them", some said to me. "It makes you wonder why they want to know everything about you so quickly. That is why we are scared to tell them much about ourselves." Others had other concerns: "These people are as unpredictable as their weather."

One thing I seldom did was ask personal questions. Instead, I engaged in general conversation, shared stories of my time in Ireland if need be, and listened to both what was said and what was left unsaid. Over a long period of relating to a person or family in this way, they became more and more open and willing to share their stories and sometimes even their strictly guarded secrets with me. But I soon discovered that the privilege of being let into other people's hidden places came at a cost.

Ministry in Galway brought me into contact with people who impacted my life for better and for worse. I have never, for example, ceased to be amazed by the tireless and selfless efforts of Stephen Smith, his wife Heather, and their friend Frances Joyce in giving everything they possibly could to support asylum seekers and refugees. Very staunch Methodist rural farmers from Gort, Stephen and Heather partnered with Frances, a local Galway woman who was passionate about social justice issues, in this service. Not wealthy people by any means, these three Irish people considered nothing too valuable to deploy in the services of people who were mere strangers. Night and day they sought the highest good for the new residents regardless of creed and colour. They made endless telephone calls to service providers on their behalf, accompanied them to landlords and police stations, organized training programmes for them, sought for and made available useful information to them, organized birthday and Christmas parties for their children, sourced used clothing for those who needed them, organized outings, and drove them to places they needed to go. That was what the Friendship Club did and for which they became widely known in the city and beyond. These three people touched so many people's lives in so many positive ways that after Stephen literally dropped dead on the job his funeral service brought the city centre traffic to a complete halt. Men and women, Christian and Muslim lined up in the church to make their way up to the microphone to testify to the self-giving and sacrificial service of love and care that this man and his wife had given them.

It was as a result of their work that I once received an unexpected invitation. It was to the home of a Muslim family who were celebrating the end of one of their Muslim festivals. The man and his wife who had been blessed by the Friendship Club over several years invited me to go and conduct prayers in their home. "What way should I dress? Do I wear my clerical shirt and dog collar? What scriptures do I read? Should I just offer a prayer? What kind of prayer and in whose name—Mohamed or Jesus?" These were issues that I had never confronted in my ministry. In the end, rightly or wrongly, I went dressed with a clerical shirt and dog collar, read the story of Abraham's call in the Old Testament of the Bible, and prayed a prayer of praise and thanksgiving for all the goodness of God in everyone's life, and prayed that God would continue to use us all as instruments of his love and peace, and closed with an Amen. In that home that afternoon we experienced the genuine fellowship of humanity as we shared in a sumptuous meal, funny stories of life's experiences, and laughter. Was God there that night? What about Jesus and His Holy Spirit? My guess is that God was fully present because we were brought together by His love and were gathered in His name to celebrate the love of one for another.

African Asylum Seekers and Refugees

Working and being in constant contact with African asylum seekers and refugees, it was never lost on me that these were men and women who are true survivors. They had escaped death in childhood and survived to adulthood in countries where child mortality rates are among the highest in the world; many had crossed several international borders in at least two continents using means that could easily have ended their lives or led them to be incarcerated or seen them deported to their home countries. Indeed some had experienced imprisonment and deportation before, but still used every means available to them to leave their countries again in search of greener fields. Some had even sold their family homes and any other possessions of value they had in order to pay for the journey to leave their home countries. Others had at times being forced by circumstances to engage in, at best, shady activities in order to survive away from home. All had made the choice to fight to leave home rather than stay there and accept what they believed were not life-enhancing prospects. All had survived the struggle to leave and succeeded in doing so. Many had unsuccessfully tried their chances in other countries in Africa and Europe before deciding to try Ireland. Most had left behind mother, father, siblings, friends, and even children of their own. Such was the nature of their determination to better their life situations.

Their strong willed, competitive and innovative personalities bore abundant witness to their constant struggles for survival from birth. These undercurrents often served as perfect ingredients for constant conflicts among themselves and between them and their Irish hosts. There were, of course, exceptions; but the aggressiveness of many did not help the prospects of those who were the exception. Not surprisingly, therefore, much of my ministry in Galway was involved with peace-making between conflicting African-African and African-Irish parties.

It was while we were in Galway that my views of Africa were profoundly challenged. For all my life until that time I had lived with a notion of Africa and Africans as largely homogenous entities. Confronted with the diversity of Africans in Galway and in close proximity with them, I did not only have to review my glib notion, I also had to consciously devise a way of speaking about Africa and Africans that reflected that diversity of African-ness. Which Africa—east, west, south, north? Which country—Kenya, Sierra Leone, Morocco, Botswana, South Africa . . . ? Which ethnic group—Ibo, Creole, Yoruba, Xhosa, Meru,

Arab, Kikuyu . . . ? What colonial history—French, British, Portuguese, American, Spanish, German, Dutch . . . ? What language—English, French, Portuguese, German . . . ? What religion—Christian, Muslim, Jewish, or some form of African Traditional Religion . . . ? What Christian tradition—Roman Catholic, Protestant, Pentecostal, Evangelical, Spiritualist?

It was in Galway that I also first came to realize how these different realities of Africa and Africans have impacted deeply and differently on the psyche and attitude of Africans towards each other and to the world at large. I discovered that there was no such thing as African food, music, clothes, religion, Christianity, language, or attitude. There was Ibo food, Xhosa attire, Nigerian Pentecostalism, Creole language, Wolof music, or French African psyche. And these realities in no small way also affected the ways Africans related to each other. So in Galway I became keenly aware that generalizations about a continent and people so varied in every way only betrayed my ignorance and created unfortunate stereotypes of the continent and her peoples.

An Unsuspecting Messenger of God

"Always remember that the people you relate to are part of God's purpose for your life." These, according to Selwyn Hughes who founded the Crusade for World Revival, were the words of his pastor to him when he was a teenager. In Galway I discovered in an extraordinary way that even those who enter our life for a short while may play a crucial role in influencing us or moving us to where we should be.

That was my experience with an African-American, Derek (whose surname I can't even remember now), who attended our church in Galway over a very short period of time. One day in the beginning of August 2004 we were having Sierra Leoneans to dinner. That was about two years after the civil war in Sierra Leone had been declared over by the United Nations, combatants disarmed, rehabilitation started and a democratically elected government installed. At the last minute we invited Derek along. He patiently listened to conversation about Sierra Leone for a long time but then he deftly started a little game in which everyone was to say what they would do if they could do whatever they wanted. The other guests enjoyed dreaming up fantastic ideas but when it came to my turn I said I didn't know. Derek discreetly led me out to the kitchen. There, he explained that he discerned from my answer that deep down I believed what I wanted wasn't feasible so I was afraid to admit what it was even to myself. Derek soon drew from me that my dream was to help people in Sierra Leone more than my wife and I could afford to. Eventually Derek convinced me that since I desperately wanted to do that, help would appear.

A few weeks went by after that visit and conversation with Derek. Then one Sunday after service, I had a short conversation with an Irish-American and American couple who were members of our church. It was about my dream to contribute towards rebuilding my war-torn country. A couple of weeks later, I got offered the possibility of setting up a charity with them in Sierra Leone. That was in November of 2004. The following January Jimmy Lavin—an Irish-American business man with strong family connections in Mayo—and

I travelled to Sierra Leone to buy the land in order to build a Vocational Skills Training Centre to teach war-affected teenagers agriculture, building, dressmaking, computers and basic literacy as well as how to set up their own businesses.

Today, nine years later, a block manufacturing facility, a skills training centre, a secondary boarding school, school staff quarters, and a reasonably comfortable bungalow for accommodating overseas volunteers have been built. As I write, an orphanage is in the process of being constructed. Yet, from the time we bought the land to setup that project, my wife and I never had the opportunity to share the story with Derek. This is because we never saw him again. I see Derek like an angel, a messenger from God, especially to me. Like a flash he came into our lives and left again, leaving positive crucial and indelible footprints in his trail that will impact not only on our lives but also the lives of people thousands of miles away in a small West African country. He never really told us why he was in Ireland or in Galway, even though we did try to find out from him. An elegant, tall giant of a man, Derek taught me again to never let my lack of resources stand in the way of my dreams.

A Minister Turned Taxi Driver

By mid-two thousand and seven, about three years after Derek left, I came home one night and told my wife that I wanted to try my hand at part-time taxi-driving. Our daughter had gone to Trinity College Dublin to study speech and language therapy and was going to live in rented accommodation for the four years duration of the course. Then, of course, there was the traditional and cultural obligation to support family and friends back at home. This involved sending money home every month to pay for their food, educational, clothing and medical needs. Indeed, it is not an obligation that I can discard of that easily. To do so would be seen as a rejection of my obligations. Nor would I want not to, because I have come to see it as my duty. Indeed, I have come to see it as my own little way of paying back for all the kindness and generosity of other people towards me in my life.

Earning only a stipend from the church, the need for an extra source of income could not have been clearer. I figured out that as a self-employed taxi-driver, I could work anytime I was able to without having to answer to anyone. And because my wife is also a Methodist Minister and worked with me in joint ministry she could do the work of pastoring and preaching when needed. So it was that I set about fulfilling the regulatory requirements to qualify as a public vehicle driver. In less than six months, I managed to fulfill all the requirements, put money together, and buy my license, ID, roof sign, and a taxi car, which was fully kitted out. With everything in place, I stepped out into my new and additional role of taxi-driver.

I do still remember vividly the night before the morning I had planned to start taxing. I timidly washed, hoovered, and polished the car, rehearsed the regulations, practiced using the meter and receipt printer, and got enough petrol—all the time wondering whether I was going to be able for it. My main worry was that some of the African taxi drivers I had told about my plans had not only told me how difficult and dangerous it could be, but also added that it was not a job for as respectable a person as a Minister of Religion. Both of their concerns played equal part in my questioning of my person and ability as a taxi driver. But I had gone a long way down the road and I was in no way going to turn back. To what, in any case, even if I could turn back? "Necessity", they say, "is the mother of invention." The invention in my case, I thought, was a special and unique creature who was both a Methodist Minister and a Taxi Driver at the same time. Some might call it a dragging into the mud of an all-time august and respectable profession, rather than an invention.

Be that as it may, the long-and-well-prepared-for-morning came. The night before, I had planned to be up at 4am, get ready and drive down to one of the city centre taxi ranks for 5am. I had been told that was the time people needing a taxi to work or from work to their homes normally come to the ranks.

Nervously, I opened the door of the car, gingerly sat down, and unenthusiastically started the engine. With the gear still in neutral, I prayed: "Lord, Jesus Christ, you once calmed the stormy waters that threatened the lives of your disciples; calm the storms of fear within me and steady the hands and feet that drive this car. You provided a miraculous catch for Simon Peter, James and John after they had fished all night and caught no fish; I am going trusting in your power and will to provide for me today. For now, this is my fishing boat, Lord Jesus; come in and sit by me so that I may experience your protection from every harm and danger within and around this car. Let me go now in your name. Amen."

The gear changed and hand brake down, off I drove straight to the Eyre Square taxi rank. There were already a few taxis there when I arrived. So, like a fresher on their first day in school not quite sure about anything except their own uncertainties, I cautiously joined the queue. About twenty minutes had gone when I had reached the top of the queue. "I am next." I whispered to myself. "Soon I will be driving my first passenger and collecting my first fare." As I was thinking aloud, my passenger door opened. This lady had come from behind me and I did not see her coming. "Good morning. Where do you want to go?" I asked. "Bon Secours, in Renmore." On the way the lady told me she was going to get her tooth removed and had not slept all night. I had wondered why she was so nervous earlier coming in to the car. So I was able to tell her my own story and source of nervousness. In fact, I was so nervous that I gave her the wrong change. She did not notice either, perhaps because she too was nervous about the prospects that awaited her. I had to go back to the hospital, look for her, and give her what remained of her change. "God has a sense of humour, eh?" I said as I was still parked on the grounds of the hospital. "Of all the taxi using public in Galway this morning, whom does He bring into the car of a first time and nervous taxi driver? Another very nervous person." I read that incident as God's way of settling me in the job.

What Taxi Driving Taught Me

For the next two years and a bit, working mostly between 10pm and 5am, I was to learn so much more about life in Ireland that no university education or simply pastoral work could have afforded me. Before that I never knew how vastly different night life was from daytime life. Sometimes I carried home well dressed and seemingly intelligent and respectable men and women who turned out to be the complete opposite. They'd puke in the car and deny they did it, use the most lurid language without any bother, seek to evade paying the fare by making false accusations, engage in behaviour with the opposite sex that no respectable person could entertain, and demonstrate grave ignorance in the way they speak to and about other races. I witnessed men and women comfortably urinating in the middle of streets as though they were celebrities highly paid to perform for the nation; others meticulously inspected taxis to see whether they were driven by a white or black person so as to avoid getting in a taxi that was driven by a black person. I knew all Irish taxi companies in the city barred black taxi drivers from registering with them. Some of those companies even painted an Irish flag or Irish language on their taxis to distinguish them from taxis driven by 'non-nationals' as they called people like me. I debated through the printed and oral media with some local politicians who sought to support these behaviours for purely cheap political gain. I was aware that some black taxi drivers' behaviour did not help the situation either. I was reliably informed that some overcharged, took longer routes, refused short runs, jumped cues, and spoke roughly to passengers. Often, consequently, I was involved in advocacy and conflict minimization between peoples in the taxi industry in the city.

Yet, some of my most cherished experiences were got in the taxi business. I remember, for example, once nearly avoiding stopping for a man who had flagged me down, thinking he looked a bit like a head case. But when I did stop and let him in the car, this man proved to be one of the most intelligent, respectful, amiable, and well read persons on global issues I have ever met. Within minutes of coming into the car he struck up a conversation with me; and for about half an hour after we had got to his destination he engaged with me in a very interesting and non-patronizing conversation on global cultural, economic, historical and social issues. As I left him that night, I could not but wonder for a long time at the real risk which we all run daily of missing out on being blessed by others purely because we inadvertently bar them out of our lives by our unchallenged prejudices.

Then there was one afternoon when I decided to go driving for a couple of hours. As it turned out, my first fare was a young man who had been at work and received a call that his mother who lived in Limerick had been found hanging in her home. She had committed suicide. He was the eldest son and was rushing home to get ready to leave for Limerick. I always had the habit of greeting people as they came into the car and asking, 'how are you today or tonight' as the case may be. As I drove out of the taxi rank this man, in reply to my question, just broke down in tears and, through his sobs, told me his story. I spent the rest of the journey listening to him as he sought to put his utter grief and pain into words that would make sense to a mere stranger. On arrival at his destination, I asked if I could pray with him, and he agreed. For at least a quarter of an hour both of us, as I prayed for him, wept together in the car. As I watched him leave the car, walk to the door of his house, and go in and shut it behind him, I continued quietly but uncontrollably sobbing for him and praying that he would know the love, strength, and healing of God for him and his family. It took me a few more minutes before I could compose myself and start driving back into the city again. I have often wondered if God had not made me go out to work that afternoon uncharacteristically just so that I could be in the company of that man.

And that was not the only time I had to pray with a customer. One dry and warm evening, just after 10pm, I picked up a young lad in his early twenties who asked me to take him to Douhiska. Many hours later, I was brought to the same area by other customers. As I was turning the car to return to the city centre, I saw somebody trying to flag me down. On stopping and letting him in, I suddenly realized he was the young lad I had brought to the area earlier on in the night. As I spoke to him to confirm my recollection, he recognized my voice. Something else he remembered which I was not conscious of was the Christian music that was playing in my car on that trip. "I really know God wanted us to meet again." He told me. "After you dropped me off earlier tonight, I began wishing that I would see you again." "Why?" I asked. "I wanted to talk to you about my life so that you can pray with me." I was a little taken aback. But after a short pause, I asked if he still wanted to. He did.

This was now about 4am, and he wanted me to go into his house with him so that he would talk to me. On one hand, I knew that it was not part of the protocol of my business to go into houses of customers. Apart from being accused of wrong doing in somebody's home, one could just voluntarily walk oneself into a death trap. Yet, my pastoral instinct kicked in, reminding me that I could be turning my back on someone who genuinely needed someone to talk to. So I rang a friend to tell them where I was and what I was doing so that he could check on me if need be. For the following two hours I listened to a young man tell me his story of how he lost his parents when he was very young, was adopted by a family that loved him, but still struggled hugely with the fact that a big part of him was still a missing jig-saw without which he was finding it very difficult to find any real purpose in life.

"What did you say to him?" You might be wondering. Not very much, really. I only listened a lot, attempted to answer honestly any direct questions he put to me, pointed him to some scriptures that I believed sought to nurture faith and hope in God, and prayed with him before I left to go home. Of what help my visit with him was, I do not know. But I went home knowing that I gave him a little of what he had asked of me: time and a listening ear. And I prayed on the way that it was of some help to him.

Scary Experiences in the Taxi Business

Driving a taxi by night anywhere is not the easiest thing. It is doubly difficult in a city. Indeed, what I had been told by those with whom I shared my intention before embarking on it was absolutely true. Racial abuse, getting drunks home, listening to meaningless conversations and chatter, sitting out in the cold for hours on end, sleepless nights, dopey days, you name it. They are all to be experienced in the taxi business.

On at least a couple of occasions I found myself in what I believed were impossible situations. One of them was to do with a young man I had picked up in the city centre who said he was going to Menlouch village on the west side of the city. Within a very short time I realized this man looked very drunk but hadn't a smell of alcohol on him.

Several kilometres outside the city, he began telling me how many people he has killed by slitting their throats. He turned towards me and said, "But don't worry I am not going to kill you." As he said those words my hands and feet grew cold. This was about 3am and in what felt like a remote place far from houses or traffic and I was alone with this man. Suddenly, I had a thought. "Say good things to him and about him anytime he says anything negative." That is what I did. As I continued to drive—and very uneasily—I countered every bad thing he said he does with words like, "You are a good man; you don't do things like that." As I was doing that I was repeatedly praying under my breath saying: "Lord Jesus, I cover this man, this car, and myself with your saving blood." This, indeed, was part of the prayer I said every time before I drove the taxi from my driveway to work.

Another few kilometres in the journey, he suddenly turned to me and shouted, "Stop the car here." On hearing that, my heart nearly fell out through my mouth. "What, Lord, is this? I spluttered tremblingly. Before I could think or say anything more, he told me he had some friends in the area and he wanted to walk to them. This was in the middle of nowhere. But who was I to tell him he could not go to his friends, especially if it meant him leaving the car? I stopped the car and impatiently waited for him to step out. Finding out he was not sure how to open the door, I leaned towards him, stretched my hand and opened the door. "How much do I owe you?" He asked. On telling him, he sat still for what seemed like many anxious hours for me. Eventually, he put one foot out, gave me the fare, and several minutes later stepped out of the car. By this time I could feel the flow of the adrenaline all over my body. I leaned over again towards the open passenger door, this time nearly falling over, grabbed and closed it with what seemed to be an almighty bang, and activated the central locking system.

Before the incident I never thought I could do the three point turn so perfectly on a narrow rural road. But that night I realized I could. Moving the car forward a bit away from him, I still cannot remember how quickly and accurately I got it turning the opposite way towards the city. "My phone is still in the car", I heard him shout as I sped towards the city, shaking and saying, God knows how many dozen times, "Thank you Jesus." I shouted back to him, "Go to the police station tomorrow morning and ask for it."

The other incident happened on the east side of the city. A couple of men came into my car and asked me to bring them to Oranmore village. It was about 11.30pm and I decided to take the coast road. As we left the city centre I found out from conversations we were having that they had come to Galway that night from Limerick. On approaching Galway Crystal on the edge of the city, they offered me cocaine, which I turned down saying, "I don't do that". This apparently angered them. Their friendliness immediately changed into animosity. The one sitting by me in the passenger seat deliberately leaned towards me so that my left elbow could touch the handle of the knife he was carrying tucked in his trousers under his overcoat. As before, I started praying underneath my breath as there was now no communication taking place between them and I except that of body language. He shouted to his friend in the back that he did not have money to pay the taxi driver. "Nor do I have any", his friend replied. Fearfully and nervously, I continued to drive in silence under the cover of night outside the car and darkness inside. Arriving in Oranmore, they got out, left the doors open, and proudly walked away as if they owned the universe, and without paying the fare. I got out, closed the doors, turned the car, and drove back into the city, praising God that even though I did not get paid, I was not hurt.

Fun Times Too

But there were good experiences as well. I remember once taking a young couple from the city centre to Tyrrellan Heights about 3am on Sunday morning. They both decided to sit in the back where they spent much of their time snuggling. A short time before we got to their home, the young man asked: "Hey, taxi driver", he shouted forward, "what do you do for a proper job?" "I am a priest". I replied. Suddenly I saw him sit up straight, almost choking as a result of what he heard. "Let us out here", he sternly told me. "No." I replied. "I won't let you out until you confess your sins." On hearing that he became even more agitated. By this time we had got to where they were going. When I announced the fare, he gave me a ten euro note shouting, "Keep the change for the collection," as he ran away towards the door.

I often enjoyed times when black taxi drivers got together for social occasions. They were quite entertaining times as one taxi driver after another told stories of their experiences in the taxi business. Everyone without exception had a story of how they dealt with people who ran away, or wanted to, without paying their fare. One taxi driver who found himself in that situation chased the man into his yard until the man called his giant dog out to settle the matter. Another decided to scare the passenger into believing that he could change himself into a baboon through African magic and beat his difficult customer into a pulp. Getting out of his car, he started beating his chest frantically with both fists and making king-kong sounds in the middle of nowhere in the Irish countryside. Thoroughly afraid of what he had seen, the passenger ran towards the car, threw on to the seat more than he owed, and ran away from his African driver as fast as he could. Still another had to resort to swearing the culprit in his ethnic language which he believed had more power to affect the culprit even though he knew the culprit could not understand the language. Several others told stories of how they got beaten up by customers they had brought far away in the country because they did not want to pay the fare. And all of us, from time to time, experienced racist behaviour and abuse from both customers and fellow white Irish taxi drivers. Sometimes these experiences made me question the validity of the notion of 'Ireland of the Welcomes'.

All Things Are Possible

For me, among the things I most cherished about my taxi work was that it in many ways was an extension of my pastoral vocation. Not only that, my taxi was also often used as my study. I recall many times bringing books, Bible commentaries, and Christian teaching on CDs that I wanted to read, look up and listen to respectively. I also prepared many a sermon sitting at the taxi rank, with relevant ready illustrations playing themselves out right there in front of me. While colleagues would sometimes be complaining that the rank was quiet, I would be sitting down fully engaged in preparation for my other work, and not noticing whether or not the rank was slow. Indeed there were many times when I was so engrossed in what I was doing that I did not realize that the taxi in front of me had moved. It was the driver behind me who would call my attention to move by blowing the horn.

There was also, of course, the satisfaction the additional needed cash raised through that work brought to me and my family. As a matter of fact, I actually used part of my taxi earnings to build a house for my parents in our village to replace the one destroyed during the decade long civil war.

Angels, the good, the bad, the struggling, dreamers, chancers, and all manners of men and women: I met them in the city of tribes. They taught me many a good lesson for my own journey of life. They brought me into worlds I would otherwise never have travelled to. They reminded me that if I am flexible enough to embrace whatever life throws at me, I can conquer and transform it into something good for me and for others. In Galway, like never before, I often came face-to-face with the 'jungle' and 'civilized' in humanity—the noble savages known as human beings.

FOURTEEN

THE HUMAN CONDITION

Facets of Christian Ministry

C hristian Ministry often brings one face-to-face with both the goodness and weakness of human beings. Pastoral visiting is not exactly a relaxing job, although it can sometimes be an amusing experience. I recall, for example, a time when I visited an old lady who began to tell me the story of her two cats that were always looking for her attention. One was black and the other was white. The gist of the story was that the white cat was gentle and adorable and the black cat was anything but. I smiled as I listened to her. Looking at me and seeing me smile, something changed suddenly in her demeanor. She must have realized that I was, like her troublesome cat, black too. Suddenly she started to say a few good things about her black cat; but the look on her face could not hide her embarrassment. At another visit an old lady was telling me about how hard her parents worked in those days to scratch a living for themselves. "They worked as hard as a black." Suddenly, as in the case of the other lady, she became all embarrassed as, I suppose, she realized I was a black man.

Little awkward moments like these apart, pastoral visits have always afforded me great opportunity to learn about life's joys, dreams, struggles and sufferings listening to the stories of other people's experiences during a meal, over a cup of coffee, in a hospital, or during a time of bereavement. Some stories are simple heart-breaking, others inspiring and uplifting, some funny, and still others down to earth stories about the ordinary stuff of life and living. In each of these situations, I am always humbled by the privilege of not only being let into the lives of people that I am related to only by reason of the faith we share, but also of the sheer capacity of people to weather storms of life. Some of the storms are caused by nature and others by challenging human relationships. But all of them, sobering reminders that hardship, pain, suffering and death know no social, racial, religious, spiritual, sex and age boundaries. Here, all human beings and societies are in the same boat.

Like pastoral visiting, conducting services and administering a church are more often than not taxing activities. They take a lot of time and energy in preparation and the results may also not always be as envisaged. A service and sermon that looks well on paper may in the actual process of delivery be a disaster. The heartache and self-beating that result from such times can be very significant. Yet people have sometimes come to me a while after such a service and told me how they were blessed by it. The fact of anyone being blessed by what

I reckoned was a disaster of a service has convinced me of the fact that it is God who ministers to people, albeit through unworthy channels like myself. I believe now, more than ever, the words of the Psalmist that "Unless God builds the house, those who build it labour in vain."[20]

People who know me well enough know that administration is not my forte; especially not meetings. Yet meetings are an important part of running any organization especially a church; and some people really like them—God bless them. But for someone like me, I just about survive the official meetings of the local church. Anything else after that is pure drudgery, even if there is coffee and sandwiches afterwards; and ". . . all good Methodist meetings", someone said to me once, "must end with a cup of tea and goodies."

In ministry, thus, I am reminded always of my strengths and weaknesses and those of others. I am also reminded of the fact of each of these helping me learn what it really means to be a human being.

Finger-Pointing

'Every time one points a finger at another, three more are pointing back at one', I have often heard said. This is so true. Yet more often than not we all as individuals, groups and whole societies engage in this somewhat pharisaic act. I recall once scolding my daughter for shouting the word 'stupid' at

---

[20]   Psalm 127:1

her brother. This happened as I was walking them to school. "Shhh . . ." I silenced her putting my finger tightly on my lips. "Don't you ever talk that way to your brother again!"

This was in Wicklow Town in 1996. My daughter's response could not have been more appropriate and revealing. "But you do that all the time, dad." I was gob-smacked. I stood for what seemed like a whole five minutes without moving an inch, reflecting on the truth of what she said, her honesty and fearless rebuke of me. The penny dropped. She was right. I had fallen into the habit of telling my children not to be stupid when they were doing things that I did not approve of. She had learnt from me that it was the way to speak to people that you disagreed with. So, that morning when I scolded her, she was just simply being her daddy: "But you do that all the time, dad." Those words rang in my ears for a long time to come. They reminded me of the famous searching question that Jesus Christ once asked His listeners: "How can you say to your brother, 'Let me take the speck out of your eye,' when all the time there is a plank in your own eye? You hypocrite, first take the plank out of your own eye, and then you will see clearly to remove the speck from your brother's eye.[21]

We arrived at the school on time. However, the exchanges with my daughter that morning alerted me to how easy it is to be a hypocrite, especially for those of us who are employed in what I call 'the business of conversion.' As a Christian, I believe that I have been given the task of preaching the gospel of repentance and the forgiveness of sins. In my experience

---

[21]   Matthew 7:4-5

on this journey of faith, however, I am discovering daily that to be faithful and effective in that task, I, more than any other, am the one who daily needs conversion to the ways of Christ. Humbling and frustrating as I find this, it has alerted me to the fact that too often I fall into the trap of pointing fingers at others for shortcomings that I myself suffer from. And, my experience of Church, for nearly fifty years now, tells me that this problem is not unique to me.

Christian people and different Christian Churches are often prone to pointing fingers at Christians, Churches, doctrines, practices, worship, dress codes, and even demeanour of those who are different. Stories and attitudes pointing to this fact are not difficult to find in any church. Fingers are also pointed at adherents of other religions. Yet there is no 'sin' present in the non-Christian world that is absent in the Church of Christ, whatever its name, nature and colour. Nor is there any 'virtue' in the non-Christian world that is not present in the Church of Christ.

In my experience, the danger of finger-pointing is not unique to the Church. It is a human problem. It is found in homes, among peers, in the academic world, in the work place, on the playground, and in all sorts of relationships. As I write, there is a radio discussion programme going on about Irish women who change the wardrobe of their husbands because the latter's dress taste is allegedly poor. What is missing from the discussion, however, is what husbands think of the wardrobes of their wives.

The West's Representations of Africa

As an African, I have found finger-pointing especially in the representations of Africa and her peoples by the West a phenomenon. In her print and oral media, the West often represents Africa and her peoples as the complete opposite of the sum total of what she is and stands for. She defines Africa and her peoples by lack of one kind or another of what she has in abundance. The result of this has been that the West's relationship with Africa and Africans is always informed primarily by her desire to make Africa like the West. Like Christians in their relationship with the non-Christian world, the West is in 'the business of changing' Africa and her peoples into the image and likeness of the West. The goal is 'development'; and 'development' essentially translates as Western value systems and ways of life.

As such, the West's relationship with Africa and her peoples is not a relationship built on true respect for and value of Africa for what she is; but one informed by what Africa has to become in order to be regarded and related to as an equal with the West. I have come to liken it to a person who marries in the hope of changing their partner before they can truly value and love them. Such a relationship would not be a relationship of respect and love; but of finger-pointing and abuse. I have often wondered if this is not the reason why the West's predominant story of Africa is one of negatives which, some would argue, ultimately results in racial and cultural abuse.

Yet a casual analysis of the wealth the West prides herself on readily reveals downsides that she often fails to admit. Most Africans I know who have lived in the West for any reasonable length of time have come to realize that in spite of so much in her favour, the West is also a deeply flawed society. Her peoples suffer immensely from loneliness even though they live in the midst of many. She is a society of peoples who are able to buy everything they believe will make them happy, but they are among the most discontented people in the world. The latest gadgets allowing for communication with every part of the globe are easily accessible, but people do not know their neighbours. More and more time-saving equipment is manufactured and purchased but the West has the most stressed people on the planet for lack of time.

The West's contributions to environmental damage are second to none. She preaches freedom, justice and the value of human life to the rest of the world, but sees no problem with manufacturing, exporting and deploying killing machines for economic gain. She advocates the end of poverty and even gives development aid towards this end, but puts into place unfair trade laws and dumps her surpluses and toxic waste on other peoples to deepen their poverty. In the West, homelessness thrives whilst there are numerous unoccupied houses and under-occupied homes. The old are relegated to the margins of society—silenced and routinely discarded into the care of mere strangers. Broken families are a norm in Western society where there is so much talk about love and romance. Indeed, psychologists now describe the 'dysfunctional family' as the typical family in the West.

In the West, suicide is common place. People are murdered routinely in the absence of visible civil wars which are common in Africa. Addictions of various kinds and their consequent enslavement are a common phenomenon even though the society prides itself on the values of freedom. Only recently I read that on average, a child in the West is first exposed to pornographic material at the age of eleven.

As I write, much of the West is reeling with the pain of a recession arguably unlike any other in the past. Many agree corruption, the stick which the West uses to beat Africa into shame with, played a big part in bringing it about. Consequently, corporate and individual greed for economic gain continues to heap immense debt burdens on the next generation. The list goes on.

In her **Ancient Futures**[22], Norberg-Hodge is aware of this shadow side of the West's abundance. She writes: "We forget that the price for never-ending economic growth and material prosperity has been spiritual and social impoverishment, psychological insecurity, and a loss of cultural vitality. We think ourselves as 'having everything', and are surprised when young people turn to drugs or strange gurus to fill the void in their lives . . . we have lost our sense of community . . ."[23]

The human, ecological, and spiritual costs of the West's wealth are truly enormous. And they are costs to both the West and the rest of the world. Indeed thousands of babies,

---

[22] (1991) Sierra Club Books
[23] P.181

women and men are killed, dispossessed and disadvantaged every day in the so called developing world as a result of Western development policies imposed upon their countries. Africa's debt burden in the bid for her to mimic the West's development model remains among the few most detrimental causes of Africa's poverty and relegation to the prison of human misery. It is this that has led me to discover that ignorance and underdevelopment are not the only causes of human pain, suffering and death. Knowledge and development also do.

Yes, there is much in the West which is good for all of humanity. Strides in education, science, technology, economics, arts and culture in the West have and continue to benefit much of the world. But the values of the West's development model are not simply to be lauded and accepted as though it was some divinely appointed way forward for everyone. I have discovered as I have lived in the West that while development has the capacity to deliver some good, it also equally has the capacity to undo other indispensable good for humanity. Yet, the West is often so absorbed with her ways of life that it often speaks and acts as though her way is the ONLY way of life worth knowing, talking about, and living. How right was Chinua Achebe, the African novelist of blessed memory, when he noted that 'travellers with closed minds can tell us little except about themselves.'

Africa is Not Blameless

Africa and her peoples are not, however, without their own problems. As my people say, "If you warn the dog (to keep away from the bone), you should also warn the bone (not to tempt the dog)." One of the salient lessons of history is that a people who settle for consuming other people's products can always only expect to be followers rather than leaders in a world of competing interests in the race for power, significance, influence and control. In a world of innovation and creativity in all fields and levels of human life and experience, Africa and Africans cannot expect to influence the rest of the global community in any significant developmental way if they are only always satisfied with consuming other people's ideas, policies, and material goods. They need to create and promote their own cultural values, material goods, ideas and the environment that enhances life and living on their continent. 'Development' is not in the gift of other people to give to Africa and her peoples, neither is it a pre-defined finished product of one culture to be handed over to others. Only Africa and her people can develop Africa and in ways that foster the kinds of values they cherish and interests they have.

This would mean not just accepting and reproducing other people's ideas and realities of 'development' as though those ideas and realities are an unalterable given. To do so would not only continue to spell disaster for the people of Africa but also keep her perpetually in the position of catch-up where the West is happy for her to remain forever. Yes, now and again, the West will make positive noises suggesting evidence of 'green shoots' indicating Africa's 'development'. I have often wondered if this is not just a ploy to encourage Africa to keep believing that .her divine destiny lies in modelling Western capitalism. But even if those 'green shoots' were to grow into proper fruit-bearing plants, I still am not sure if the end results would be as enhancing of life for Africa and the world at large as is been talked about so very often. If the situation in the West is anything to go by, I doubt it.

Indeed, critical eyes and discerning minds are already seeing a new take-over of Africa by the West's and East's multi-nationals in the name of development. As it was in the first take-over, so this new one. Africa's land is been taken over again to grow food to feed 'hungry Africa'. So they say. In actual fact, however, it is for the feeding of the West's and East's economies. Those in Africa who have ears to hear and abilities to act, let them hear and act. 'Development' talk about Africa is often more about the West's need for Africa's resources for her own development than it is about love and concern for the wellbeing of Africa and her people.

As in the basic day-to-day interactions of people, so in the major global economic, political, and cultural exchanges: there is no such thing as a free lunch. Self-interest is always at the heart of most human interactions, especially when it comes to planned and managed development: capitalism. Not only that, in those exchanges, respect from others is earned not demanded; the same is true with regard to being considered significant in the global playing field. The onus is on Africa and her peoples to shape their own destinies. Only Africa and Africans can make this happen. Nobody else can, even if they were ready to give Africa and her peoples all the money and ideas the world can afford them. Development aid (tied up and influenced as it often is) with the liberal economic and political interests and goals of its givers will certainly never do it.

I have often wondered why it is that a Westerner could generally go to my country and not just readily work in the field of their expertise but also in the highest position and without being able to communicate to the locals in their language. Yet, the same is not the case for an African in the West. Even if an African had their qualification in a Western University and could speak the language of the country very well, they could still not be guaranteed readily a job in their area of expertise if they were to apply for one with citizens of the country they are in. In Ireland I have heard ridiculous excuses like 'he could not be given the job because he has an accent'. Who speaks without an accent? And why do people with Irish accents easily get good jobs in Africa?

To those who may want to suggest that this is just simple racist discrimination I would beg to differ. To my mind, the real issue has little or nothing to do with racist discrimination. Instead, it is Western people saying to Africans in and outside Africa that every person and people can and do choose to do what they want to do with their resources. They are therefore free to choose who they want to benefit from their resources. The truth is that when a Westerner works in Africa, they are more often than not working in jobs created by Westerners and paid for by them. The same is not often the case with an African in the West. The African who comes to the West comes essentially to benefit from the resources of the West. Why should Africans expect to be given priority of choice for a job over a Western person? I am pretty certain that if Africans were faced with the same realities of life as Westerners, they would do no better. This realization should teach Africa and Africans that they, as it were, have to work out their own salvation instead of expecting others to do it for them, or thinking that others owe them an obligation to do so.

Africans Are Their Own Worst Enemies

I have always being intrigued by the fact that when many of us Africans are in the West, we admire the infrastructural, economic, and democratic developments there. Yes, we may be aware of the downsides of those developments. But we see and value the disciplined orderly way things are done. We are even educated in some of these ways of the West, often excel, and acquire degrees and certificates as evidence of our achievements. But immediately we go back to Africa, many of us often behave as though we never left the place or were never exposed to better ways of doing things. How true it is that you can take a person out of the bush but you may never be able to take the bush out of them!

I once confronted a Sierra Leonean who was on the same flight with me from London Heathrow to Freetown Lungi. In London, this man, like all of us, patiently and orderly queued through all the processes of clearing passengers through various checks. He seemingly saw and accepted that this was the best way to do things. But on arrival at Lungi Freetown, I saw him blatantly ignoring the system that was in place there, like in London Heathrow, to clear passengers through various checks. He apparently knew some airport authorities and so sought to jump the queue through their aid. Realizing what he was trying to do, I left my place in the queue, went straight to him, drew to his attention the anomaly between his behaviour in London and that in Freetown, and asked him why? As I expected, he suddenly became furious with me because I had the guts to challenge him; but when he saw that other people in the queue also started to challenge him, he walked to the back of the queue and waited for his turn.

It would not be so bad if that was just an isolated incident. However, it is not so. Truth to be spoken, that little incident is unfortunately a microcosm of the attitude and behaviour of many of us Africans when we return home from the West. It is as though we never left the jungle where survival of the fittest is the norm. The only difference is that we may now wear suits, ties and shiny Italian shoes, drive four-wheel drive vehicles, speak a European language (especially when we want to cover-up our ignorance by silencing those who dare to challenge us), and have some foreign currency to buy our way through any obstacles that have the potential to stop us from having what we want to have or doing what we want to do. And when we eventually manage to bribe our ways to the top, only our bodies and work are in Africa; our hearts and interests, on the other hand, are in the West—where we educate our children and relations, access health facilities, and have our Western benefactors and electors (especially if we are politicians of any significance). That scenario, of course, excuses us from doing anything to better the services and lives of people in our countries. So returning from the West we bring with us both the jungle we brought to the West and that which we have acquired while in the West, so that our state is twice as bad as what it was before we ever left our home countries. Yet we take every available opportunity to blame Africa's poverty and sufferings on Western colonialism and neo-colonialism. To crown it all, we would decry ignorance which we more often than not equate with not being able to read, write and speak a European language, unaware that one who knows what is right but fails to do that right displays a worse form of ignorance.

Talking to people about leadership in my country has more often than not left me simply sad and hopeless. The discussion will often start with condemnation of politicians and other leaders for their corrupt practices. Yet, the same people would, as the discussion progresses, suddenly say things which clearly show that they admire people who have enriched themselves with ill-gotten gains. They refer to them as 'sensible' and 'wise' because 'they have done well for themselves'. Those in leadership positions who served selflessly and honestly without enriching themselves, they call 'foolish' because 'they did not do well for themselves'.

Leadership for many Africans in Africa is not something one aspires to primarily to serve, but to be served. It is firstly for the benefits that accrue to oneself when one becomes a leader; serving the needs of those one leads is only a secondary matter. That is why in Africa women and children are treated as though they were not as fully human as men, using culture as a convenient defence; politicians and other leaders in society see their positions as a divine right that should not only remain unchallenged but should be passed on down their family line; public resources are used as though they are private possessions; public servants demand to be bribed for doing jobs that they are paid to do; and the poor, disabled, mentally ill and disadvantaged are treated as disposable entities. And when a Western person comments on this, they are accused of having racist views and attitudes. Yet, those same people would value and respect that Western person more than they would value and respect their own people.

For over two hundred years the value of Africa and her peoples have been staked on the West's idea of 'development'. This has been called different names—civilization, progress, Christianization, globalization, human rights, and so on—but essentially informed by the same idea. And, for over two hundred years, Africa and her peoples have largely failed to be what their Western teachers and benefactors wanted them to be. Is it that something is desperately wrong with us Africans? Are we simply stupid, incapable of learning and so of being educated, or are we just very slow learners? Are we just bold pupils who do not want to do what we are told, or have we found out that both our Western teachers and the 'development' product they sell to us is not quite what we want? Whatever it is, perhaps it is time for us to declare either that we are able but do not want to because we prefer to be who and what we are, or want to but cannot. In the case of the former, we would need to set out clearly who and what we are, the values that inform that reality, ways of pursuing and enhancing the further development of those realities, and selling them to the rest of the world. In the latter case, we may have to declare simply, openly and honestly our inability to 'develop' ourselves, invite the West to re-colonize us or China to take over the continent, and cede to the West or China every decision and execution of the same towards our development.

A Word of Caution

In either case, however, we should never fool ourselves by thinking that there is a way of life and a system of living that is devoid of serious weaknesses and challenges: Western, Chinese, or African. So-called 'development'—African, Western or Asian—like 'under-development'—impoverishes and invariably also causes suffering and death. For better and for worse, the human condition—need, poverty, ignorance, tragedy, wrongdoing, fear, and so on—are not just African, Western or Asian realities. Nor are wealth, strength, and goodness—which exist in different forms and are experienced in different ways. Poverty is not just about lack of money. Neither is ignorance just about those who are not educated in Western ways. Nor are hope and initiative to humanize life just Western realities. All these are seemingly intrinsic human realities, which human beings seek to address in their own ways, however inadequately. Over the years, the realization of this human condition has made me keenly aware of the nonsense of finger-pointing. I think it was Albert Camus who said that "Once you begin to think, you begin to undermine yourself."

FIFTEEN

A PARABLE AND A STATEMENT

Change Yourself

Weaknesses are not a monopoly of any particular peoples or societies or cultures; nor are strengths. There is no person or society whose make-up is solely of weaknesses or strengths. Strengths and weaknesses are realities of every human being, society and civilization. Yes, in the West people are aware enough about these realities with regard to their people that they put structures of accountability and transparency into place for holding the general public and leaders to account for their attitudes and actions. Rules are put into place and they are generally policed. This is true also of non-Western societies—traditional or modern. But the very fact that such structures need to be put in place is an acceptance that no person or society of human beings is without its own weaknesses. Being aware of this would not only help us nurture humility—a strength that most of us lack to our detriment and that of others—but would keep before us the primary need of our own continuing reformation, conversion, transformation and change.

It was Bayazid Bastami, a Persian Sufi of the ninth century, who is said to have expressed this human reality in the following way: "I was a revolutionary when I was young and all my prayer to God was 'Lord give me the energy to change the world.' As I approached middle age and realized that half my life was gone without my changing a single soul, I changed my prayer to 'Lord, give me the grace to change all those who come in contact with me. Just my family and friends, and I shall be satisfied.' Now that I am an old man and my days are numbered, my only prayer is, 'Lord, give me the grace to change myself.' If I had prayed for this right from the start I would not have wasted my life."

Many years ago, I heard somewhere these words which I jotted down in my notepad. "Anyone who has so little knowledge of human nature as to seek happiness by changing anything but his own disposition will waste his life in fruitless efforts and multiply the grief which he purposes to remove." I can't remember who said them, but they seem to echo the experience of Bastami.

Jesus Condemns Finger-Pointing

In this matter of the human condition, I am reminded of the story of Jesus which I believe unveils the ignorance of finger-pointing. It is commonly known as the parable of the

Pharisee and the Tax Collector.[24] Luke's introduction to this story is relevant: "To some who were confident of their own righteousness and looked down on everyone else, Jesus told this parable."[25]

There are three characters in the story: a Pharisee, a Tax Collector, and God. The first two are the actors in the human drama; and God is the spectator and judge. The Pharisee and the Tax Collector meet in the place of prayer. They are both there to pray. "God, I thank you that I am not like other people—robbers, evildoers, adulterers—or even like this Tax Collector. I fast twice a week and give a tenth of all I get."[26] This is the prayer of the Pharisee in the hearing of the Tax Collector.

Reflecting on his words, I cannot help but ask the following questions: Are all human beings not ultimately the same: embodied creatures, who feel hunger, thirst, fear, and pain; who reason, hope, dream, and aspire; who are vulnerable? Was the Pharisee above any of these? Do not all human beings as individuals, groups, and societies have their shortcomings and strengths? Was the Pharisee in this story any different? Granted, as he himself claimed, he was a good man, was he also not a self-righteousness man, uncharitable in his representation of other fellow human beings? How come then that this man denies he is not like other people? In assuming that he was not like other men, was this man being truthful? Was he also revealing his ignorance of the true and total

---

[24] It is recorded in the Gospel according to St. Luke 18:9-14
[25] Verse 9
[26] Verses 11-12

reality of what it means to be human? Did his being a human being not imply that he was like all other human beings in every sense of the word?

These are some questions that this man's assertion about himself raise in my mind. Yet it also occurs to me that this man was right in recognizing and saying that he was not like other men? After all, he was a Pharisee. And, like other Pharisees, he was intent on keeping the Jewish religious tradition meticulously and scrupulously pure. So he was what he said he was. He was unlike others who were different from him—others who were not Pharisees—and so did not necessarily see their life's goal as one of guarding and preserving Jewish orthodoxy.

This acknowledgement of his uniqueness, and by implication the uniqueness of the group he represented vis-à-vis other people in Jewish society and beyond, is something that I think the Pharisee should be commended for. In acknowledging that he was different, this man put his finger on a reality that describes and is a part and parcel of all human existence—the need for boundaries of distinction. And the creation of boundaries of distinctions between oneself—as group or individual—and others is not bad in itself. It is, in fact, necessary and essential to life. Otherwise, we would never be able to know what we are fighting for or against.

Yes, the Pharisee was not like other men because he did not do the evil that other men did: steal, murder, commit adultery, and so on. Indeed, his own sin, though he did not know, was called by other names: self-righteousness, pride,

self-centredness, and critical spirit. That is not all. He
described his goodness in terms of obedience to the law,
discipline in fasting, and generosity in paying tithes; but not
in terms of humility or acknowledgement of need—both of
which constituted the Tax Collector's 'goodness' who simply
prayed, unable even to lift up his eyes, "God have mercy on
me, a sinner."[27] Yes, in these—the difference in the names
of their sins and virtues they had—the Pharisee and the Tax
Collector were different.

Also, the Pharisee, unlike the other people he condemned
condescendingly, was the only one who was not aware of
his own shortcomings. But neither was the Tax Collector
aware of his own strength for which Jesus recommended
him—humility. That was another significant difference
between these two men. Add to that the fact that one was a
Pharisee—with all that meant—and the other was not; and
you see how very right the Pharisee was in saying that he was
not like other people. Important differences distinguished him
from the other people he had in mind.

But knowing and declaring that he was different from other
people gave him no right to think, as his prayer insinuated,
that those other people were worse than he was. Doing so,
he demonstrated his ignorance in three ways: firstly, his
ignorance of the invaluable human values those people had;
secondly, his ignorance of the shortcomings of his own ways
of life; and thirdly, his ignorance of the fact that he too,
like the Tax Collector and others, was a person with needs,

---

[27] Verse 13

strengths, and weaknesses. For, while there were differences between the Pharisee and the Tax Collector, the differences were not in **what** kind of people they were, but in **how** they were **what** they were. Both represented true humanity in which 'fair is foul and foul is fair'.

Had the Pharisee and Tax Collector recognized this, it would have freed them both from any delusions of total goodness and so self-righteousness (on the part of the Pharisee), or of total depravity and so self-depreciation (on the part of the Tax Collector). Evil is among the good, and good among the evil. The strangeness we see in others that makes us discriminate against them, is a strangeness that also resides within us, if we cared to look for it. This parable of Jesus clearly demonstrates this.

What Jesus does in this parable is that he puts his finger on what I believe is the perennial issue at the heart of human responses to other humans beings as different: the uncritical acceptance of our own ways of life as normal and essential while we seek to deny or ignore or even label other people's ways of life as abnormal, and wish, consciously or otherwise, that their own differences should give way to our own. Taking this stance, we not only display our ignorance of the weaknesses that might be present in the worldviews, beliefs and practices we take for granted within ourselves, but we also display our ignorance of the strengths and values that other people's worldviews, beliefs, and practices may have that we could benefit from.

Jesus recommended the self-view of the Tax Collector not, I would suggest, because he was better or worse than the Pharisee in actual fact; but because he had the attitude of mind and heart that in the end, mattered most: "God be merciful to me a sinner", he prayed. His disposition characterized him as a man open to new ways of seeing and being. In this man reposed the humble recognition that he is nowhere near being what he could be as a human being created in the image of God. In this man was real hope for change for the better. You see, we never begin to be good until we can feel and say that we are bad.

On the other hand, the Pharisee no longer saw anything good in different others to emulate; at least not in the Tax Collector whom he perceived as being below him; perhaps not even in God because he sounded totally self-liberated and self-dependent. He had arrived so to speak. His standard was himself, and no other. The Pharisee saw himself as the master exemplar that everyone else must imitate. Such a person would find no reason to learn from others, or change for the better. No wonder the Tax Collector, and not the Pharisee, according to Jesus, 'went home made right with God'. Then Jesus concluded: "For all those who exalt themselves will be humbled, and those who humble themselves will be exalted."[28] This underlines the significance of St. Paul's warning to Christians in Rome: ". . . I give each of you this warning: Don't think you are better than you really are. Be honest in your evaluation of yourselves . . ."[29]

---

[28]   Verse 14
[29]   Romans 12:3

A Jungle in each of Us

A friend of mine Rodney Croly, an insurance broker of Church Town in South Dublin, once said to me in a matter-of-fact way that "There is a jungle in each of us." Rodney's assessment of the make-up of every human being is no different from what my daughter reminded me I was, or from the realities of the stories of finger-pointing I have told, or Jesus' parable of the Pharisee and the Tax Collector which I have reflected upon. It is an acknowledgement of the capacity of human beings to be noble and savage at the same time. In essence, Rodney was saying that the untamed, wild, undomesticated, uncontrollable place which we call jungle is not just out there in the bush; it is also within each and every human being. But in what he said, Rodney also affirmed at least by implication that there is 'the domesticated' in each of us. "There is", he said, a jungle in each of us", and not "Each of us is made up of jungle". These two realities of what it means to be a human being, I believe, was the message he was conveying to me. If Rodney was right, as I think he was, why then do people still talk about the 'civilized' and the 'uncivilized' as though they were two totally unrelated and distinct groups of people?"

This Pharisaic stance, I have come to conclude, has the stuff from which ethnic, national, religious, gender, age, economic, cultural, political, and skin colour discriminations, exclusions, and conflicts are made. The stuff is called 'superiority complex'. It is the "I am better than you" syndrome that has always plagued this world and continues to do so. It is present in both the Church and outside of it. It is the attitude that says unless you are like me, or until you become like me, I am not prepared to value you as a human being like me, nor the way of life you represent. It is the finger-pointing attitude which does not accept and value people for who they already are but for what they will become as a result of our interventions. And backed up with money, military might, policy-making power, and control, this stuff has in it the seed from which injustice of every kind is born: slavery, colonization, the holocaust, apartheid, ethnic cleansing, sectarianism, the oppression and exploitation of women and non-white people, and religious intolerance in our world.

Jungle is Not All Bad

Yet, even these acts and behaviours should not be considered as totally purposeless. Life has taught me that the 'jungle' in us and others which we so often deplore may after all have a good reason for existing. Imagine a world without a moral, emotional, and spiritual jungle! It would be a world with no heroes and heroines to admire, no achievers of anything to celebrate, no histories of men and women who sought to tame the jungle in their lives and societies so as to make life more bearable, and no stories that would challenge, encourage, or urge caution about how to treat our jungles. It would be a world of people with nothing to work for, nothing to hope for, and nothing to expect. Who, I have often asked myself, would like to live in such a world? What sort of life would one live in it? Who would bear living in such a world of purposeless, hopeless, and boring existence?

The weaknesses in each of us and in each society have often served as the site where great battles have been fought, great struggles taken place, great discoveries and inventions made, great victories won, and life made worth living. On this site, on this margin dividing 'civilization' from 'savagery', also exists not only the possibilities for a new and better humanity and creation, but also of the goals that give meaning to life.

Indeed, sometimes it is the very existence in us of jungle, in thought or behaviour that also creates and strengthens in us both the desire for 'civilized' behaviour and the urge to work towards translating that desire into some semblance of reality. I have come to understand the Tax Collector's "Lord be merciful to me, a sinner" request as an expression of that desire.

Yet, at other times, we long to cultivate and exhibit the jungle in us at the slightest possible opportunity we get to do so. The Pharisee in this parable of Jesus does this as he seems to say immediately he sees the Tax Collector, "I am the fittest here, God, and so I alone and those who decide to be like me deserve a claim on your providence."

More often than not, though, we have a much better propensity to see and deplore other people's jungle than we do our own. And almost always, we demonstrate a much better ability to pity others for their jungle than we do ourselves for our own.

When I first arrived in the West from Africa, I had many illusions which I now question. Coming from where life in general was characterized by obedience to and control by

347

authority, for example, one of the earliest things I was attracted to in the West was freedom to think, choose and do what one wanted as long as one did not cause others any harm. It was only after many years I realized what very little freedom there actually was in the West in the face of the kind and extent of control the media, multi-nationals, the economy and growth had on our thoughts and decisions. What seems to me a clear example of this reality is the passionate debate that is going on in the Irish media as I write. A politician, Clare Daly, has just lashed out in parliament against President Obama and his family who are in Ireland for the G8 summit. Ms Daly has accused President Obama of being a 'war criminal' for his increased use of drones to kill thousands of people and his decision to arm the Syrian Opposition. She has also criticized his wife and children for having lunch with Bono (lead singer of the Irish band U2) whom she accuses of being a 'Tax Exile'. She does not want Ireland to be a 'lap-dog of US Imperialism' and is unhappy with the 'sycophantic falling over' the Obamas by sections of the media.

I mention this issue not because of its rights or wrongs, whatever these may be. But I do so especially because this is the year of The Gathering when many Irish-Americans, after a huge amount of advertisement and encouragement, are coming to Ireland as a way of boosting the faltering Irish economy. As a result, little or nothing is being said about the truth or otherwise of the issues that Ms Daly has raised. Instead, most of the comments are concerned about the economic damage to Ireland that her comments may cause. So I find myself asking, 'What is more important; money or justice, truth or politics? Outside of this particular incident, I have found in the West that even though we talk so much—even lecture others—about justice, human rights, the sanctity of human life, telling the truth and fair play, we are prepared to sacrifice any of them on the altar of political and economic expediency.

Long ago before I was exposed to this reality, I thought idol worship happened only in non-Christian and non—Western countries. As I daily witness worship in the West at altars other than that of the God of our Lord Jesus Christ, I now know better.

All this taught me that the 'strengths' and 'Weaknesses' in each of us are what unite all human beings. There is no person or society totally bad or totally good. Every person and society is a mixture of both. And it seems that no amount of effort and resources on any of our parts is ever going to change that. Yet it is the presence and experience of both of these realities in our lives that help us recognize 'good' and 'bad' when we see them.

Sober Judgment

St. Paul instructs the Christians in Galatia that ". . . each one examine his own work, and then he will have rejoicing in himself alone, and not in another."[30] Rejoicing in oneself for one's own work is different from rejoicing in another for one's own work. When we look at what is good about our own

---

[30] Galatians 6:4

personal achievements and those of our societies and rejoice solely because of them, we are rejoicing in ourselves for our own work. But when we look at those same achievements and rejoice because we know or believe others lack those achievements, we are not rejoicing in ourselves alone, but in something else. We are rejoicing because we think we are better than another and not simply because we have achieved something good. That is to say we are rejoicing in what we believe or know is the misfortune of another. And this is what the Bible says about the latter: "Do not gloat when your enemy falls; when they stumble, do not let your heart rejoice . . .[31]"

'Jungle' and 'tamed' living are two worlds between which all of us constantly live. This is an inescapable human condition. Aware of this we do well to again heed the advice of Albert Camus who allegedly warned his fellow human travellers in life saying: "Don't walk in front of me, I may not follow. Don't walk behind me, I may not lead. Just walk beside me and be my friend." Real friends are those who honestly tell each other stories of both the good fruits of their ways of life and the thorns on the plants that produce those fruits.

---

[31]   Proverbs 24:17-18

SIXTEEN

FREEDOM

An Innate Human Desire

O ne of the things life has taught me is the eternally present desire in me to better my life socially and spiritually. I have reason to believe that this is not something unique to me. I have come to believe that the desire and capacity of human beings to better their life situations no matter how good their present life circumstance is, perhaps, one clear example of how we all often live life as though in prison of one sort or another, always yearning to break out and be free. We never ever seem to arrive at a place in our lives where we experience total freedom from the need to be and feel better.

The desire to be free is a basic human impulse. It is one of the milestones in the human march in history. It was there in Martin Luther King's vision for America when he declared "I have a dream." It was the basis of Muhatma Gandhi's non-violent protests against British rule in India. It was obvious in the jubilation of countries emerging from colonial rule; in the collapse of communism; and in the street parties which accompanied the black vote in South Africa and the ending of apartheid there.

> The desire for freedom, it seems, is written into the very core of the make-up of human beings—young and old, male and female, black and white, rich and poor, one and all. Some years ago I read Nelson Mandela's story of how he first became conscious of the fact that he and his people were slaves and how this discovery signalled the beginning of his political consciousness and gave him a mission. "It was only when I began to learn that my boyhood freedom was an illusion, when I discovered as a young man that my freedom had already been taken away from me, that I began to hunger for it. At first . . . I wanted freedom for myself: . . . But then I slowly saw that not only was I not free, but my brothers and sisters were not free . . . . That is when I joined the African National Congress, and that is when the hunger for my freedom became a hunger for the freedom of my people . . . .[32]

In this experience of Mandela, we can discern something of our own yearning for the kind of freedoms that he sought

---

[32] Mandela, Nelson, (1995:750-1) Long Walk to Freedom. Cornwall: Abacus Books

for himself and for his people, a yearning echoed in other struggles for freedom in human history.

The quiet but desperate yearning of human beings to be free is a message at the heart of the widely known country song 'Green, Green Grass of Home'. It is about an imprisoned man yearning to be free. He will get his heart's desire, but not perhaps in the way he would have loved it. He is going to be freed from one prison, but only by walking through the door of another prison—death: the ultimate and only freedom that there is for human beings, some would say. He will go home or, more accurately, he will be brought home, but only as a dead man. He will go home a different man in many ways from the one that left home.

Putman Junior's character in the 'Green, Green Grass of Home' is representative of all human beings. It is our desire for freedom from the unwanted in our lives that make us the people we ultimately become. Many parts of us die in that process of becoming, so that on arrival 'home' we are never the same people we were when we first left home.

Decades ago my desire to be free encouraged me to leave my home village and country. That decision set me off on a mental, emotional, spiritual, and physical journey that has led me to cross many borders in order to be free from the prison of my then perceived limitations. I envisioned that freedom in terms of a destination—a place where all that was not well with me would be made well. Yet, no sooner when I have ever arrived at any envisaged ideal place, I have sought to make it better. It is as though every finishing line for me has often become the beginning of a new race. In this sense, I have often lived and felt like a displaced person—always on the move to, as it were, a new and better 'home'.

My desire to Return Home

Today, it baffles me that at fifty-five years of age and after living in Ireland for eighteen years, my greatest desire is to return to my home country. Hardly a day passes without me thinking about going back home one day. This desire is born out of the feeling that my life and ministry would be a lot freer and better at home. Yet many considerations including family and means of support often frighten me when I think about it. On the faces of those with whom I share this dream, I often see wonder about my sanity, even though many never voice their opinions. Will it happen? I don't know. But this much I know: if the strength of my desire is matched by the will of God, it will happen.

This, I must hasten to say, is no reflection on Ireland and her peoples per se. On the contrary. Eighteen years ago, Ireland provided me with a home away from my home. She offered my family and me safety and security, provided me with a job, and facilitated me in several other ways to pursue my interests and live as fulfilled a life as possible. The same, in fact, is true about all the time I have spent in the West beginning from when I first arrived here in 1985. This is a blessing I will be grateful for forever.

Then there are a whole host of other blessings: easy availability of light, water, food, transport, healthcare, and educational facilities, to name a few. These often taken-for-granted services and comforts here are not so in my country; and even when they are available, it can often take a huge amount of money, time and energy to avail of them. I often tell my friends, for example, about the blessing of being in Ireland where I am able to read and write whenever I want to: two of my most cherished hobbies which I feared I might have lost had I, a night person, stayed in Sierra Leone all these years with sporadic electricity supply. Then there is the blessing of humility that has come not only from knowing that anything I do here can be done by hundreds of other people and better, but also from the awareness that I am an outsider both in and outside the church and, so, always dependent on the good will of insiders for my needs and interests to be addressed. In all these ways and more, Ireland and her peoples have not only provided me a home from home, but they have also reminded me of home.

My Two Homes in Ireland

In the last few years, I have become a man of two homes in Ireland: one in Carlow in the South East and the other in Bray about one hundred and fourteen kilometres away on the East Coast. This is so because my wife and I are Methodist ministers and are assigned to two different Circuits. From Tuesday night to Sunday afternoon I live at home in Carlow from where I serve the Methodist Churches in Carlow and Kilkenny. Then I travel home to Bray to be with my wife and children from Sunday night to Tuesday afternoon. This situation has made talking about home a very interesting phenomenon for me in recent times.

Is home a warm house where I stay, cook my meals, keep my belongings, wash and am alone by myself? Is it not possible to do all of these things in a place that is not necessarily home: perhaps in a rented accommodation on holiday, or visiting with somebody? My home in Carlow affords me these possibilities and more. It is a place where I can be myself: do what I want to do when I want to do it; say what I want to say as I want to say it; watch TV or listen to the radio when I want to; not feel the need to say anything if I don't want to. These, perhaps more than anything else, are what make me refer to where I live in Carlow as home. There, at the end of my working day, I can just be—without needing to say, do, or be anything else other than what I want. I do not have to listen to anybody. There, I am able to go to my own bed and, sometimes, sleep. These are things I cannot do when I am on duty.

There are many times, though, when I go into my own bed in Carlow and do not sleep. They are the times when I bring the demands, conflicts, and needs of being a pastor, and administrator, and a preacher home with me. One of the difficulties of being a minister is the fact that I have people in my churches who think, for whatever reason, that they can do my job better than I am doing it: they presume to know the Bible better even though they have never been to a Bible school; they know better than me how to conduct a service, what hymns to sing at a service, how to pray, how to chair a meeting, what to preach, and so on. Of this group, there are some who are upfront with their opinions and, when they are, most of us conclude they are trouble-makers. Yet they are no worse than some of their accusers who want to control what the minister does but in subtle and circuitous ways. But these would-be-ministers of both groups agree on one thing: it is on the fact that a minister is not allowed to be angry or complain because he or she is a minister—as if a minister is some emotionless plastic creature from outer space who is not affected by what he or she hears and sees and experiences.

As a result, my experience of ministry here, more than anywhere else in the previous twenty-eight years, has often being one of patient painful listening to half a dozen or so people suggesting passionately not only what ideas I should hold and what Christian views I should promote, but also how to do my job in a dozen different and contradictory ways. I have often wondered what those same people would think of me telling them how to do their own jobs.

Yet, I do sympathize with these people, not least because the curious thing about Christianity is that the moment one becomes a Christian, one becomes one with all; and because it is the Holy Spirit who teaches all Christians what true religion is, it is not surprising that some Christians immediately presume to be experts in the faith of Christ and as God's emissaries. What makes this way of seeing, understanding and doing Christianity a little more concerning than it might otherwise be is when such people begin to introduce their opinions with "God clearly told/showed me . . ." or words to that effect. When you add to this the fact that many Christians think and feel that until others' understanding and experience and practice of Christianity is like theirs those others are not proper Christians, you have a proper recipe for conflict. Little wonder that there are many times when I come home to Carlow, drag myself into my warm and comfortable bed, but not go to sleep. Instead, I am awake mulling over the day's goings on and seeking to make some sense of them.

But there is another group of people in the church who let you do your job as you choose to do it. One of this group once typically told me to wear whatever I feel comfortable to church and not feel obligated to wear a suit and a clerical shirt and collar. "We don't mind what you wear as long as you are comfortable," she said to me in a very friendly and loving way. This group makes little or no demands on me outside the ordinary. Neither do they allow me to make any demands on them outside the ordinary. They come to church when they want to and participate in what extra church events they choose, and contribute towards the finances of the church through the offerings they give when they come to church. Outside of that, they are not able to do anything else: not Bible studies, prayers, youth work, Sunday school teaching, coffee mornings, and so on. And yet they are most sincerely Christian in their attitudes towards all. I still recall with a smile and great joy a letter written to me by one of these thanking me for my ministry. "I aim to save my soul through faith in my Lord Jesus Christ, by the grace of God. The core is that Christ is Risen! . . . I have to accept it emotionally as well as logically. I have to lean on God . . . Our family enemies can cheat us out of our possessions, but they cannot cheat me out of the promise of eternal life with the Lamb of God . . . . I am a soft gentle person, but I get strength to cope through prayer . . . I find your sermons great. You make the books of the Bible alive. I look forward to service every Sunday . . . God bless your work." This group is in the majority.

The rest, which is often not more than half a dozen and some of whom belong to the first two groups above, are genuinely interested in both your physical and spiritual wellbeing, and so endeavour in different ways to support and encourage you. "If there is anything I can do to help you in your ministry please do not hesitate to ask. I would only be very pleased to help in any way I can", they would say to me at different times. "I do pray for you and your family every day." "Be sure not to overdo things; find time to rest." "Drop by for a cup of coffee anytime." These are the kinds of things they say to me as I go about doing my work. I wonder sometimes if they know how much strength and inspiration their words give me in both good and challenging times when I am home in Carlow mulling over the goings on of the day in my bed.

"He has gone home to Bray," the people in my churches in Carlow and Kilkenny say when I go to be with my wife and children every Sunday to Tuesday afternoon. Unlike Carlow, when I am at home in Bray, I am with my family. In Bray, my family know my likes and dislikes. I can shout across the room or house, and somebody will hear me and hopefully help me do what I want to be done. I sit in my favorite chair and everyone knows it is my chair. I can do all the things I do in my home in Carlow. I can benefit from the opinion of my wife and children when thinking things through. I can go to bed and almost always sleep. Nevertheless, Bray is in many ways not my home. If and when my family is no longer living there, I do not think I will miss it. I know nobody in Bray apart from a handful of people who go to my wife's church. There is no place of particular interest or significance to me there. Like Carlow, Bray is just a home of convenience. So when I refer to both homes as 'my village' to the amusement of those listening to me, it is a mental effort on my part to make them more acceptable to me than they are in actual fact.

This is true also with regard to how I see Ireland. For the many years I have lived here, I still do not feel at home in Ireland; and I do not think any number of years I end up living here is going to change that. Ireland, for me, is a stop-gap home—a place of transition—from where I hope to one day depart for my actual home destination.

My Home is Sierra Leone

If and when I eventually do go home to Sierra Leone, I will be able to eat what I want all the time—all my favourite traditional dishes from I was a child—prepared to specification and organically grown. I will speak my mother and father tongues without any worry of speaking them wrongly, or being misunderstood, or accused of mispronunciation or speaking with an accent. In my home country I will be free not only to speak my native tongues but also to enjoy heart-to-heart communication. How right Nelson Mandela was when he said that when you speak to someone in their mother tongue, you speak to their heart and when you speak to them in a learned language, you speak to their head!

At home in Sierra Leone, I will be free to walk in and out of my neighbours' homes without asking for permission or making an appointment. I can shout across the yard, compound, road, village without been considered mad or uncivilized or a public nuisance. I can play the music of my choice in my house as loud as I wish without been accused of noise pollution by my neighbours. I will not stand out, nor will I be looked down upon, laughed at, and judged purely on the basis of my skin colour and even before I say or do anything. My name and family name will be very well-known and pronounced properly. I will not have to give reason for being there, justify my right to be present, or prove that my being there is of benefit to the country. If I am not up and out of my bedroom at a certain time in the morning people will knock on my door to make sure I am all-right; and they won't be considered nosy or told to mine their own business. Children are not warned against talking to strangers for fear of being abducted and harmed; and, unless there is a war going, people are seldom shot and killed. I will be honestly angry if I need to without someone thinking that I need psychiatric help. I will not have to second guess the boundaries of relationships and behaviour. When I buy a product I will always pay for it upfront and so do not live a life of indebtedness. In my village again, I will be able to see children learning important employable skills of life through observing their older ones and participating in what is being done, without being expected to pay fees. I will be free to walk into the nearby bush and access herbal health remedies without being charged ridiculous sums of money, or barred from doing so for lack of patenting rights, or some expert telling me that the remedy needs to be licensed by some authority before I could use it.

What Makes a Place Home?

In the face of the freedoms my home country affords me, Carlow, Bray and Ireland are simply just pale reflections of what it really means for me to be at home. So I often wonder when I tell people I don't consider Ireland home whether they understand these realities of what I consider home! It is not the absence of needs that makes a place home, nor just the presence of loved ones. Instead, it is history, memory, the sense of belonging, a feeling of innate familiarity of what you see, hear, and do, a connectedness that goes beyond one's individuality and reaches back to the unknown distant past that nonetheless impacts on your present and determines your future. Home is a place that takes on a personality like no other. That personality reflects something of the stories that have turned you into the person you are—your stories, the stories of your ancestors and the stories of your community. For me, home is where my umbilical cord is buried; and that cord, essentially my birth certificate, ties and draws me to it as long as I live. Friends and relations may die, loved ones may move away, worldviews and values may change gradually, but the residues of memories and nostalgia of connectedness with home never really lose their potency. They never die; and as long as they stay alive, home is alive no matter where else I am in the world and how much more well-off it is perceived to be. A feeling, smell, sound, sight, gesture, and touch can easily bring all that home represents flooding into the present.

The idea of the Promised Land found in the Bible always comes to mind when I reflect on the realities of home I have depicted above. On first hearing about it as a child, the Promised Land conjured up for me images exclusively of a destination of bliss. ". . . a land flowing with milk and honey" is how the Bible depicts it[33]. As I grew up and started reading the Bible for myself, I came to realize increasingly that it is not as simple as I had thought. The rub is in the word 'promised'. There is no question about whether or not the land was there. It was. Neither was there any question about the truth of God's word to give that land to the Hebrews as their permanent home. In fact, from the moment God promised it to them, it was their home. But it had to be claimed before the promise could become a reality. The truth of this is made clear by the fact that alongside the promise the Bible says that the land is already inhabited and occupied by different nations[34]. They were not just different but they were also enemy nations; some of them were not just inhabited by ordinary people, but by giants[35]. We all know the fear that enemies, especially giant ones, can cause us. But they need to be defeated before the land could become home; not all at once, as God told His people, but gradually.[36] This, as it turned out to be, was the work of more than a lifetime, and for generation after generation. While on the one hand the Hebrews arrived and made the Promised Land their home, on the other hand, their experience of life in their homeland has never been free of threats and difficulties of one kind or another. Some of those are of the making of the Jews themselves. Yet, though enemies and giant enemies still abound, so also is a place that they call and know as home which was promised to them by their God.

---

[33] Exodus 3:8b & 17b
[34] Read Deuteronomy 19:8-9
[35] Numbers 13
[36] Exodus 23:29-30

The Journey 'Home'

I recently heard on the John Creedon music programme on the RTE Radio1 a song titled 'Wading deep waters trying to get home'. When I arrived home that night, I looked for the lyrics of the song on the search engine, Google. The lyrics express the deep need and desire to get home amidst challenges which presented as serious and risky obstacles along that way. These are characterized in terms of 'deep waters', 'high mountains', and 'deep valleys'. I watched a rendition of the song on You Tube against the background of images of musicians, a pub, wheelchair, crucifix, church, plain cross, waterfall, boat on water, welcome sign, light, an angel, mountaineers, firefighters, black faced coal miners, guns, words from the Bible, flags, skyscrapers, steel bridges, baptism by emersion, and Christ. I understood all of these as symbols representing the different ways human beings have always sought to fulfill their desire to get home in both the real and metaphorical senses, the mixed bag of need and satisfaction in their experiences on that journey, and the results they achieved.

Perhaps there is a message here for all who seek to get home in the real or metaphorical sense. The road is not without obstacles. The journey is neither simple nor straightforward. The destination may not be wholly as expected. Yet the fulfillment of the desire is also in the journey and not just in the destination.

The Promised Land of which we read in the Bible can perhaps be also read as a parable of human life in general and of ideas of home in particular. Wherever any of us could call home and feel at home, there is also always something about life and living in that place that does not quite reflect our ideal of home. So there is a 'now' and 'not yet' reality of every place we call home. This is not something we need to shy away from or apologize for. It is just the way life on this imperfect earth is and will always be.

The adequacies and inadequacies of my Irish and Sierra Leonean homes outlined above, perhaps point to a deeper reality that this world will never be my home, no matter how much and which part of it I seek to make home. The faith I profess says so: someday, Christ will return and bring us to the home which he has gone to prepare for us. That is the hope of Christians. It is my hope. It is based on the promise of Christ. It is hope in that promise that informs Odetta Chorale's Negro spiritual[37]: "Oh freedom . . . over me; and before I'd be a slave I'll be buried in my grave, and go home to my Lord and be free. No more moaning . . . No more crying . . . There'll be singing' . . . There will be glory over me."

The Bible says that human beings come from God. That is what I read in the creation stories in Genesis.[38] If I originally come from God, then my home is in God. And if home is the place I belong, then it is with God I belong now and forever. In God alone, therefore, will I ever feel truly at home and free in this world and the next. At home in God, every place is home, waiting to become my ideal home.

After I had fled to Ireland from my home country, I shared my story at the 2002 Annual Conference of the Methodist Church in Ireland in Enniskillen, Northern Ireland. On returning

---

[37] A post-Civil War African American freedom song. Date unknown
[38] Genesis 1 & 2

home from the conference, Brian Callan, a scientist and poet, reflected on my story. It was only very recently that he made me aware of a poem he wrote about it in one of his many volumes of published poems:

You left so much
When you sought this home,
There, you were somebody
They knew your name,
Acknowledged your worth,
You taught deep things
And they walled your life with respect
Hanging on to your words
Making you a part of who you are.

It was more than cultural change
To arrive with only your written name,
Waiting in the shadow of all you left
Your PhD a devalued currency.

You reached that inner crisis of faith,
Standing at an Athlone bus stop,
Washed in an Irish rain,
Feeling like a piece of straw
Blown in the autumn wind,
Your name parked in another place
Waiting for you to come back,
But you were home.[39]

---

[39] 'Seeking Asylum', by Brian Callan in his, Journey of the Soul (2006:94). Oxford: Trafford Publishing

SEVENTEEN

THE BEST IS YET TO COME

A Utopia that Has Not Materialized

'Veni, vidi, vici' ('I came, I saw, I conquered')
are the words of Gaius Julius Caesar when
addressing the senate in Rome after conquering
King Pharnaces II of Pontus after the battle of Zela in 47 BC.
Long before I was born, my father had, so to speak, embarked
on a mental, social and spiritual journey towards the West. I
suspect it was a journey of exploration. He had hope that it
would lead him and his people to experience the best that was
on offer in life for them.

As I have sought to demonstrate, I was enrolled on that
journey long before I had any chance of deciding for myself.
It was while I was already on the journey that I not only
discovered what it was about, but also believed and dreamed,
like my father before me, that it would lead me to a paradise
of life where I would experience total satisfaction.

In many ways the story I have told here is a story of that journey. It has exposed me to Western ways of thinking, living, believing, and speaking. Sometimes it takes people who have not travelled the road I have travelled to remind me how Western I have become. I remember visiting my home village a few years ago and talking passionately about the terrible economic recession we were experiencing in Ireland. On finishing and waiting for a sympathetic response, one of the men listening laughed me off saying he did not understand what I was talking about. "We have always lived in recession, but life goes on," he remarked as he walked away to attend to another seemingly more important business than listening to me. That man made me think a lot about the kind of person I have become since I embarked on the journey towards the West. I thought to myself: "Here is a man who has no mortgage to pay, no credit card debts to settle, no electricity, telephone, water, gas, bin collection, petrol, and transport bills to pay. He lives in a house he built from his own resources, grows his own food, and engages in economic activities that provide him with the money he needs to take care of the basic needs of his family. Yes, he has problems too. So do the rest of the people in his community. But he does not see the need to broadcast his problems to the world. He deals with them as they come his way. Yet, it is people like this man that the world in which I live pity and look down upon. I may not now choose to live the life he lives. But I envy the relative freedom his way of life affords him.

Yes, indeed, I have come a long way towards the West. But with regard to this my journey of exploration, I wish I could say at this stage, "I came, I saw, I conquered." But that is not the case. Indeed, I have come and I have seen. But conquering? That is another story altogether. For, I cannot by any means say that I am anywhere near experiencing the paradise I had envisioned when I first set out on this journey. There is still a lot in my life that I do not want and therefore takes away from my satisfaction with life. There is a lot that I am ignorant of, that I want, and that I fear. There are unfulfilled potentials and the constant awareness of my inability to change what I do not like. Yes, I have in many ways succeeded in realizing the ambitions that I suspect inspired my father long ago and drew him to align himself with the ways of the West. But, no, I am a long way away from being able to say as a result of my experiences of the West that I have conquered life. I believe this would be the case even if I had never embraced the ways of the West.

Bewildered

What I can honestly say at this moment in my life is that I am bewildered. The experiences of my journey between the various worlds depicted in this story sometimes make it difficult for me to know who I am. It is not just simply about being neither African nor Western, though this might be part of the cause of my bewilderment. But it is also because I no longer believe that any of those ways of being human satisfy my longing and search for an ideal life. What long ago seemed to be so straightforward and clear a path to the life of bliss has turned into a myriad of roads suggesting themselves to me. What once seemed to be one voice directing my steps has now turned into many inner and outside voices shouting out to me their preferences of the best road I should travel. Their directions are often not as clear as I would like. Consequently, I no longer know what an ideal life would really look like.

Yet, in my bewilderment, I have one certainty. It is my belief and hope, as lyricist Carolyn Leigh wrote in 1959, that "**the best is yet to come**". A realist, I suppose, would laugh off the idea of being certain in things as non-concrete as belief and hope. Yet it is my conviction that they are the only things that are certain in this life. Communities in Japan, Indonesia, and Oklahoma which in recent times and as a result of tornados and tsunamis have seen disappear in a twinkle of an eye what seemed to be concrete and verifiable realities in their lives would need no convincing about this. For, they know that the only things that are certain are belief and hope: belief and hope that whatever life may bring our way, the best might yet come. It is that belief and hope that make them rise to their feet and do what they need to do towards making that future possible.

My Belief and Hope

This is my belief and hope as I continue to live between and within the worlds of my experiences: that the best is yet to come. They are founded on much more than I can do to know and have what I will recognize as ideal life. Instead, they are rooted in the promise of God to me in Christ that one day He is going to make all things new[40]. I take the 'all' to mean everything: the world, people, my experiences, expectations,

---

[40] Revelation 21:5

anxieties, and knowledge. Only then will I know and live a truly unencumbered life—free and shot through by the love of God which knows no boundaries, heights, and depths.

The founder of the Methodist Church, the Reverend John Wesley, is alleged to have said on his death bed that 'the best of all is, God is with us . . .' It is this reality, I believe, that has made my journey thus far in life possible. Looking back on how my life has unfolded, I can say without a doubt that in good and bad times God has been with me throughout, even though I was not always aware of it. Yet in this world of sin and suffering, the ideal life that I long for is, and will, never be possible. It is awareness of this that made St. Paul say that, "If only for this life we (Christians) have hope in Christ, we are of all people most to be pitied."[41] That is why I believe and hope in the world to come when Christ shall return, make all things new and restore to us our heritage in God.

As I wait for that time, I dwell on the words of Anna Laetitia Waring written in 1850:

> "Green pastures are before me, which yet I have
> not seen.
> Bright skies will soon be over me, where darkest
> clouds have been.
> My hope I cannot measure, my path to life is free.
> My Saviour has my treasure, and He will walk with
> me."[42]

---

[41] 1Corinthians 15:19
[42] Hymns and Psalms (1986:No. 678). London: Methodist Publishing House

Meanwhile, I will continue to enjoy and endure life as best as I can, aware of the truth that life is not a problem to solve, but a mystery to enjoy in the knowledge that my life and times are God's hands.[43]

---

[43]   Psalm 31:15

APPENDIX 1

A Historical Timeline of Sierra Leone to Independence

1787—British abolitionists and philanthropists establish a settlement in Freetown for repatriated and rescued slaves.

- Freetown, the capital, is a port city and commercial hub
- Settled by freed and rescued slaves in 18th century
- 1821: Made seat of government for British territories in West Africa
- Became capital in 1961

1808—Freetown settlement becomes crown colony.

1896—Britain sets up a protectorate over the Freetown hinterland.

1898—The Hut Tax War took place as hinterland people refused to pay tax to the British Administration

1954—Sir Milton Margai, leader of the Sierra Leone People's Party, appointed chief minister.

1961—Sierra Leone becomes independent.

APPENDIX 2

Map of Sierra Leone showing some places mentioned in the book

APPENDIX 3

Map of Africa showing Sierra Leone

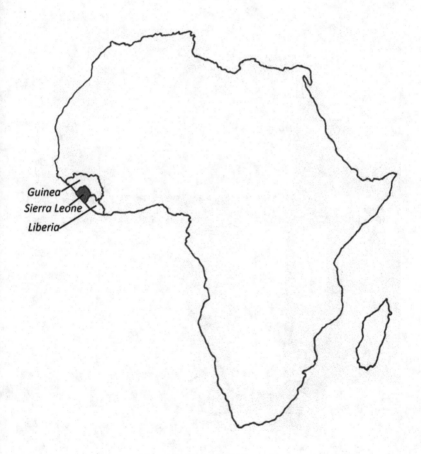